Sustainable Operations Management

Sustainable Operations Management applies the principles of sustainability to all strategic decisions of operations: capacity management, supply network, process technology, and development and organisation. This book extends the existing literature of operations management that for years has been paramount in creating economic value with little consideration of environment and social dimensions. Whilst based on robust theoretical frameworks, some developed by its own authors, the book is enriched by international case studies and real-world illustrations throughout, to demonstrate how this theory translates to practice. Each chapter begins with learning objectives and ends with a summary, activity, or questions for discussion. Readers will gain a comprehensive and in-depth knowledge on how to manage operations for sustainability. They will learn the ways to formulate a sustainable operations strategy and the elements involved in managing tactical and operational activities to enhance sustainability performance over time. The book covers all aspects of the new business sustainability paradigm from an operations perspective, including sustainable development goals, the circular economy, and digital transformation. With international agreements and national policies in place around themes such as climate change, ocean plastic pollution, loss of biodiversity, water scarcity, and zero landfill targets, this book will be a must for any university abiding to the Principles of Responsible Management Education (PRIME). The text is suitable mostly for MSc and MBA students on sustainable supply chain and operations management modules as well as broader operations management courses, but it can also be used for final-year undergraduate students as part of advanced operations management modules.

Breno Nunes is Senior Lecturer in Sustainable Operations Management and Deputy-director of the Centre for Circular Economy and Advanced Sustainability at Aston Business School, UK. He is currently President of IAMOT – the International Association for Management of Technology. Breno has published his research in high-impact journals and delivered several keynotes worldwide on SOM and related topics.

Luciano Batista is Director of the Centre for Circular Economy and Advanced Sustainability (CEAS) at Aston Business School, UK. He is also Chartered Member of the Chartered Institute of Logistics and Transport and affiliated faculty member of the Microeconomics of Competitiveness group at Harvard Business School, USA.

Donato Masi is Deputy-director of the Centre of Cybersecurity Innovation at Aston Business School, UK, and Reader in Operations and Supply Chain Management in the Operations and Information Department.

David Bennett is Affiliated Professor at Chalmers University, Sweden, and Emeritus Professor at Aston University, UK. David's research interests are concerned with issues relating to management of technology, operations systems design for manufacturing, and the transfer of technology between industrialised and developing countries.

Sustainable Operations Management

Key Practices and Cases

Breno Nunes, Luciano Batista, Donato Masi, and David Bennett

Routledge
Taylor & Francis Group
LONDON AND NEW YORK

Cover image: Getty Images

First published 2023
by Routledge
4 Park Square, Milton Park, Abingdon, Oxon OX14 4RN

and by Routledge
605 Third Avenue, New York, NY 10158

Routledge is an imprint of the Taylor & Francis Group, an informa business

British Library Cataloguing-in-Publication Data
A catalogue record for this book is available from the British Library

ISBN: 978-0-367-44379-5 (hbk)
ISBN: 978-0-367-44383-2 (pbk)
ISBN: 978-1-003-00937-5 (ebk)

DOI: 10.4324/9781003009375

Typeset in Bembo
by Deanta Global Publishing Services, Chennai, India

Access the Support Material: www.routledge.com/9780367443832

Contents

Preface

For more than two decades the United Nations has held numerous workshops, meetings, conferences, and summits related to climate change and sustainable development. The most important event concerning climate change is the annual COP (Conference of the Parties), the first of which was held in Berlin in 1995. And among these COP conferences perhaps most significant have been COP 3 in Kyoto, Japan, held in 1997, which established legal obligations for developed countries to reduce their greenhouse gas emissions, and COP 21 in Paris, France, where a general path towards climate action was agreed. We finished writing this book shortly after COP 26, held in Glasgow, United Kingdom, in November 2021. This was attended not only by political leaders of several nations, but also by representatives of businesses and civil society, to discuss an action plan to mitigate and adapt to climate change and its impact on societies and economies.

In contrast to previous COP meetings, countries were asked for COP 26 to come forward specifically with more ambitious targets and commit to clear initiatives for curbing emissions and reducing global warming until 2030. These included a faster phasing-out of coal, curtailing deforestation, speeding up the switch to electric vehicles, and encouraging investments in renewable energy. In addition, COP 26 also included discussions on how to finance such transformations in both developed and developing countries.

Much attention inevitably focused on whether the COP 26 agreements would deliver significant changes after the conference ended. Certainly, in some nations several sectors are already going through a process of transition, particularly with respect to investments in renewable energy and electrification of urban mobility. At the level of industrial sectors and industries these changes will ultimately require companies to rethink their business values and functions. From strategic decisions (related to location, supply networks, and product development) to tactical and operational levels of management, the operations function is likely to be the most affected area of business. Pressures to reduce energy consumption and greenhouse gas emissions of products, services, and processes will surely increase in the coming years.

However, the pressures from climate change policies are not alone as drivers to improve businesses' sustainability performance. Many companies are also directing their environmental and social contributions more widely based on the UN Sustainable Development Goals (UNSDGs) established in 2015 and ratified that year at the UN Sustainable Development Summit in New York. The UNSDGs, which include climate action as one of the goals, cover all three dimensions of sustainable development. Thus, it is expected that they will also affect the management of operations. Rather than focusing only on greenhouse gas emission reductions, and consequently creating potential impact on other areas, organisations aligned by the UNSDGs will address issues related to water, waste materials, land contamination, and biodiversity, among other things. The magnitude of such tasks impacts upon companies after a challenging period, during which many were forced to shut down operations because of the COVID-19 pandemic. In short, we are likely to experience a simultaneous stimulus for economic growth and job creation, while restrained by stricter environmental regulations.

The coming years will be, without doubt, a very challenging time for businesses. It is also a very exciting moment from which many new opportunities will emerge. This combination of challenge and excitement has driven us to write this book. We have written it with our students and practising operations managers in mind, as well as other people involved in learning, applying, and developing ways to make business operations more sustainable.

What sustainable operations management means within business may be getting clearer, but is also potentially more complex. New concepts such as net zero carbon dioxide emissions and circular economy models are still in their early stages for the majority of the firms. Increased transparency, particularly in the social dimension, has negated the value and coherence of capitalising on low labour costs and using unaudited suppliers in distant locations.

Whether you are an undergraduate or postgraduate business student, or a practising operations manager, we hope this book will widen your views on how to manage operations for better sustainability. You will find original concepts, international examples, and case studies laid out within a clear structure for you to conduct your studies or for general reading.

We want to thank all those who supported us in writing this book: our families, colleagues, and operations managers who took part in our various research projects; but mainly, our students, who drove us with their passion and interest for sustainability and making businesses a part of the solution for a sustainable future rather than a burden for the next generations.

Breno Nunes,
Luciano Batista,
Donato Masi, and
David Bennett

Glossary of abbreviations and special terms

5G communications	The fifth generation standard for broadband cellular networks
AI	Artificial intelligence
Blockchain	A ledger or database that stores and links encrypted blocks of data
BOP	Bottom of the pyramid (refers to the poorest part of the economic human pyramid)
BREEAM	Building Research Establishment Environmental Assessment Method (UK)
BSI	British Standards Institution
BSO	Business Services Organisation (Northern Ireland)
C2C	Customer-to-customer (or consumer-to-consumer)
CEO	Chief executive officer
CO	Carbon monoxide
CO_2	Carbon dioxide (CO_2)
COO	Chief operating officer
COSHH	Control of Substances Hazardous to Health (UK)
CSR	Corporate social responsibility
DfE	Design for environment
DfS (or D4S)	Design for sustainability
DHSSPS	Department of Health Social Services & Public Safety (Northern Ireland)
DIN	Deutsches Institut für Normung (German Institute for Standardization)
EOQ	Economic order quantity
EPA	Environmental Protection Agency (USA)
EPOS	Electronic point of sale
EUR	EU euros
FM	Facilities management
GBP	British pounds
GDP	Gross domestic product
GHG	Greenhouse gas
GPS	Global positioning system
HSE	Health and Safety Executive (UK)
ICT	Information and communications technology
IDSA	Industrial Designers Society of America
ILO	International Labour Organization (United Nations)

Industry 1.0 (etc.)	The waves of technological evolution
IoT	Internet of things
ISO	International Organization for Standardization
IT	Information technology
Last-mile	The final part of a journey (logistics and supply chain terminology)
LCA	Life cycle assessment
LCI	Life cycle inventory analysis
LCIA	The life cycle impact assessment
LED	Light emitting diode
LEED	Leadership in Energy and Environmental Design
MHRA	Medicines and Health Care Products Regulatory Agency (UK)
NAE	National Academy of Engineering (USA)
NGO	Non-governmental organisation
NHS	National Health Service (UK)
NI	Northern Ireland
NOX	Nitrogen Oxide (NO_X)
NZEB	Nearly-zero energy building
ODS	Ozone depleting substances
OECD	Organisation for Economic Co-operation and Development
OEE	Overall equipment efficiency
OHS	Occupational health and safety
OSF	Operations sustainability fitness
PLA	Product life cycle analysis
PPE	Personal protective equipment
PV	Photovoltaics
R&D	Research and development
REACH	Registration, Evaluation, Authorisation and Restriction of Chemicals (EU)
RES	Renewable energy system
SCOR	Supply chain operations reference model
SDG	Sustainable Development Goal
SMEs	Small and medium-sized enterprises
SO_2	Sulphur dioxide (SO_2)
SOM	Sustainable operations management
SVI	Sustainable value innovation
TBL	Triple bottom line
UAV	Unmanned aerial vehicles (or drones)
UNEP	United Nations Environment Programme
UNU-IHDP	United Nations University International Human Dimensions Programme on Global Environmental Change
USD	United States dollars
WBCSD	World Business Council for Sustainable Development
WCED	World Commission on Environment and Development (United Nations)
WDO	World Design Organization
WiFi	Wireless fidelity

Part 1

Setting the scene

1 Introduction to sustainable operations management

This chapter presents the topics of sustainability, sustainable development, and related concepts. It also provides an overview of the operations function, its role and importance for business sustainability. The concept of sustainable operations management (SOM) is then defined alongside its implications for the management of operations in respect of its traditional roots.

The key learning objectives of the chapter are:

- to develop awareness of the key concepts of sustainable development and sustainable operations management;
- to recognise the elements and trade-offs within the dimensions of operations sustainability, namely: economic, environmental, and social;
- to identify the areas of operations which are related to the improvement of sustainability performance.

This book comprises three parts: Part 1 Setting the scene, Part 2 Sustainable operations management practices, and Part 3 Cases in sustainable operations management (see Figure 1.1). The first three chapters belong to Part 1 (Introduction to sustainable operations management; Towards a circular economy; Sustainable operations strategy). Chapters 4 to 8 are in Part 2 (Sustainable facilities; Sustainable supply chains; Sustainable production; Process technologies for sustainable operations; Sustainable design and product development), and the cases that comprise practical examples in sustainable operations management comprise Part 3.

Introduction to sustainability and sustainable development

Before becoming mainstream in the operations management discipline, sustainability had been discussed for a long time in other academic disciplines such as philosophy, history, sociology, and biology. For example, philosophers, historians, sociologists, and biologists have extensively analysed the collapse of ecosystems, societies, and economies. Besides analysis based on military power, which includes the relationship between allies and enemies, other studies on the resilience and collapse of ancient civilisations were usually linked to use, degradation, and availability of (natural) resources, strength of social institutions, and individual and collective behaviour (Nunes, 2011). In economics, for instance, a landmark sustainability study (although not using the term 'sustainability' as such) is the Essay on Population by Thomas Malthus (Malthus, 1798). At the time, Malthus

DOI: 10.4324/9781003009375-2

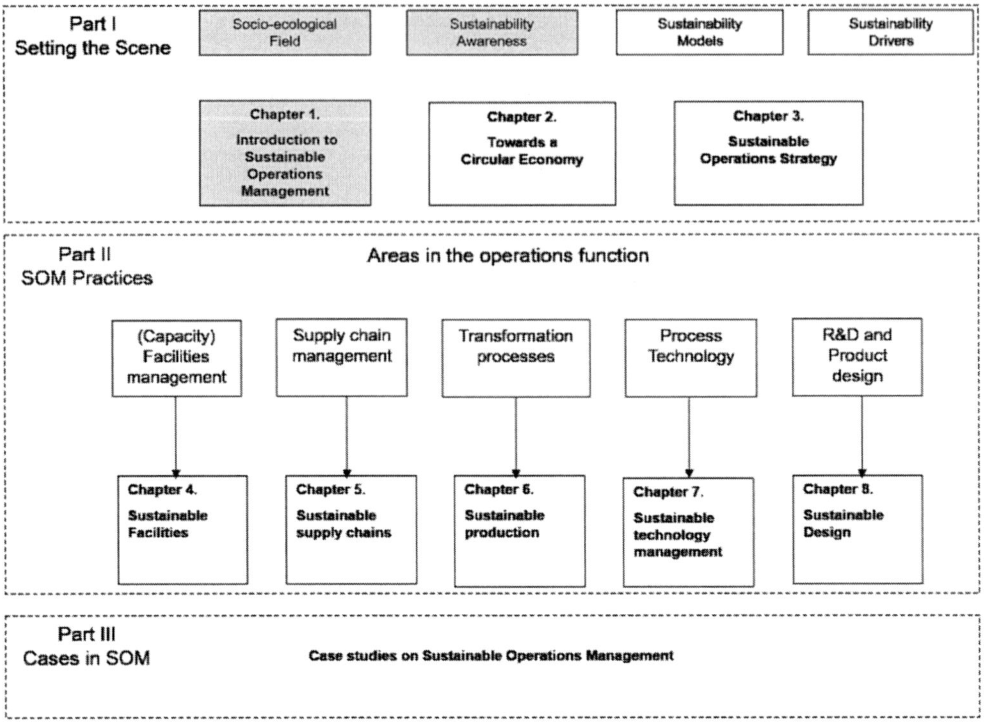

Figure 1.1 Chapter 1 within the book structure

was unable to predict both stable population growth in developed countries and new techniques for cropping. However, despite the agribusiness sector now being able to supply enough food, concerns about environmental impacts of how we actually produced the food have gained attention, together with the threats to 21st century society. Deforestation, loss of biodiversity, pollution of the air, water, and soil, animal welfare, health implications of food (mainly regarding the use of chemicals) are nowadays included in the environmental agenda of agribusinesses together with other issues (Nunes, 2011). In the social agenda, agricultural supply chains are among the key sectors where modern slavery and child labour often take place (Lalwani et al., 2018).

Thus, scholars continue to be concerned about the impact of human economic activities on environment and societal relationships – furthermore, food supply is not alone in the list of concerns. With the industrialisation of countries after the 1800s and clear abundance of food in rich nations, attention was drawn from agricultural systems to manufacturing industries and their harmful emissions. Indeed, the manufacturing sector is currently the largest source of environmental impacts due to the use of toxic substances, large consumption of water and energy, and disposal of dangerous wastes. While the environmental impacts were primarily from production and confined to local areas, environmental legislation became stricter and pollution control took place to avoid wasteful activities. Later, pollution prevention and process improvement proved more economic and effective in responding to legislation targets (Klassen and MacLauglin, 1996; Klassen and Whybark, 1999). Nevertheless, with the current globalisation of markets and production, the sustainability debate is leading towards a more holistic approach, which includes both production and consumption systems (Clark, 2007; Tukker et al., 2008). Hence, the modern studies of sustainability analyse the location of factories, production processes, logistics routes, product use, and consumer behaviour, and ultimately, the final disposal of waste, be it in the form of an end-of-life product or residues of production.

According to the United Nations, the World's population will rise from the current 7 billion to 9 billion people by 2050. As most nations focus on and celebrate success in reducing poverty, a 'neo-Malthusianism' reality is again raised by scholars, i.e. the global population's desire for consumption will not be met within the Planet's carrying capacity, leading to environmental degradation and social inequality. In this scenario, social unrest due to shortages of water, food, and energy is only a matter of time. The current high levels of consumption (and waste) in developed nations have already caused them to create an ecological footprint larger than their own ecosystems can support (Wackernagel and Rees, 1998). Developing economies are likely to follow historical development patterns leading to increased motor vehicle ownership, material consumption, land use, and finally, higher use of air travel. For developing nations, the initial increase in consumption addresses essential needs and provides important improvements in individual and collective productivity (e.g. organisational, local, regional, and national). And as several developing countries are finding, this can still be done without sacrificing other species' existence on our planet, and with a harmonious relationship between people and nature.

A definition that encapsulates the values of sustainability is provided by John Ehrenfeld:

> Sustainability is the possibility that humans and other life will flourish on Earth forever.
>
> (Ehrenfeld, 2008a)

For Ehrenfeld, sustainability needs to be attained not managed (Ehrenfeld, 2008b). The pressures presented today for economic growth in both developed and developing nations rely on various sustainability initiatives such as:

- tackling climate change and its causes, including:
  - reduced consumption of fossil fuels, even eliminating the use of coal to produce electricity;
  - electrification of mobility as a replacement for diesel and petrol to fuel vehicles;
- rational use of water, and protection of marine areas;
- conservation of biodiversity and native forest areas;
- reduction of waste to landfill;
- health and quality of life;
- decent working conditions;
- equality of opportunities for women and minorities groups.

In 2020, the COVID-19 pandemic created a health crisis which led to a global economic downturn for most countries. So, much emphasis is now put on making economies more resilient to socio-ecological crises. The European Union, as well as the United Kingdom, the United States, and other countries have all announced green recovery plans. These plans will have an impact on various sectors, but structural changes are expected in energy, buildings, and transport. Fostering science and innovation, and respecting the natural environment, will be at the centre of the transformations.

BOX 1.1 ANNOUNCEMENT BY THE UK DEPARTMENT FOR BUSINESS, ENERGY & INDUSTRIAL STRATEGY AND THE PRIME MINISTER'S OFFICE, NOVEMBER 2020

www.gov.uk/government/publications/the-ten-point-plan-for-a-green-industrial-revolution/title

UK aims at a Green Industrial Revolution

Two centuries ago, the UK led the world's first Industrial Revolution. Powered by innovation and private investment, this transformation gave birth to many of our great cities and effectively created the modern world. Today we will mobilise the same forces to level up our country and enable our proud industrial heartlands to forge the future once again. By investing in clean technologies – wind, carbon capture, hydrogen, and many others – Britain will lead the world into a new Green Industrial Revolution.

As the world begins to recover from the devastating impact of the coronavirus on lives and livelihoods, a broader transformation is taking shape. We will create hundreds of thousands of new jobs by investing in pioneering British industries while simultaneously protecting future generations from climate change and the remorseless destruction of habitats.

Britain is already leading the way. Over the last 30 years, we have shown that economic success and environmental responsibility go hand in hand. We expanded our GDP by 75% while cutting emissions by 43%. Our low-carbon industries already support over 460,000 jobs, from electric vehicle manufacturing in the Midlands and the North East to our thriving offshore wind industry centred on the Humber and the Tees. In 2019, we became the first major economy to adopt a legally binding obligation to reach net zero greenhouse gas emissions by 2050.

This year, our Ten Point Plan will lay the foundations for a Green Industrial Revolution. We will start by supporting 90,000 jobs across the UK within this Parliament, and up to 250,000 by 2030. Engineers, fitters, construction workers, and many others will be engaged in harnessing British science and technology to create and use clean energy and forge great new industries that export to new markets around the world. Our Lifetime Skills Guarantee will equip people with the training they need to take advantage of these opportunities.

The government has announced over £5 billion to support a green recovery. This plan mobilises £12 billion – and potentially more than three times as much from the private sector – to place green jobs at the heart of our economic revival.

As the world goes green, we will seek to put the UK at the forefront of global markets for clean technology. One measure of the opportunity is that 83% of the $13.3 trillion of global investment in electricity systems by 2050 could be in zero-carbon technologies.

For businesses, the green recovery plans will mean a constant reflection on their societal value and environmental impact. Conceptually, this will need to start by taking a real representation of the sustainability dimensions. These dimensions have been presented in various ways and do not always show the actual reality of how they operate. Instead of disconnected pillars or overlapping ellipses, the systems approach with spheres is more appropriate because it shows the hierarchical levels of reality (Nunes et al., 2016).

Fundamentally, the economy belongs to a society, which itself belongs to the ecological environment. In addition, rather than it being a static relationship, there is an inter-dependency of the economic sphere with the other spheres of the social and ecological system (see Figure 1.2). It is the balance between these systems that allows sustainable creation, growth, and welfare. This inter-dependency exists between the environment, society, and its economy, which makes each sphere create positive and negative impacts on the others. For example, the environment may harm the

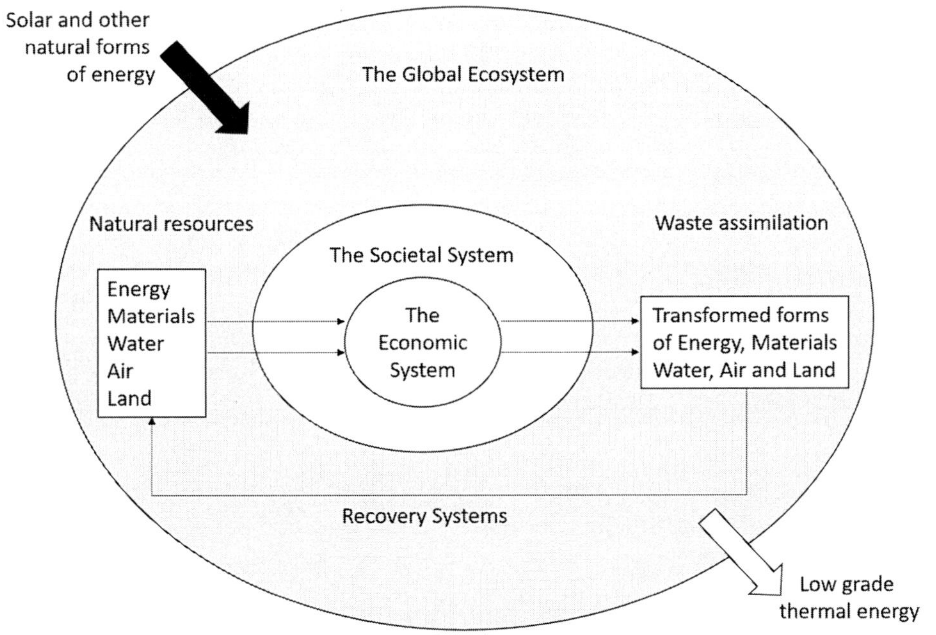

Figure 1.2 A simplified representation of natural resources flows across the global ecosystem, society, and the economic system. Source: adapted from Hammond and Winnett (2009)

> economy and society through an earthquake or a volcanic eruption, while society may harm the economy due to the lack of trust and weak public institutions. On the other hand, economic activities and anthropogenic actions may damage the environment with pollution and depletion of natural resources. It is also possible for the environment to create a positive impact on the socio-economic system and vice versa. Consider the natural resources available to nourish people and grow economies, and from the opposite direction, economic activities that help societies (e.g. educational institutions, hospitals, etc.) and conserve or enhance the environment (e.g. water treatment stations, soil and vegetation management, etc.). Sustainability is therefore not only the need to respect the bottom line of the three "Ps"– planet, people and profit – (Kleindorfer et al., 2005), but also the harmonisation of resources to meet people's desires for a fulfilling life.
>
> (Nunes and Bennett, 2010, p398)

In the next section of this introduction to sustainable operations management, the concept of sustainable development will be presented and discussed.

Sustainable development: the process to increase sustainability?

The concepts of sustainability and sustainable development are often highlighted as the ways forward in which societies, economies, and the environment can coexist and thrive in harmony. Sustainability and sustainable development are concepts that are often used interchangeably. In fact, they hold their values and principles based on three dimensions: economic, social, and environmental. But in terms of conceptualisation, sustainability is much older and with several definitions and various interpretations. Sustainability is a multidisciplinary, complex, and wide concept relating to avoidance of collapse, biodiversity conservation, ecological integrity, and the role of humankind as another species in nature (Mebratu, 1998; Olawumi and Chan, 2018).

Sustainable development (SD) is defined as the development that "*meets the needs of the present without compromising the ability of future generations to meet their own needs*" (Our Common Future, WCED, 1989).

As a concept, SD received much criticism for its vagueness despite its simple, clear, and elegant message. Its anthropogenic style and lack of explicit inclusion of other species have also received negative remarks. It is, nevertheless, a bureaucratic or technocratic step that responds to the path of unsustainability that economic growth impinges on nations. Furthermore, it has popularised and formalised sustainability into the development plans which were later refined and fashioned into 17 Sustainable Development Goals (SDGs) by the United Nations (UN, 2015):

(1) No Poverty,
(2) Zero Hunger,
(3) Good Health and Well-being,
(4) Quality Education,
(5) Gender Equality,
(6) Clean Water and Sanitation,
(7) Affordable and Clean Energy,
(8) Decent Work and Economic Growth,

(9) Industry, Innovation, and Infrastructure,
(10) Reducing Inequality,
(11) Sustainable Cities and Communities,
(12) Responsible Consumption and Production,
(13) Climate Action,
(14) Life below Water,
(15) Life on Land,
(16) Peace, Justice, and Strong Institutions,
(17) Partnerships for the Goals.

The SDGs attempt to balance the predominant focus on economic growth (GDP growth) by ascribing more attention to socio-economic development and environmental preservation. Consideration of additional measures to GDP growth is taken as a key step to meeting the SDGs. The Inclusive Wealth Index is suggested by the United Nations as an alternative.

Beyond GDP: the Inclusive Wealth Index

For many, the roots of unsustainability are in the pursuit of endless economic growth. The measure of GDP itself has also received a fair share of criticism for not including externalities, the value of other species, and ecosystems services.

The Inclusive Wealth Index (UNU-IHDP and UNEP, 2012) includes more realistic measures of wealth using three macro-indicators: natural capital, human capital, and manufactured or produced capital.

Manufactured capital is the physical capital produced by humans – transport infrastructure, vehicles, roads, buildings, etc. Human capital is often defined as the stock of knowledge and skills possessed by a population, and the health status of that population. Investments in education, training, and health are called investments in human capital. Natural capital can be viewed as the stocks of natural assets, ranging from soil, water, and air to all living things.

BOX 1.2 THE INCLUSIVE WEALTH REPORT (UNEP, 2018)

www.unep.org/resources/report/inclusive-wealth-report-2018

The Inclusive Wealth Report (IWR) is a biennial effort led by the UN Environment to evaluate the capacities and performance of the nations around the world to measure the sustainability of the economy and well-being of their people. The existing statistical systems in countries are using the System of Environment and Economic Accounts which are geared to measuring flow income. The flow would critically depend upon the health and resilience of capital assets like manufactured capital, human capital, and natural capital.

A country's inclusive wealth is the social value (not dollar price) of all its capital assets, including natural capital, human capital, and produced capital. The IWR 2018 builds on previous versions of the report (IWR2012 and IWR 2014) and advances methods of measuring the base of economy–capital of all types.

The results of the IWR 2018 covering 140 countries indicate that the inclusive wealth (IW) in 135 countries was higher in 2014 compared to the level in 1990 and the global growth rate of IW was 44% over the indicated period, which implies an average growth rate of 1.8% per year. However, during the same period the global GDP growth per year was 3.4%, which is close to double the annual growth rate of IW.

In terms of IW per capita and IW per capita adjusted, 89 and 96 of the 140 countries saw increases over the study period compared to their levels in 1990.

The global level of growth of each of the three capitals over the study period indicates that produced capital was growing at an average rate of 3.8% per year and health and education induced human capital was growing at 2.1%. By contrast, natural capital was decreasing at a rate of 0.7% per annum.

An overview of the basis for wealth estimation explores how various types of conservation and development policies recognising the trade-off can be understood better with the help of IW. The findings also suggest that over the past 20 years the negative wealth effects of a decline in natural capital have been offset by growth in human and physical capital.

The IWR 2018 demonstrates that assessing and valuing natural capital and the change in per capita inclusive/comprehensive wealth over time has the potential to keep track of progress on most SDGs.

Global concerns towards unsustainability

It is important to understand the key global challenges societies are currently facing.

In the environmental dimension they refer to how human activities might have gone beyond consuming their 'own share' of natural resources and imposed a negative impact on ecosystems. Sustainability naturally implies setting up limits to guarantee individual survival and that of others whom a person interacts with. Therefore, environmental sustainability implies identifying limits within a given environment and respecting those limits.

In fact, the concept of 'ecological boundaries' is not new. The use of environmental limitations for socio-economic activities is considered part of a more complex assessment done by Meadows et al. (1972). King (1995) also suggested that environmental conditions should be constantly monitored to avoid ecological surprises (i.e. sudden changes that encourage environmental collapse). The idea of 'planetary boundaries' extends the argument in this direction and can influence the management of corporations (Whiteman et al., 2013) and their operations.

The planetary boundaries are:

- stratospheric ozone layer
- biodiversity
- chemicals dispersion
- climate change
- ocean acidification
- freshwater consumption and the global hydrological cycle
- land system change

- nitrogen and phosphorus inputs to the biosphere and ocean
- atmospheric aerosol loading.

The literature on sustainable development and sustainability management indicates the need to manage and measure sustainability performance by identifying system characteristics, e.g. its boundary and resource availability (Enfors, 2013), followed by the assessment of interventions to promote higher levels of resilience.

The importance of identifying thresholds within socio-ecological systems is vital to reducing their vulnerability to socio-economic and ecological crises (Young, 2010). Prior to the planetary boundaries approach, Meadows et al. (1972), Wackernagel and Rees (1998), and Meadows et al. (2004) used similar methods to assess the carrying capacity of our planet and the tipping points. Such studies sought to understand the complexity of societal, economic, and ecological systems and give an idea of the magnitude of the challenge of achieving sustainability at the global level.

Global sustainability can only be achieved by recognising political, legal, social, as well as technological challenges. As part of a study by the US National Academy of Engineering, an international group of leading technological thinkers were asked to identify the "Grand Challenges" for Engineering in the 21st century. They listed 14 game-changing goals for improving life on the planet, which were announced in 2008 as the Grand Engineering Challenges (NAE, 2008). These challenges cover the four broad themes of: Sustainability, Health, Security, and Joy of Living. They are:

- make solar energy economical
- provide energy from fusion
- develop carbon sequestration methods
- manage the nitrogen cycle
- provide access to clean water
- restore and improve urban infrastructure
- advance health informatics
- engineer better medicines
- reverse-engineer the brain
- prevent nuclear terror
- secure cyberspace
- enhance virtual reality
- advance personalised learning
- engineer the tools of scientific discovery.

Note the 14 challenges proceeded the SDGs by eight years but both have a large overlap and in practice the SDGs address some of these grand challenges.

Thus, organisations will need to rethink and adapt to foreseeable business and technological trends, sustainability policies and legislations, as well as being able to (quickly) react to unexpected changes that can hurt their business bottom line, their aptitude to respect environmental limits, and maintain a harmonious relationship with stakeholders.

Urgent sustainability pressures that can influence operations management include:

- climate change
- water, food, and energy

- waste materials
- biodiversity loss
- increasing social inequality
- premature health issues and preventable diseases (e.g. childhood obesity, diabetes, etc.)
- employment and work conditions
- quality of jobs.

The next section of this chapter introduces the concept of sustainable operations management.

Managing operations for sustainability

In its widest sense the operations function of an organisation is responsible for sourcing and transforming materials and other resources into goods and services that are delivered to end-customers. In most cases, it is the function that employs most people in an organisation. It is also considered to be the one with the largest negative environmental and social impacts, particularly in the manufacturing sector.

However, the operations function does not exist in isolation. There is a large interface between the management of operations and all the other organisational functions such as marketing, finance, human resources, and research and development (R&D). But, as a rule of thumb, it is the operations manager who will work on the allocation of resources to produce goods and services that meet the standards and objectives set within the organisation. This is because the operations function is concerned with transformation processes that consume large quantities of energy, water, and materials, and sometimes create risky working environments. Undesirable outputs of the operations function may include toxic and non-toxic wastes and pollutants.

The first important point to clarify is that operations management should not simply be reduced to the management of short-term operational activities. The management of operations includes three management levels: strategic, tactical, and operational. Strategic operations management refers to the development of resources and processes that impact the organisational capabilities and develop its long-term competitiveness. It is concerned with resource allocation in the areas of capacity management, supply networks, process technology, 'development and organisation', as well as how these areas impact on key performance objectives such as quality, speed, dependability, flexibility, and cost. The tactical level usually refers to monthly or weekly production planning and the operational level is concerned with daily routines and procedures. Decisions and actions within these management levels need to be aligned when seeking a robust improvement to the operations function.

The scope of what is called the operations management function varies from company to company and even between authors and commentators. In this book, we will consider the wider perspective of operations management in which the scope of the function includes product design, facilities, supply chain and logistics, production (also called internal operations), sales and after sales, process technology, and reverse logistics. Other areas such as human resources and stakeholder management are also very important for sustainable operations management, although they do not have their own dedicated chapters in this book.

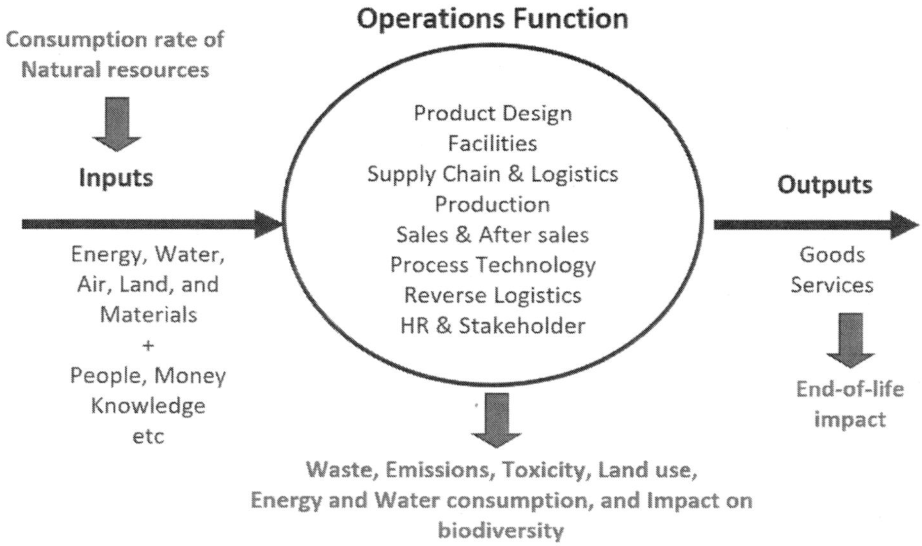

Figure 1.3 Input–output model for the sustainable operations function

The best way to represent the operations function is as an input–output model. The operations function is the transformation process that will take inputs such as people, money, raw materials, knowledge, energy, water (among others) and convert them into outputs that will be goods and services for consumption by customers (Figure 1.3).

The way sustainable operations management differs from traditional operations management is by considering sustainability elements as part of this input–output model. For instance, in a sustainable operations management model we will consider, in addition to the traditional operations management variables, other issues such as the consumption rate of natural resources on the input side. We should also be concerned with undesirable outputs such as waste, emissions, toxicity, energy and water consumption, and the impact processes and products have on biodiversity and the well-being of internal and external stakeholders. Last but not least, sustainable operations management will consider the environmental and social impacts as well as end-of-life of facilities, equipment, and products.

It is important to note that the scope of sustainability in operations management has been expanded from internal operations to the entire value chain. Thus, it is common that researchers in this area will investigate issues such as energy consumption or waste within links of the supply chain such as exploration and procurement of raw materials, and processing of virgin materials, beyond internal operations such as fabrication of key components and assembly. Some companies will pay particular attention to the sustainability performance of the product's use in the hands of customers. Finally, the destination of end-of-life products to reusing, remanufacturing, recycling, or their final disposal may also impact the way companies manage their operations. This is quite daunting in terms of management because, since the 1990s, there has been immense pressure to seek economies of scale and extend market reach, leading to globalisation of operations and supply chains.

BOX 1.3 ESSENTIAL CONCEPTS

Environment is the surroundings in which an organisation operates, including air, water, land, natural resources, flora, fauna, humans, and their interrelation (ISO 14001).

NOTE: surroundings in this context extend from within an organisation to the global system.

Environmental aspect: element of an organisation's activities, products, or services that can interact with the environment.

Environmental impact: any change to the environment, whether adverse or beneficial, wholly or partially resulting from an organisation's activities, products or services.

BOX 1.4 IS GLOBALISING OPERATIONS BAD FOR SUSTAINABLE DEVELOPMENT?

Whether or not to globalise their operations is a crucial and strategic aspect for organisations. Companies can globalise operations by procuring from foreign suppliers, exporting their own goods and services, establishing licensing or franchising agreements, developing partnerships, joint-ventures, or wholly owned facilities (e.g. warehouses, production plants, distribution centres, retail stores, after-sales support, etc.). The motivations to globalise operations are usually linked to overcoming market imperfections such as high tariffs on imports/exports. It is also justified as a reason for accessing new markets or resources (e.g. low-cost labour), in a country which differs from your own. Global companies are often 'accused' of promoting rapid degradation of pristine environmental areas in developing countries, lacking commitment to the preservation of environmental resources, and increased transport emission. The media also often voices how foreign operations exploit vulnerable communities, reduce cultural diversity, and contribute to instable economic growth.

The relationship of globalisation and sustainable development is, however, not one-sided and much more complex than what it may appear. By globalising operations, organisations are creating jobs where they are most needed. In addition to job creation, when working conditions are globally standardised, companies provide improved productivity and efficiency in various industrial sectors and act as a key element for skills development and give wider access to essential products. Responsible companies can promote and share knowledge and technologies for sustainability globally, so enhancing their contribution to SDGs in various locations.

The OECD view on the impact of globalisation on the environment

Source: www.oecd-ilibrary.org/economics/economic-globalisation/what-is-the-impact-of-globalisation-on-the-environment_9789264111905-8-en

What is the impact of globalisation on the environment?

There's no single answer to that question. As a growth-stimulating factor, globalisation impacts on the environment. At the same time, thanks to globalised information and knowledge, the public is considerably more aware of ecological issues and this has generated greater mobilisation. Theoretically, resources can be used more rationally because of increased trade and investment. But for the moment, it seems that globalisation's negative environmental effects are more apparent. For example, increased pollution linked to transport immediately comes to mind.

Globalisation helped accentuate the major environmental damages we're experiencing today, even though it's only indirectly responsible. Some national, regional and international policies have attenuated the negative effects of globalisation on the environment. Some solutions can also be found in the mechanisms of globalisation itself. But while vital, political regulations and incentives are still lacking compared to the breadth and urgency of the challenges ahead.

(Brendan Gillespie, Head, Environmental Performances and Information division, OECD Environment Directorate)

BOX 1.5 TASK:

Research and reflect on the question: Can a company be 'sustainable' in an unsustainable national environment?

Complete the tasks below and answer the question:

Choose one of the following countries: Indonesia, Morocco, or Colombia.
List the benefits and negative impacts globalisation has brought into those countries. Use all dimensions of sustainability (economic, social, and environmental).
Which sectors would benefit from wider adoption of SOM practices? If you were an operations manager or sustainability manager in one of these sectors, what would you recommend for improving your organisation's sustainability performance?

So, what is sustainable operations management (SOM)?

Having consideration for the social, economic, and environmental dimensions of sustainable development, the literature offers the following definitions for sustainable operations management:

- Sustainable operations management (SOM) is the set of skills and concepts that allow a company to structure and manage its business processes to obtain competitive returns on its capital assets without sacrificing the legitimate needs of internal and external stakeholders and with due regard for the impact of its operations on people and the environment. (Kleindorfer et al., 2005)

- Sustainable OM as the pursuit of social, economic, and environmental objectives – the triple bottom line (TBL) – within operations of a specific firm and operational linkages that extend beyond the firm to include the supply chain and communities. (Walker et al., 2014)

In addition to providing an understanding of sustainable operations management, this book also offers a unifying concept of operations sustainability fitness which connects the purpose of SOM to space and time dimensions. Here, SOM is understood as the process to increase or maintain operations sustainability 'fitness' at appropriate levels according to the contextual requirements imposed by geographical and temporal aspects. Thus, operations sustainability fitness (OSF) can be defined as:

> The ability to meet their own needs to survive in the short and long term while respecting the environmental limits of both global and local systems when creating socio-economic value and addressing local and global societal needs.

The OSF concept is strongly influenced by the notion of collapse. So, it is the role of SOM to avoid contributing to undesirable corporate collapse as well as the collapse of the social–ecological field which it inherently depends upon. For this notion, SOM also has a role in creating a better alignment between the needs of the organisation (e.g. profit, market share, technology development, learning, and innovation) and the needs of society.

The OSF concept not only gives a more dynamic view of external and internal demands but also explicitly inserts the needs of society and the limits of the environment as crucial inputs for sustainable operations strategy and management.

Implications for operations performance

For companies, this implies rethinking established methods of production and consumption, as well as relationships with suppliers and customers, among other changes. Naturally, the way performance is measured will also need to change. A popular way to measure corporate performance and connect it to strategy implementation is the 'Balanced Scorecard' proposed by Kaplan and Norton (1996). A Balanced Scorecard is composed of four perspectives, namely: Financial, Customer, Internal Processes, and 'Learning and Innovation'. Each of them has key specific performance metrics that are linked through a logical cascading method that starts from the Finance perspective and ends at Learning and Innovation.

Internal processes and development perspectives are the ones most relevant to operations management. Historically, there are five traditional operations performance objectives at strategic level: Quality, Cost, Speed, Dependability, and Flexibility. These are then cascaded into key performance indicators at the tactical and operational levels, such as percentage defective products, unitary cost, percentage of on-time delivery, etc. The traditional approach to measuring performance also covers the economic dimension. But to incorporate the values of sustainability into operations management, performance objectives, and key performance indicators, environmental and social factors must also be added within a formal performance measurement system. Examples of these measures include but are not limited to:

Environmental	*Social*
Total water use	Wage level
Fresh water use	Work satisfaction
Recycled water use	Gender and ethnic equality
Quality of water	Number of employees
Total material use	Number of high-skilled employees
Hazardous material use	Accidents
Toxic material use	Injuries
Total energy use for production	Fatalities
Total energy use not for production	Absenteeism
Renewable energy use for production	Noise
Fuel, gas, coal use for production and non-production activities	Dust
	Toxic substances
Air emissions (GHG, NOX, SO_2, ODS)	Safety expenditure
Volume of waste water	
Hazardous and non-hazardous solid waste	
Environmental accidents, fines, certification	
Cost of compliance	

Conclusion

It is important to locate and study operations management within its actual physical context. The operations of an organisation often happen within, and impact on, a local community which exists in the natural environment. The interdependence between environment–society–economy–firm is a key issue to consider when managing operations for sustainability.

While the addition of environmental and social measures is an imperative for sustainable operations management, the understanding of macro trends and direction of travel precedes the choice of practices and selection of performance indicators. The next two chapters on circular economy and sustainable operations strategy will complete Part I of the book, and thereby reinforce the awareness of those macro processes and long-term plans that organisations need to navigate, and also to survive, the social–ecological changes.

References

Clark, G (2007). Evolution of the global sustainable consumption and production policy and the United Nations Environment Programme's (UNEP) supporting activities. *Journal of Cleaner Production, 15*(6), 492–498.

Ehrenfeld, J. R. (2008a). *Sustainability by Design*. New Haven, CT: Yale University Press.

Ehrenfeld, J. R. (2008b). Sustainability needs to be attained, not managed. *Sustainability: Science, Practice and Policy, 4*(2), 1–3, DOI: 10.1080/15487733.2008.11908016

Enfors, E. (2013). Social–ecological traps and transformations in dryland agro-ecosystems: Using water system innovations to change the trajectory of development. *Global Environmental Change, 23*(1), 51–60.

Hammond, G. P., & Winnett, A. B. (2009). The influence of thermodynamic ideas on ecological economics: An interdisciplinary critique. *Sustainability*, *1*(4), 1195–1225.

ISO. (2004). *ISO 14004:2004 Environmental Management Systems: General Guidelines on Principles, Systems and Support Techniques*. Geneva, Switzerland: International Standards Organization.

Kaplan, R. S., & Norton, D. P. (1996). Linking the balanced scorecard to strategy. *California Management Review*, *39*(1), pp.53–79.

King, A. (1995). Avoiding ecological surprise: Lessons from long-standing communities. *Academy of Management Review*, *20*(4), 961–985.

Klassen, R. D., & MacLauglin, C. P. (1996). The impact of environmental management on firm performance. *Management Science*, *42*(8), 1199–1214.

Klassen, R. D., & Whybark, D. C. (1999). The impact of environmental technologies on manufacturing performance, *Academy of Management Journal*, *42*(6), 599–615.

Kleindorfer, P. R., Singhal, K., & Wassenhove, L. N. V. (2005). Sustainable operations management. *Production and Operations Management*, *14*(4), 482–492.

Lalwani, S. K., Nunes, B., Chicksand, D., & Boojihawon, D. K. R. (2018). Benchmarking self-declared social sustainability initiatives in cocoa sourcing. *Benchmarking: An International Journal*, *25*(9), 3986–4008.

Malthus, T. R. (1798). *An Essay on the Principle of Population, as It Affects the Future Improvements of Society, with Remarks on the Speculations of Mr. Godwin, Mr. Condercet, and other Writers*. London, UK: J. Johnson in St Paul's Church-yard.

Meadows, D. H., Meadows, D., Randers, J., & Behrens III, W. W. (1972). *The Limits to Growth: A Report to the Club of Rome's Project on the Predicament of Mankind*. New York: Universe Books.

Meadows, D. H., Randers, J., & Meadows, D. (2004). *Limits to Growth: Limits to Growth*. London: Earth Island Ltd.

Mebratu, D. (1998). Sustainability and sustainable development: Historical and conceptual review. *Environmental Impact Assessment Review*, *18*(6), 493–520.

NAE (2008). *NAE Grand Challenges for Engineering, National Academy of Sciences, on behalf of the National Academy of Engineering (Updated 2017)*. http://www.engineeringchallenges.org

Nunes, B. T. (2011). *Greening Operations: An Investigation of Environmental Decision Making* (Doctoral dissertation, Aston University).

Nunes, B., & Bennett, D. J. (2010). Green operations initiatives in the automotive industry: An environmental reports analysis and benchmarking study. *Benchmarking International Journal*, *17*(3), 396–420.

Nunes, B., Alamino, R. C., Shaw, D., & Bennett, D. (2016). Modelling sustainability performance to achieve absolute reductions in socio-ecological systems. *Journal of Cleaner Production*, *132*, 32–44.

Olawumi, T. O., & Chan, D. W. (2018). A scientometric review of global research on sustainability and sustainable development. *Journal of Cleaner Production*, *183*, 231–250.

Tukker, A., Emmert, S., Charter, M., Vezzoli, C., Sto, E., Munch Andersen, M., Geerken, T., Tischner, U., & Lahlou, S. (2008). Fostering change to sustainable consumption and production: An evidence based view. *Journal of Cleaner Production*, *16*(11), 1218–1225.

UN (2015). *The Global Goals for Sustainable Development*. New York: United Nations. https://www.globalgoals.org/

UNEP (2018). *Measuring Sustainability and Well-Being, Inclusive Wealth Report 2018*. Nairobi, Kenya: United Nations Environment Programme.

UNU-IHDP, & UNEP (2012). *Inclusive Wealth Report 2012. Measuring Progress Toward Sustainability*. Cambridge: Cambridge University Press.

Wackernagel, M., & Rees, W. (1998). *Our Ecological Footprint: Reducing Human Impact on the Earth*. Philadelphia: New Society Publishers.

Walker, H., Seuring, S., Sarkis, J., & Klassen, R. (2014). Sustainable operations management: Recent trends and future directions. *International Journal of Operations & Production Management*, 34(5). https://doi.org/10.1108/IJOPM-12-2013-0557.

WCED, World Commission on Environment and Development (1989). *Our Common Future*. Oxford: Oxford University Press, 1987.

Whiteman, G., Walker, B., & Perego, P. (2013). Planetary boundaries: Ecological foundations for corporate sustainability. *Journal of Management Studies*, *50*(2), 307–336.

Young, O. R. (2010). Institutional dynamics: Resilience, vulnerability and adaptation in environmental and resource regimes. *Global Environmental Change*, *20*(3), 378–385.

2 Towards a circular economy

This chapter presents the topic of circular economy and its main associations with the sustainable operations and supply chain management discipline. It is a relatively new area within the subject of operations management that is based on the principles of designing out waste and pollution, keeping products and materials in use, and regenerating natural systems. It contrasts with the traditional view of a linear economy based on "make", "use", "dispose".

The key learning outcomes of the chapter are:

- to develop awareness of the economic, environmental, and social sustainability dimension of the circular economy;
- to highlight the differences between circular and linear economy practices;
- to understand the challenges of implementing the circular economy.

Introduction to the circularity principle

At the end of the 18th century, the French chemist and biologist Antoine de Lavoisier concluded from his many studies that "in nature, nothing is created, nothing is destroyed, but everything is transformed". At that time, little did he know that this very important finding would become the classic Law of Conservation of Mass in modern chemistry, which helped us to understand how nature works in terms of maintaining its resources.

Although Lavoisier was probably not thinking about economics, nor the modern concept of sustainable development, the conservation principle of his classic law provides a fundamental inspiration for the idea of a circular economy: an ideal concept where the *materials in everything we produce are not discarded or wasted, but reused or transformed for further use, in the form of either the same product or a different one, in many circular cycles of production and consumption* (EM Foundation, 2013).

This circularity principle is still far from being the predominant basis of the way our industries and societies produce and consume material resources. The reality is that the current economy and related production and consumption systems are still predominantly linear, rather than circular.

The linear economy

The Industrial Revolution started at the end of the 18th century prompted radical changes in the economy, transforming agricultural and artisanal production eventually into

DOI: 10.4324/9781003009375-3

large-scale manufacturing systems enabled by highly mechanised factories. Since then, demand for industrialised products has been continuously growing, not only because of the natural growth of populations, but also because of the practicalities, convenience and innovations that come together with them.

As a response to increasing demand, industries focused on developing their capacity to produce at high volume and speed. To achieve such capacity, companies developed fast-paced production systems based on linear sequences of raw materials extraction, standardised production, and disposal methods after use. Centuries ago, the environmental impact of such systems was not a major concern. Over three centuries, this linear 'take–make–use–dispose' system of production and consumptionbecame the predominant standard for industries and societies, shaping the 'linear economy' context in which we live.

As shown in Figure 2.1, in a linear economy the material resources available at the end of a product's life cycle flow into landfill or incineration, instead of flowing 'back' into the economy for further cycles of reuse or reprocessing. The worrying reality is that our predominantly linear economy is generating too much waste as well as consuming too many resources. Taking agriculture as an example, about one-third of all food produced in the world ends up in landfill (Ishangulyyev et al., 2019). The waste from plastics in the linear economy is another major problem. The disposal of substantial amounts of plastics, including "microplastics", has achieved alarming levels of global pollution, making up 80% of all marine debris (Galafassi et al., 2019). The acclaimed BBC series Blue Planet II, narrated by Sir David Attenborough, provides vivid evidence of this problem, pointing out that marine life is seriously threatened by the 8 million tons of plastic waste that enter the oceans every single year.

Besides the problems mentioned above, there is the fact that the world's population is growing very fast, creating a continuous increase in the demand for food, durable goods, consumables, energy, etc. However, the Earth's resources are finite. This means that the availability of arable land, raw materials, water, fossil fuels, and other resources necessary for the production of food and all the items essential to our daily lives is limited. We are also consuming and polluting natural renewable resources such as clean water, air, timber, and so forth faster than the Earth's capacity to renew them.

In this context, relying on a predominantly linear economy is no longer a viable option. On one hand, we cannot carry on polluting the Earth's renewable resources at the current pace and volume. On the other hand, we cannot keep depending excessively on finite non-renewable resources such as fossil fuels, minerals, iron, and other metals. Many economies are realising that a shift from the linear to the circular economy is necessary to tackle these major problems.

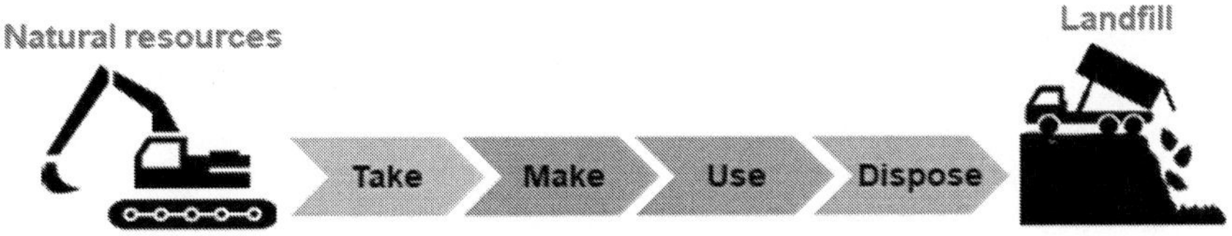

Figure 2.1 A linear production and consumption system

ADVANCE LONDON – STIMULATING AND SCALING CIRCULAR BREAKTHROUGHS

Adapted from Ellen MacArthur Foundation (www.ellenmacarthurfoundation.org)

To support small and medium-sized enterprises in the transition to a circular economy, London Waste and Recycling Board has created Advance London – a circular economy programme that offers business advisory services and investment guidance to SMEs that meet specific size, turnover, and focus criteria. Engagement with the SMEs is tailored to their individual activities, and includes exploring new circular economy markets, revenue streams, and business models. By transforming waste challenges into business opportunities, the work of Advance London also contributes to meeting the city's goal of zero waste to landfill by 2026.

Advance London is a three-year programme, running from January 2017 to December 2019. It will likely seek further funding to scale up support over a longer term following positive SME demand and impactful results.

Participating SMEs are addressing the five focus areas that were identified in London's Circular Economy Route Map issued in June 2017: built environment, food, textiles, electricals, and plastic.

By the end of 2018, Advance London had held five collaboration events with the aim of brokering relations between SMEs and corporates, as well as 20 technical learning workshops on topics such as an Access to Finance Masterclass, Compelling Communications for your Circular Innovations, and Design Thinking.

Advance London has also provided 700 hours of bespoke support to 112 SMEs. By December 2019, the programme aims to provide:

- 100 SMEs with at least three hours of bespoke support in the early stages of the programme, which includes eligibility assessment and circular diagnostics;
- 80 SMEs with at least 12 hours of bespoke support further along the programme, which includes growth and transition support for one in three SMEs engaged in the programme having secured grant, equity, or loan funding within 18 months of first receiving advice.

The programme also helped to facilitate 20 product–market collaborations which by the end of 2018 had generated five new circular products or services. These are:

- Pluumo, a unique thermal packaging material made from surplus feathers;
- CupClub™, a returnable packaging service designed for hot or cold drinks;
- expansion of OLIO, the food sharing app, to include local shops so that surplus food and other items can be shared rather than thrown away;
- launch of a refillable scheme for perfume bottles by 4160 Tuesdays, a London-based perfume manufacturer;
- launch of Biohm's small-scale production of mycelium (branching filaments of fungi) based construction products.

All businesses that become part of Advance London's programme receive between a minimum of three hours and ten days of bespoke support, ranging from advice on business models, to how to market and scale, or ways to obtain the finance appropriate to their goals and development stage. SMEs also receive invitations to workshops to build their capacity, and benefit from a range of networking and collaboration opportunities. SMEs that want to move forward with securing investment are put in touch with expert investors from the relevant stand-alone funds or are signposted to other funding opportunities.

Sustainability and the circular economy

Due to the problems mentioned above, a strong emphasis on developing the sustainability of organisations has been gradually changing the way businesses operate in the economy. Improving the sustainability of production and consumption systems is the main purpose of the circular economy. And to understand the circular economy it is important to first have a good understanding of 'sustainability'.

An important point to understand about sustainability is that it is not just about the environment. Sustainability, in its full meaning, involves the three important areas listed below:

1. **Economic sustainability**: Initiatives targeted to improve the financial health of organisations. Examples: cost minimisation; creation of income streams; improved cash flows; expansion of customer base; customer satisfaction; etc.
2. **Social sustainability**: Initiatives targeted to improve society. Examples: health and well-being; job creation; employee satisfaction; quality of life; equality and diversity; community engagement; etc.
3. **Environmental sustainability**: Initiatives targeted to improve the environment. Examples: minimisation of waste and pollution; preservation of materials and natural resources; energy conservation; better land use; etc.

John Elkington, a British entrepreneur and author who is well known for his works on corporate responsibility and sustainable development, coined the term 'triple bottom line' (TBL) (Elkington, 1998) to represent integrated business approaches that take into account the three key sustainability areas which overlap, as shown in Figure 2.2. Thus, the sustainability of a company should be measured not only in terms of its 'profit' performance (how financially healthy an organisation is), but also in terms of its 'people' (how socially responsible an organisation is) and 'planet' (how environmentally friendly an organisation is) performance.

The circular economy seeks to improve sustainability to its full extent across the three sustainability areas, minimising the trade-offs between them as much as possible. For example, *economic* improvements should not come at the cost of the environment and society. Similarly, *environmental* improvements should not come at the cost of the economy and society, and *societal* improvements should not come at the cost of the economy and the environment.

Circular economy practices

In contrast to the linear economy, the circular economy is a general approach to economic development aimed at eliminating waste and dissociating economic growth from the consumption of finite resources.

Figure 2.2 The triple bottom line dimensions of sustainability (based on John Elkington, 'Cannibals with Forks')

In practice, the circular economy is regenerative and restorative by purpose, where materials are kept in the economy at their highest utility for as long as possible (Webster, 2015). This places a crucial importance on the industry capability to recover used materials for further use or reprocessing cycles. More specifically, the restorative and regenerative capabilities of businesses refer to their capacity to restore (impart new life and vigour, promote recuperation) and regenerate (recuperate to a new, usually improved, state) materials (Esty and Simmons, 2011). Both concepts entail the 'recuperation' or recovery of materials for further use (Batista et al., 2018).

From a circular economy perspective, it is critical for industries to reduce the use of non-renewable resources and minimise the generation of waste across their production systems. There are many industrial sustainability practices encouraged by the circular economy; among them, recycling is one of the most well-known materials recovery activities that is largely associated with the circular economy. However, it is important to realise that the circular economy is not just about recycling products; other recovery practices are also critical. Table 2.1 provides a comprehensive list of key materials recovery practices encouraged by the circular economy, which include the traditional 'R' approaches of sustainability (Dossa et al., 2020).

The circular economy attaches a degree of preference to the recovery activities mentioned in Table 2.1, according to the impact they have on the Earth's resources. For example, recycling materials may require heavy industrial processing, which may involve substantial use of energy, water, heat, fuel, transportation, etc. In this case repairing products as many times as possible, before sending them for recycling, is a preferable option. This applies to all the other 'R' approaches. A general axiom of the circular economy is 'do not repair what can be reused, do not recycle what can be repaired, do not dispose what can be recycled'. This follows the classic hierarchy of waste materials shown in

Table 2.1 Restorative or regenerative practices in the circular economy (Batista, 2021)

Approach	*Practice involved*
Reduce	• Reduction of energy, water, and non-renewable raw materials in production processes. • Reduction of pollutants emission and generation of waste.
Refuse	• Refuse the use of materials that are difficult to repair or recycle. • Refuse the use of energy inefficient products. • Refuse products based on scarce natural resources.
Rethink (Redesign)	• Redesign processes to minimise generation of waste materials. • Design out waste from production and distribution processes. • Improve product utility, e.g. maximise utilisation via collaborative consumption. • Redesign products to use more recyclable components and resources.
Reuse	• Simple reuse of products and components as they are, with no modifications apart from cleaning processes before reuse.
Repair (including Refurbish and Remanufacture)	• Simple adjustments made to fix a fault in a product in order to bring it back to working order. • Aesthetic improvements (refurbishing) in a product in order to bring it to a renewed state, but with no addition of functionalities. • Application of manufacturing activities on an 'end-of-life' product (remanufacturing), through the reuse of as many parts as possible, in order to bring it to a 'like-new' state, which may involve improved functionalities.
Remanufacture	• Apply manufacturing processes to bring a used product to its 'as-new' state.
Recycle	• Transformation of used materials and waste into similar or different types of materials that can be used in the production of further products.
Recover (for energy)	• Conversion of waste into general energy resources such as heat, electricity, compost, fuel, and so forth, through thermal and biological transformations. It takes place after the traditional 3R approaches (reduce, reuse, recycle) have been attempted.

Figure 2.3. The pyramid is intentionally inverted to suggest that most of the activities in the circular economy should first aim at reducing the generation of waste and the use of non-renewable materials.

Not all activities mentioned above require manufacturing processes to be implemented. While remanufacturing and recycling processes usually involving industrial processing, reuse activities can be implemented through service-based businesses involving active participation of end consumers. There is a growing number of businesses creating opportunities for individuals to make their used assets available for further use by other individuals. Airbnb, eBay, Zipcar are typical examples of businesses facilitating consumer-to-consumer (C2C) transactions based on the 'reuse' practice. Through these businesses, consumers can rent or sell used assets (cars, rooms, apartments, electronics, clothing, etc.) to other consumers. The proliferation of such C2C business platforms enables the emergence of the 'sharing economy', which is an economic system based on the shared use (usually involving a fee) of underused assets or services directly from individuals (Belk, 2014). The sharing economy is an important movement towards consolidating the shift to a circular economy.

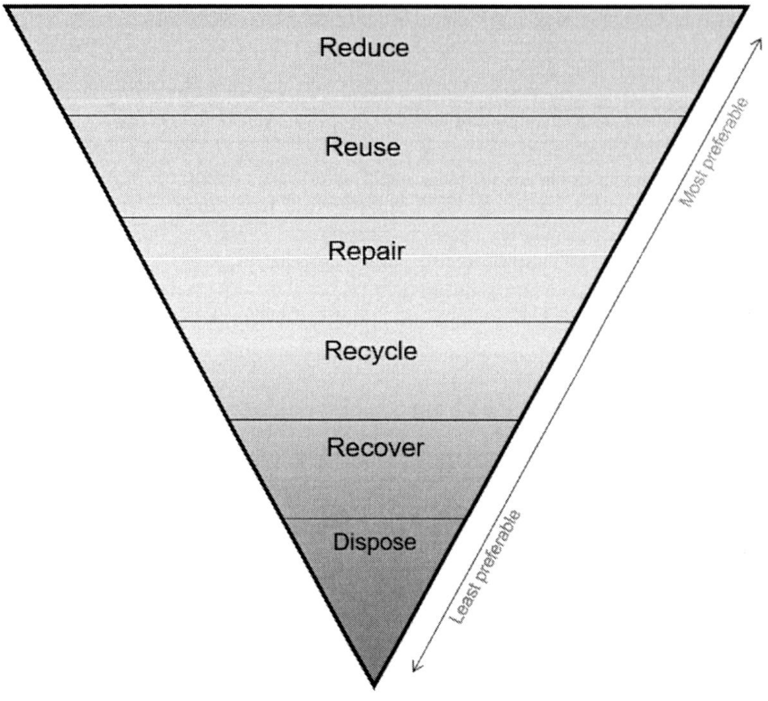

Figure 2.3 The waste hierarchy model

Circular flows in the circular economy

The materials recovery activities discussed in the previous section involve 'circular flows' of materials (products, by-products, components, waste, etc.) back to the economy. Such flows are preferable alternatives to material flows to landfill (disposals) and they are technically termed 'closed-loop' flows. Overall, they represent the essential 'circularity' feature that is characteristic of the circular economy.

In practice, the circular flows of materials in the circular economy are regenerative and restorative value chains which take place to recover two generic types of materials, namely: biological materials (of bio-organic nature) and technical materials (metals, minerals, and any other products of non-bio-organic nature) (EM Foundation, 2015). Such universal sub-division of circular flows in the circular economy are associated with specific 'R' approaches that are more commonly applied to implement closed-loop flows for biological and technical materials.

Key points (Batista, 2021)

1. The world's population is growing very fast, creating a continuous increase in the demand for food, goods, consumables, energy, etc. However, the Earth's resources are finite and we are consuming and polluting natural renewable resources faster than the Earth's capacity to renew them.

2. Relying on a linear economy is no longer sustainable. We cannot carry on polluting the Earth's renewable resources at the current pace and volume. Also, we cannot keep depending excessively on finite non-renewable resources.
3. The circular economy is based on the ideal of an economy where the materials in everything we produce are not discarded or wasted, but reused or transformed for further use, in the form of either the same product or a different one, in many circular cycles of production and consumption.
4. The circular economy seeks to improve sustainability across the three dimension of sustainability (economic, social, and environmental), minimising the trade-offs between them as much as possible, through triple bottom line approaches.
5. The circular economy attaches a degree of preference for the recovery activities based on 6R approaches. A general motto of the circular economy is 'do not repair what can be reused, do not recycle what can be repaired, do not dispose what can be recycled'.

Conclusion

Increasing pressure from governments and societies to more effective responses to climate change, associated with significant advancements in industrial technologies and business innovations, are accelerating the adoption of circular economy practices.

However, the implementation of the circular economy is not without its challenges. There is still a long way to go for our economy to become predominantly circular. Our production and consumption systems remain strongly rooted in linear economy models, with many inefficiencies across the three dimensions of sustainability. A clear understanding and awareness of the benefits of the circular economy is an important first step towards a more sustainable economy and society.

Questions (Batista, 2021)

1. **What are the main differences between the linear and the circular economy?**

   The linear economy is based on traditional 'take–make–use–dispose' models of production aimed at fast production systems based on linear sequences of raw materials extraction, standardised production, and disposal cycles after use. Quick cycles of production and consumption are key priorities. The material resources available at the end of a product's life cycle flow into landfills, instead of flowing 'back' into the economy for further cycles of reuse or reprocess.

   By its turn, the circular economy ideal is focused on the sustainability of production and consumption systems. It is an ideal where the materials in everything we produce are not discarded or wasted, but reused or transformed for further use, in the form of either the same product or a different one, in many circular cycles of production and consumption. Thus, the circular economy is regenerative and restorative by purpose. It aims to keep materials in the economy at their highest utility for as long as possible, in order to reduce the use of non-renewable resources and minimise the generation of waste.

2. **Explain why the triple bottom line sustainability approach proposed by John Elkington is relevant for the circular economy.**

The triple bottom line (TBL) approach to sustainability refers to integrated business approaches that take into account three key sustainability areas: economic, social, and environmental. From a TBL perspective, the sustainability of organisations should be measured not only in terms of its 'profit' performance (how financially healthy an organisation is), but also in terms of its 'people' (how socially responsible an organisation is) and 'planet' (how environmentally friendly an organisation is) performance.

The circular economy encourages TBL approaches, so that sustainability can be improved in its full extent, across the three sustainability areas (economic, social, and environmental), minimising the trade-offs between them as much as possible. In this sense, economic improvements should not come at the cost of the environment and society. Similarly, environmental improvements should not come at the cost of the economy and society.

3. **Discuss the main materials recovery practices encouraged by the circular economy and their relative implementation priorities.**

The materials recovery practices encouraged by the circular economy are mainly based on 6R initiatives (reduce, refuse, rethink, reuse, repair, recycle) plus 'recovery' of waste for energy if it cannot be used for the production of other materials.

The circular economy attaches a degree of preference or priority for the implementation of those activities. The reason for establishing a preference order for materials recovery activities is that some activities may require more resources than other activities to be implemented. For example, recycling materials may require heavy industrial processing involving substantial use of energy, water, heat, fuel, transportation, etc. In this case repairing products as many times as possible before sending them to recycle is a preferable option.

A general motto of the circular economy is 'do not repair what can be reused, do not recycle what can be repaired, do not dispose what can be recycled'. This follows the classic hierarchy model of waste materials.

References

Batista, L. (2021). What is circular economy? Exploring key concepts and practices. *Economic Review*, *38*(3), 2–6, Banbury - Oxfordshire: Hodder Education.

Batista, L., Bourlakis, M., Smart, P., & Maull, R. (2018). In search of a circular supply chain archetype: A content-analysis-based literature review. *Production Planning & Control*, Taylor & Francis, *29*(6), 438–451.

Belk, R. (2014). You are what you can access: Sharing and collaborative consumption online. *Journal of Business Research*, *67*(8), 1595–1600.

Dossa, A. A., Gough, A., Batista, L., & Mortimer, K. (2020). Diffusion of circular economy practices in the UK wheat food supply chain. Taylor & Francis, available at: https://doi.org/10.1080/13675567.2020.1837759.

Elkington, J. (1998). Accounting for the triple bottom line. *Measuring Business Excellence*, MCB UP Ltd, *2*(3), 18–22.

EM Foundation. (2013). Towards the circular economy: Economic and business rationale for accelerated transition. *Journal of Industrial Ecology*, *1*(1), 4–8.

EM Foundation. (2015). *Towards a Circular Economy: Business Rationale for an Accelerated Transition, Greener Management International.* Cowes, Isle of Wight: Ellen MacArthur Foundation, available at:https://doi.org/2012-04-03.

Esty, D. C., & Simmons, P. J. (2011). *The Green to Gold Business Playbook : How to Implement Sustainability Practices for Bottom-Line Results in Every Business Function.* Hoboken: Wiley.

Galafassi, S., Nizzetto, L., & Volta, P. (2019). Plastic sources: A survey across scientific and grey literature for their inventory and relative contribution to microplastics pollution in natural environments, with an emphasis on surface water. *Science of the Total Environment*, Elsevier, *693*, 133499.

Ishangulyyev, R., Kim, S., & Lee, S. H. (2019). Understanding food loss and waste: Why are we losing and wasting food?. *Foods*, *8*, 297, Multidisciplinary Digital Publishing Institute, Vol. 8 No. 8, p. 297.

Morseletto, P. (2020). Targets for a circular economy. *Resources, Conservation and Recycling*, Elsevier, *153*, 104553.

Potting, J., Hekkert, M., Worrell, E., & Hanemaaijer, A. (2017). *Circular Economy: Measuring Innovation in the Product Chain.* The Hague, available at: file:///C:/Users/batistal/Downloads/Circular (1).pdf. Accessed on 22 May 2021.

Webster, K. (2015). *The Circular Economy: A Wealth of Flows.* Cowes, Isle of Wight: Ellen MacArthur Foundation Publishing.

3 Sustainable operations strategy

Devising a strategy involves looking ahead, from beyond what can only be seen immediately within a company to what can be seen when looking beyond into the wider business environment. This chapter presents the topic of sustainable operations strategy. Sustainability issues have been regarded as an input to the operations strategy agenda for more than 20 years. The traditional operations strategy frameworks have usually addressed the sustainability dimension simply as a market requirement. However, sustainability demands are not always translated only into customer or market requirements. Therefore, this chapter will provide a unifying theory and framework that merges all the dimensions of sustainability: economic, social, and environmental. The chapter will set the scene for how all dimensions of sustainability need to be considered in the decision areas of operations strategy: capacity, supply network, process technology, and development and learning. It will also explore the formulation, implementation, and assessment elements of a sustainable operations strategy. The key learning outcomes of the chapter are:

- to assist the formulation of a sustainable operations strategy considering the context of the firm and where it operates;
- to appreciate concepts, models, and frameworks that make sustainable operations strategy more comprehensive, consistent/coherent, and robust at both local and global level;
- to develop a system of improvement and performance measurement to monitor the implementation of a strategy considering the different organisational contexts.

Introduction to the concept of strategy

What is a strategy?

We commonly used to hear the word 'strategy' in various fields of knowledge from business to sports as well as government plans to even non-human biological behaviour of animals and plants. But what does strategy actually mean?

Strategy is a word derived from the Greek *Stratēgia* or *Strategos*; which originally meant relating to 'the art of leading an army' or 'army leader'. Indeed, the origins of the word strategy are strongly related to military applications and competition in games. As a result, a good strategy is usually associated with the following characteristics:

- It focuses on long-term.
- It is hard to be imitated and creates unique value.

DOI: 10.4324/9781003009375-4

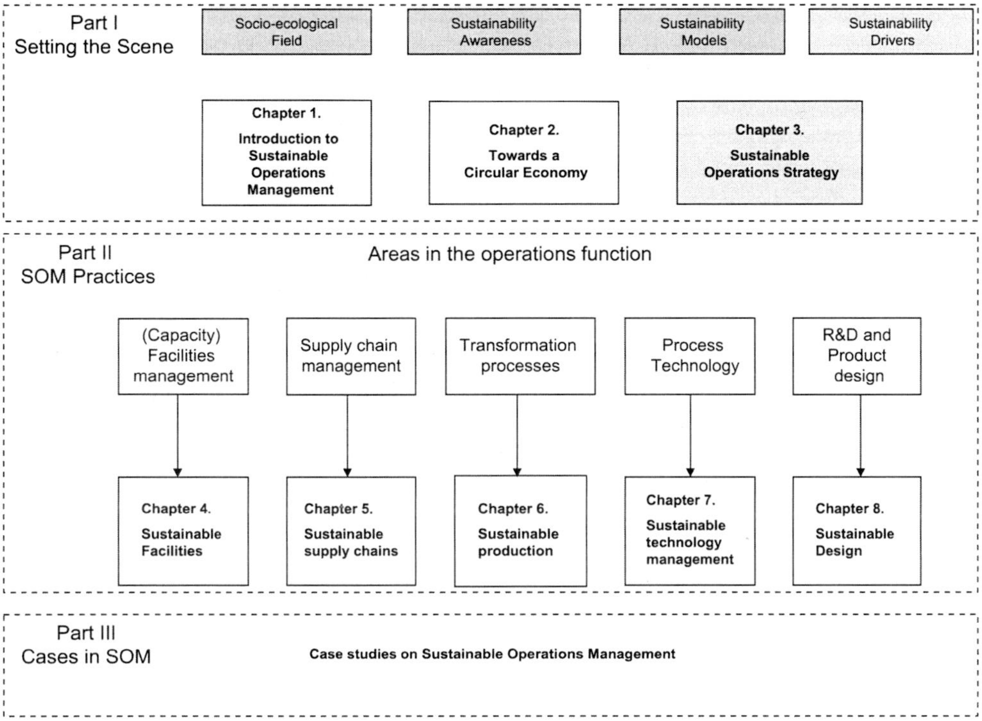

Figure 3.1 Chapter 3 within the book structure

- It provides a clear direction and permeates all levels of the entity being led.
- It makes, allocates, and develops competences and resources.
- It gives a better position against the competitors.

Although it is not so obvious from the above characteristics, strategies are not only about what to do and how to do key activities but also what NOT to do. The definition of scope and level of flexibility are part of strategic planning. Some organisations deliberately refrain from doing or becoming involved with those economic activities that are outside their core business, while others are open and embrace so-called 'unintended' or 'emergent' strategies. According to Canadian professor Henry Mintzberg, emergent strategies are key to the development of successful businesses:

> I have always argued that strategic planning is an oxymoron in the sense that strategies don't come out as formally planned processes. Most strategies and the 'interesting' strategies tend to emerge as people solve little problems and learn things.
>
> (Mintzberg in an interview at McGill University, Canada. Source: https://youtu.be/_NRWtd_SiU8).

In Mintzberg's view, the emergent strategy works as an alternative or a complement to deliberate strategy. So, how should we define a sustainable operations strategy?

Sustainable operations strategy is a deliberate or an emergent plan, focused primarily on the long-term, which aims at responding to sustainability pressures on products and production systems. It allows the organisation to meet its own needs and create socio-economic value while addressing local and global needs and respecting the environmental limits, both global and local.

A comprehensive sustainable operations strategy will consider decisions on capacity, supply networks, process technology, and the development and organisational aspects of the firm, including development of new products.

The formulation of a traditional operations strategy

Operations strategy is a functional strategy, and as such it usually derives from, and needs to be aligned to, corporate and business strategies. Corporate strategy is built predominantly upon financial measures to achieve growth, survival, profit, or return on investment. Business strategies relate primarily to business units and how they support the corporate strategy. They can be based on differentiation or low-cost competitive advantages. They are also commonly classified into two main groups – market based and resource based – as their approach to sustaining competitive advantage over time. As part of the strategy formulation process, corporate and business strategy will inform an operations strategy. Thus, an operations strategy should assess and position the operations to develop capabilities and resources and be able to deliver products and services that meet the market requirements, which in turn will sustain growth, survival, profit, or any other corporate objective.

Strategic alignment between corporate and business strategies and functional strategies is key to the successful development of a business. Ken Platts and Mike Gregory's audit procedure (Platts and Gregory, 1990) is a useful tool for the preliminary phases of operations strategy formulation. It recommends an initial evaluation of opportunities and threats alongside an assessment of what the market wants and how the operation performs in critical performance objectives, which is later contrasted against the current level of operations performance. The expected output of the Platts and Gregory procedure is a clear view of what needs to improve in the operations strategy (Figure 3.2).

Terry Hill's framework (Hill and Hill, 2009) is also a useful tool at the strategy formulation stage to align corporate objectives to marketing strategy and then to product strategy and finally to process choice and infrastructure decisions. Hill's concepts of order-winners and order-qualifiers remain relevant in the translation of customer requirements into product specifications, and hence, what characteristics (and strategy) the operation should have to meet those requirements now and in the future (Figure 3.3).

In addition to resource and market (customer requirements) perspectives, the process of operations strategy can be influenced by top-down and bottom-up perspectives (Slack and Lewis, 2020). From the top-down perspective, the vision of senior management is laid down and deployed onto the business function. On the other hand, in the bottom-up perspective, the strategy is influenced (or emerges) from day-to-day learning experiences of lower and middle managers (Figure 3.4).

Strategy can also be formulated through a performance-driven approach, considering the relative performance of the operation against key competitors. Slack and Lewis (2020) also suggest that Chief Operating Officers (COOs) should identify critical intersections between the decision areas (e.g. capacity, supply networks, process technology, and design

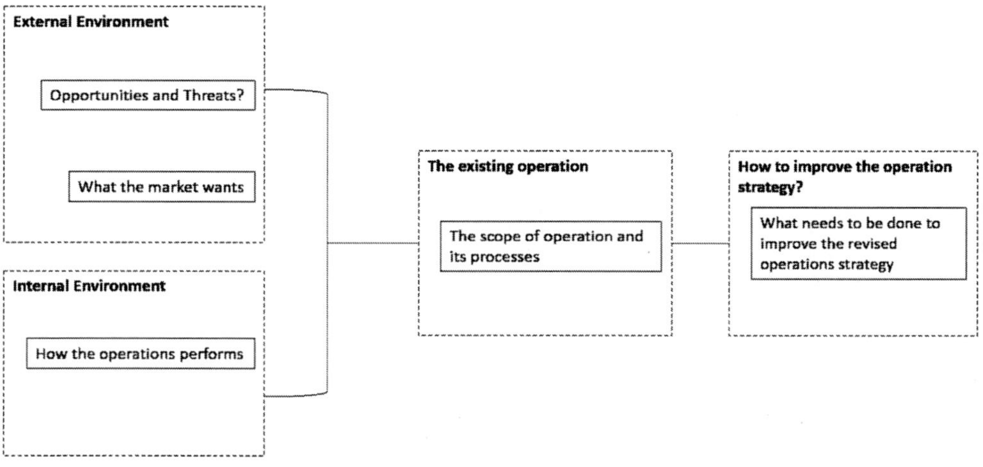

Figure 3.2 Conceptual basis for Platts–Gregory Procedure

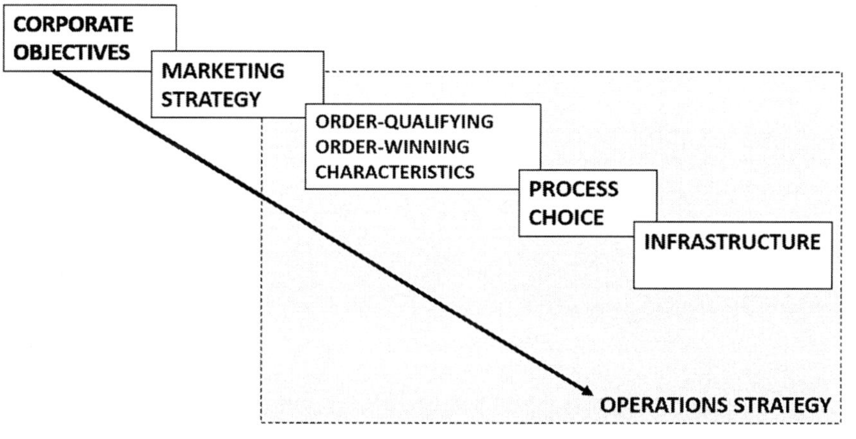

Figure 3.3 Operations strategy formulation using Hill's model

and organisation) and the traditional performance objectives (e.g. quality, speed, flexibility, dependability, and cost); while the performance–importance framework (Slack, 1994) will assist in identifying the need for urgent and critical improvement, and the operations strategy framework will help with recognising the decision areas and instructing strategic decisions and improving key performance objectives (Figure 3.5).

Making operations strategy formulation more sustainable

The traditional tools for operations strategy formulation remain important and necessary, particularly to improve operations performance and the survival of the firm, which

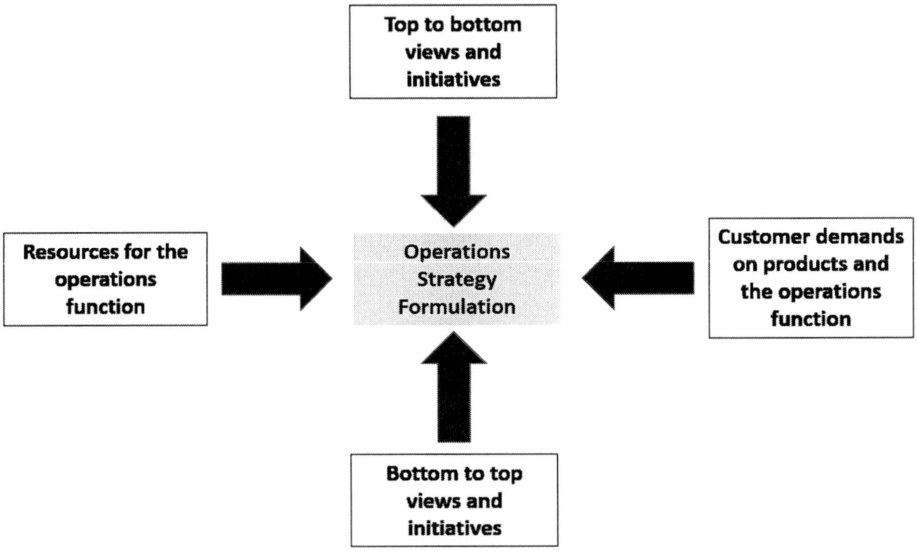

Figure 3.4 Dimensions of operations strategy

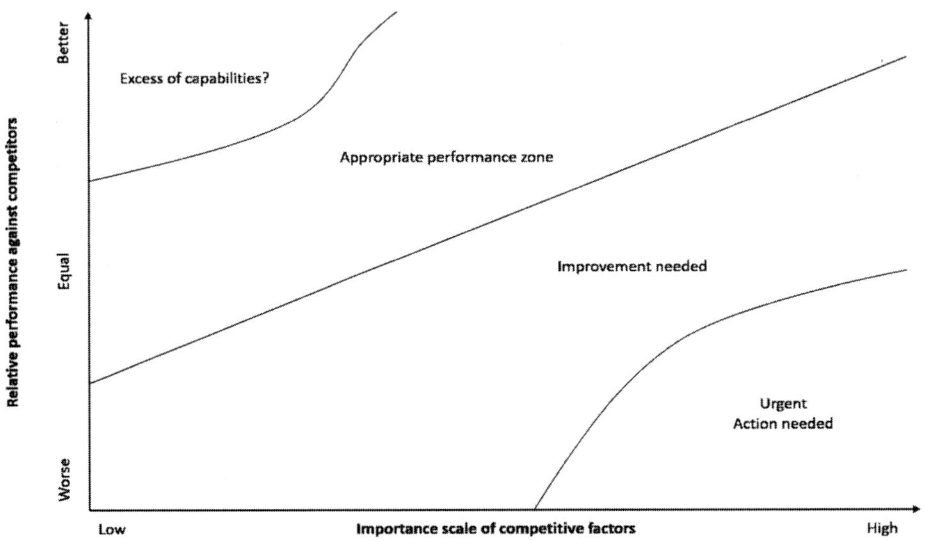

Figure 3.5 Assessing relative performance through Slack's importance–performance framework

is only one of the aspects of business sustainability. Thus, the traditional frameworks are unfortunately not sufficient to make an organisation fully aligned with the core values of sustainability, and therefore, they may limit the firm's contribution to SDGs.

The introduction of sustainability elements in the formulation process requires the use of additional tools and frameworks or adaptation of existing ones. For instance, addressing specific environmental and social opportunities and threats in the Platts and Gregory audit procedure mentioned above will make evaluation of the external environment more robust as it would cover all dimensions of sustainability (rather than solely focused on the economic dimension, i.e. market requirements).

Organisations interested in integrating social and environmental issues usually create environmental or sustainability departments and develop an environmental or sustainability policy/strategy. This is possibly a consequence of the need to adopt ISO 140001 environmental management standards which require companies to publicly commit to meeting the legislation, continuous improvement, and pollution prevention. But strategically, it is often criticised as being an 'add-on' and not aligned to corporate and functional strategies. Scholars from the field of environmental and sustainability strategy have suggested a different approach by combining business and sustainability elements into one single framework.

The Sustainable Value Framework (Hart and Milstein, 2003) is a good example of this. Four strategies are devised with consideration of the two dimensions of organisational environment (internal versus external) and time (today versus 'tomorrow') (Table 3.1).

Another widely cited business sustainability model has been developed by Professor Renato Orsato (Orsato, 2009). This builds on aspects of generic competitive advantage (differentiation or low-cost business strategies) associated with competitive focus (organisational processes or products – goods and services). Orsato suggests that organisations will build a sustainable competitive advantage by choosing their strategies based on contextual elements of their industrial sectors and internal capabilities for both processes and products. On the side of differentiation, some companies can lead the 'sustainability race' by exercising leadership in environmental and social aspects of their processes. Alternatively, they may prefer to appeal only to environmental or sustainable product niches. With the lower cost approach, they can compete by having the most eco-efficient processes or cost leadership of sustainable products. Orsato (2009) suggests a fifth strategy called a 'sustainable value innovation (SVI) strategy' aimed at new markets and influenced also by the firm's contribution to society (Table 3.2).

Table 3.1 Strategies in the 'Sustainable Value Framework' and their characteristics

Strategy	*Key drivers*	*Main objective*	*Corporate pay-off*	*Time dimension and focus*	*Perspective of firm*
Pollution prevention	Pollution Consumption Waste	Minimise waste and emissions from operations	Cost and risk reduction	Today (Present)	Internal
Clean technology	Disruption Clean Tech Footprint	Develop the sustainable competencies of the future	Innovation and repositioning	Tomorrow (Future)	Internal
Product stewardship	Civil Society Transparency Connectivity	Integrate stakeholder views into business process	Reputation and legitimacy	Today (Present)	External
Sustainability vision	Population Poverty Inequity	Create a shared roadmap for meeting unmet needs	Growth trajectory	Tomorrow (Future)	External

(Source: Hart and Milstein, 2003)

Table 3.2 Competitive sustainability strategies and their characteristics

<table>
<tr><th>Strategies</th><th>Competitive advantage</th><th>Competitive focus</th><th>Market orientation</th></tr>
<tr><td>Eco-efficiency</td><td>Lower cost</td><td rowspan="2">Organisational processes</td><td rowspan="4">Existing markets</td></tr>
<tr><td>Beyond compliance leadership</td><td>Differentiation</td></tr>
<tr><td>Environmental cost leadership</td><td>Lower cost</td><td rowspan="2">Products and services</td></tr>
<tr><td>Eco-branding</td><td>Differentiation</td></tr>
<tr><td>Sustainable innovation</td><td>Beyond the trade-off between low cost and differentiation. Based on customer needs (demand-oriented)</td><td>Beyond internal operations (upstream and downstream supply chains)</td><td>New markets</td></tr>
</table>

(Source: Orsato, 2009)

BOX 3.1 TESLA MOTORS – WWW.TESLA.COM/EN_GB/ABOUT

www.tesla.com/en_GB/blog/secret-tesla-motors-master-plan-just-between-you-and-me

Tesla was founded in 2003 by a group of engineers who wanted to prove that people didn't need to compromise to drive electric – that electric vehicles can be better, quicker, and more fun to drive than gasoline cars.

Launched in 2008, the Roadster unveiled Tesla's cutting-edge battery technology and electric powertrain. From there, Tesla designed the world's first ever premium all-electric sedan from the ground up – Model S – which has become the best car in its class in every category. Combining safety, performance, and efficiency, Model S has reset the world's expectations for the car of the 21st century with the longest range of any electric vehicle, over-the-air software updates that make it better over time, and a record 0–60 mph acceleration time of 2.28 seconds as measured by Motor Trend. In 2015, Tesla expanded its product line with Model X, the safest, quickest, and most capable sport utility vehicle in history that holds 5-star safety ratings across every category from the National Highway Traffic Safety Administration. In 2016, Tesla introduced Model 3, a low-priced, high-volume electric vehicle that began production in 2017. Soon after, Tesla unveiled the safest, most comfortable truck ever – Tesla Semi – which is designed to save owners at least $200,000 over a million miles based on fuel costs alone. In 2019, Tesla unveiled Model Y, a mid-size SUV, with seating for up to seven, and Cybertruck, which will have better utility than a traditional truck and more performance than a sports car.

Tesla vehicles are produced at its factory in Fremont, California, and Gigafactory Shanghai. To achieve their goal of having the safest factories in the world, Tesla require production employees to participate in a multi-day training programme before ever setting foot on the factory floor. From there, Tesla continues to provide on-the-job training and track performance daily so that improvements can be made quickly. The result is that Tesla's safety rate continues to improve while production ramps.

To create an entire sustainable energy ecosystem, Tesla also manufactures a unique set of energy solutions, Powerwall, Powerpack, and Solar Roof, enabling homeowners, businesses, and utilities to manage renewable energy generation, storage, and consumption. Supporting Tesla's automotive and energy products is Gigafactory 1 – a facility designed to significantly reduce battery cell costs. By bringing cell production in-house, Tesla manufactures batteries at the volumes required to meet production goals, while creating thousands of jobs.

In the words of Elon Musk:

So, in short, Tesla's "secret" master plan is:

- *Build sports car*
- *Use that money to build an affordable car*
- *Use that money to build an even more affordable car*
- *While doing above, also provide zero emission electric power generation options*
- *Don't tell anyone.*

Exercise: Discuss the connection between Tesla's strategy and SDGs. Analyse Tesla's sustainability strategy in the light of the models presented (Hart and Milstein, 2003; Orsato, 2009).

Drivers for operations sustainability

Readers of this text are now in a position to understand the motivations behind companies' sustainability initiatives. The drivers of sustainability that lead to changing products and processes may ultimately influence location choice, production capacity of plants, selection of suppliers, and development of technologies and capabilities.

The literature concerning the main sustainable operations management (SOM) drivers converges with those found in corporate sustainability studies. The literature identifies the main drivers for businesses sustainability: international, industry, or business agreements, legislation, investors, internal policy, customers, performance-related issues, competitors, reputation/image, and advocacy groups (Table 3.3).

Table 3.3 Drivers for sustainability

External drivers	International agreements
	Legislation and regulations (national, state, city)
	industry or business standards
	Investors
	Customers and consumers
	Advocacy groups
	Competitors
Internal drivers	Internal policy and employees
	Performance-related issues
	Reputation/image

International agreements and industry standards: international agreements such as the Paris Agreement to reduce the emissions of greenhouse gases can lead to both voluntary action in businesses and development of stricter national environmental legislation. Likewise, signatory countries to the Human Rights Declaration should actively avoid modern types of slavery, which in turn may change organisations' practices. Animal rights NGOs can also drive third-party assessment of organisations and propose international agreements, labels, or certifications for companies that follow certain values (e.g. cruelty-free cosmetics, etc.). In addition to international agreements, industry forums or even local business associations may create agreements and standards (e.g. organic production) that trigger the adoption of sustainable operations practices.

Legislation and regulations: In the United Kingdom, legislation is a law or a set of laws that have been passed by Parliament. The word is also used to describe the act of making a new law. In other countries, like the United States, businesses need to pay attention and conform to various levels of legislation, for example: federal, state, and local (municipal). Government regulation is also a key driver for change. The Encyclopaedia Britannica defines regulation as "a rule or mechanism that limits, steers, or otherwise controls social behaviour". According to the UK National Audit Office, regulation is used to protect and benefit people, businesses, and the environment and to support economic growth. For instance, there are more than 90 regulatory bodies in the United Kingdom, with total expenditure in excess of GBP 4 billion a year. They cover a wide range of areas, from education, healthcare, and charities to transport, communications and the media, utilities and the environment. For the US Environmental Protection Agency, regulations explain the technical, operational, and legal details necessary to implement laws. As a result, regulations should also be considered as a driver for sustainable operations strategy. In fact, meeting the relevant legislation is a key aspect of many certification schemes in the sustainability area.

Investors: An investor is understood here to be any person or entity that makes a capital investment in an organisation, including banks, governments (through incentives), independent funders, donors, and sponsors, parent companies, venture capitalists, angel investors, crowd funding sources, etc. Investments are usually allocated in the build-up of new facilities, development of new products, acquisitions, and plant improvements, among other options. Increasingly, investors are including a socio-environmental analysis or impact assessment as part of their investment decisions. It is normal nowadays that investments are tied up with sustainability requirements such as choice of greener technology and materials, or job creation for both skilled and unskilled labour force. As a driver, organisations may engage in a sustainability journey because of the values and conditions imposed by investors.

Internal policy: While agreements, legislations, clients, and (some) investors are external drivers, companies can also drive a change for sustainability from within. Visionary leaders can develop an internal policy that drives changes towards a higher sustainability performance of the operations function. A bottom-up perspective is also fairly common in which employees identify the direction in which the operations must go to be more sustainable.

Customers and consumers: Customers or clients are those who pay for the goods or services and consumers are those who use them. Both groups can require changes in products or processes. They may also request sustainability data from organisations which can lead to transformational change and improved performance in the operations function. Both groups can suspend purchase, actively suggest boycotts, and enhance societal awareness if such requirements are not met.

Economic performance and related issues: Not all sustainability initiatives are driven by ecological or social motivation. For example, several initiatives may be the result of an attempt to improve economic performance. Often companies that want to reduce cost will aim at reducing waste, which can be a part of, or overlap with, an environmental programme (e.g. water and energy conservation, waste reduction, etc). For companies at the beginning of their journey towards a higher sustainability performance, these win–win solutions are very important and strategic. There will eventually be trade-offs with traditional performance measures (cost, speed, quality, flexibility, and dependability), but frequently sustainability initiatives tend to improve productivity and efficiency while enhancing sustainability performance measures such as pollution prevention, indoor environmental quality, personnel safety, etc. Being ahead with green technology development can also be an economic driver for sustainable operations management.

Competitors: As sustainability criteria become a standard in purchasing decisions, companies also start competing through their sustainability performance measures. This is still limited as a differentiating factor, but very visible in some market niches that are strongly associated with sustainability values (e.g. sustainable cosmetics, organic food, etc.). In the mainstream marketplace, competition can lead to stricter environmental and social criteria so as to be order qualifiers, i.e. a criterion that makes a company as an eligible supplier for a given order. Leading companies play a fundamental role in both contexts. They may be able to set industry benchmarks and standards, influence legislation, and create greater customer awareness of industry sustainability issues.

Reputation/image: In today's competitive environment, companies spend large amounts of money to build a strong brand image and reputation. Several companies (i.e. mainly those listed on the stock market) have their valuation linked largely to intangible assets and brand value. Now, to be seen as a contributor to the unsustainability of the planet can have severe impact on company value. Loss of reputation can prevent firms from gaining investment, reduce chances of collaborating with competitors and suppliers, create friction with local communities, as well as impacting on their relationship with customers and regulators and other key stakeholders. Thus, firms may invest in sustainability initiatives to not only reduce their negative environmental and social impacts, but also to enhance their image and reputation. Lastly, even companies in sectors with notably significant negative contributions will make these investments as an attempt to alleviate reputational damage when possible failures happen in their operations. Such companies may include those possibly contributing to the emission of greenhouse gases, loss of biodiversity, and pollution of local ecosystems (such as mining, oil and gas, industrialised farming, etc.), as well as those that are vulnerable to child labour and modern slavery in their supply chains,

Advocacy groups: Last but not least, advocacy groups have been found as the reason why companies embark on an organisational change that includes adoption of SOM practices. Advocacy groups can expose environmental failures or poor performance on social performance metrics, which can lead to reputational damage, customer boycotts, and loss of investment. At a functional level, the chances of operations and supply chain disruption may increase due to campaigns or protests organised by advocacy groups. But not all advocacy groups' actions are aimed at exposing corporate failure and disruption of operations and supply chains. Many groups may have constructive ideas, suggestions, and recommendations that companies can use and be able to help the sustainability agenda with feasible solutions.

In practice, it is likely that companies will plan and implement sustainability initiatives based on a strategy that identifies the influence of various drivers simultaneously. So, the list in Table 3.3 should not give the impression that the drivers act in isolation. On the contrary, some issues may be entangled in a way that various drivers are involved. Consider for instance a company that for some reason has broken the legislation in an area of their operations (e.g. grey water treatment). That action can lead to loss of environmental label/certification, which in turn can make them lose customer orders. It may also create bad publicity and the firm can attract the attention of advocacy groups and therefore be more vulnerable to public exposure in future failures. Likewise, one driver may deliberately overtake the role of another driver. For example, in a company in which the internal policy or sustainability strategy is to be ahead of legislation or competitors. It is also normal that ethical behaviour of firms should be considered beyond the law, so firms relying on market niches whose customers have higher ethical standards or expectations would preferably tend to follow customers' pressures rather than be limited by legislation targets.

In addition, some stakeholders may create opposing forces for a particular organisational change. Companies that make decisions based solely on one driver or stakeholder (e.g. an advocacy group) will follow a path that may not be acceptable to other stakeholders (e.g. suppliers and customers). The views and relationship between the different stakeholders will directly influence the level of complexity in the formulation of a sustainable operations strategy.

Nevertheless, any response to the pressures from different groups is likely to impact on the management of operations or influence the adoption of sustainable practices (Figure 3.6).

Sustainable operations practices

The adoption of sustainable operations practices must support the implementation of a sustainable operation strategy. Sustainable operations practices are the response to the pressures from drivers detailed in the previous section. The terminology around these practices varies a lot, as much in academia as in business practice. Hence, before the sustainable operations practices are presented, their scope and decision rationale will be examined.

Lately, the scope of sustainability analysis has gone beyond the tactical and operational management levels and internal activities. It has become more long-term oriented (i.e. strategic), influenced by multiple external stakeholders, and finally, reaching beyond the geographical area where the internal operations take place (e.g. scrutiny of raw material supply from the least developed countries). This trend certainly increases the complexity and uncertainty of SOM decisions. Other business trends (e.g. market specialisation, offshoring, and outsourcing) can create further difficulties for evaluating and managing business sustainability performance in key operations strategy decision areas (e.g. capacity, supply network, process technology, development, and organisation).

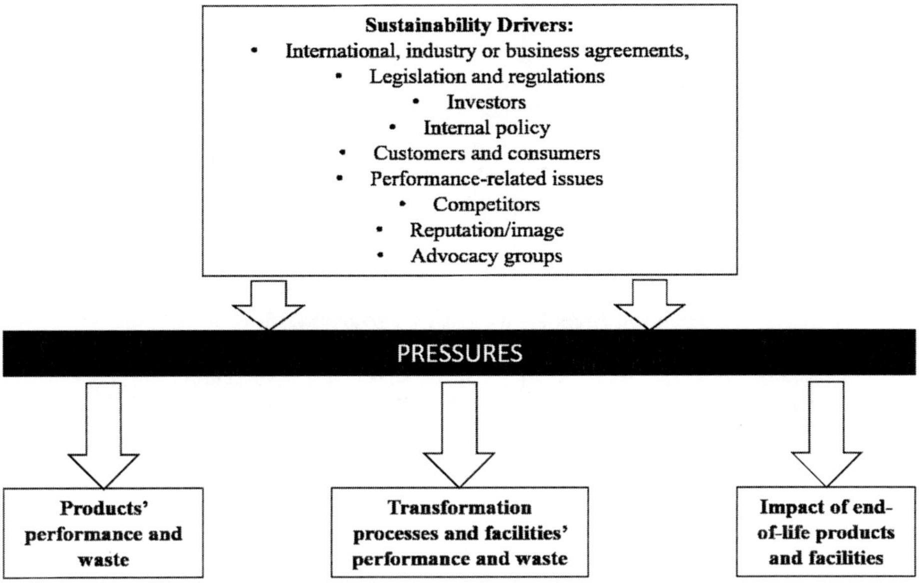

Figure 3.6 Sustainability drivers and pressures on product, process, and end-of-life

So, the first step companies need to take in making operations strategy more sustainable is to add environmental and social criteria to strategic decisions in OM (as suggested in the previous section "Formulation of a traditional operations strategy"). These socio-environmental criteria are usually linked to sustainability performance metrics and drivers, which will then instruct the implementation of the strategy through the adoption of sustainable operations practices.

Various previous authors have classified different sustainable (and environmental/green) operations practices. But by compiling their studies, sustainable operations practices can be presented into four main areas: (1) sustainable buildings (facilities management); (2) sustainable supply chains (inbound and outbound logistics, and supplier relationships, including reverse logistics – which is the backwards flow of materials and end-of-life products); (3) sustainable production processes (transformation processes, including the choice and development of process technologies); (4) sustainable design (product and process development, including innovation).

Figure 3.7 shows three decision levels for a sustainable operations strategy.

Given the increasing importance of sustainability issues, the recent development of SOM tools has led to a better accommodation of environmental and social responsibility aspects with traditional operations strategy goals, i.e. optimal capacity utilisation, long-term profitability, effective supply network, development of process technologies, and introduction of new products. However, this has also led to an increasing number of organisational trade-offs beyond the contrasting objectives of cost performance *versus* quality levels, flexibility *versus* speed, etc.

It is vital that sustainability initiatives are performed strategically and permanently in business operations. Having sustainability as a simple 'add-on' to the operations

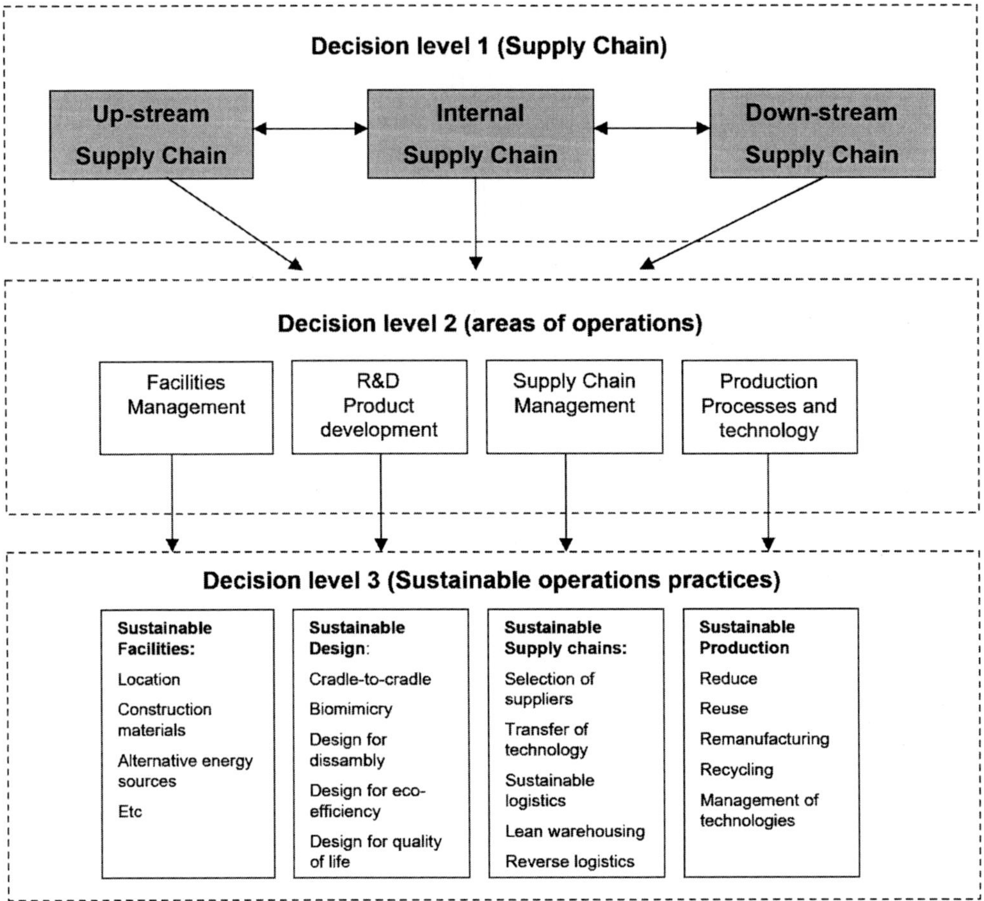

Figure 3.7 Decision levels for sustainable operations strategy

management agenda can backfire, making the organisation spend resources without obtaining the benefits.

Corporate Social Responsibility strategy

The concept of Corporate Social Responsibility (CSR) has been on the management agenda for more than 50 years. Bowen (1953) is considered one of the first to highlight its importance and it is commonly used interchangeably with the Social Sustainability of Business. In subsequent years, many theorists have continued to debate the topic and differing schools of thought about CSR still exist. There are those who believe it is an essential aspect for the longevity of firms; while others will claim the main role of the business is simply to make a profit. The latter are largely influenced by the views of Milton Friedman and his principles on neoliberalism and management (*The purpose of a firm is to increase its profits*). In their view, being profitable may be the best guarantee of the long-term survival of the firm, and as a result their social contribution in creating and maintaining jobs as well as distributing wealth is sustained. It is true that the relationship between financial performance and social responsibility actions remains uncertain and largely inconclusive. Nevertheless, companies seem to assess that the risks of not taking CSR seriously at board level are higher than the investments in the area (e.g. because of reputational risk, supply chain disruption, etc.).

Therefore, in practice, most large firms have taken steps towards accommodating sustainability and social responsibility in the strategic agenda and the top of their organisation structures.

BOX 3.2 EXERCISE

We invite you to choose one of your favourite companies in three different industrial sectors of your choice. Do they have a Chief Sustainability Officer? Do they publish an annual sustainability, environmental, or social sustainability report? Do they mention sustainability values, principles, performance, or initiatives in their websites?

Despite the uncertainties, several investors have assigned significant weight to the CSR efforts of the company and considered it as a parameter for investment. Thus, these efforts are now thought about with a strategic perspective and are among the main priorities for business leaders.

In recent times this is particularly important because of the level of information sharing between the economies of the West and the East, or the developed and developing countries. With the help of the growing globalised media and the internet, unethical social practices that may exist in global supply chains of multinational companies have been highlighted. Consequently, the general public has become more aware of the origin of goods and the conditions under which they are produced. NGOs and the media have become adept at targeting companies concerning the social consequences of their business activities and this leads to boycotts by the consumer. Nike probably represented one of the most popular cases of social misconduct in supply chains after it faced severe criticism when the media revealed the working conditions in its sweatshops in Indonesia. However, it is the agricultural supply chains that are still found to be the main source of modern slavery and child labour. The sector has reacted with labelling and certification tactics to address the problem. But these are not always enough. Associated with these solutions, there is always the risk that the certification actions are interpreted differently by other stakeholders as being a mere marketing or public relations investment which can turn into reputational damage. To avoid that happening, companies need to be transparent and avoid being inconsistent with their action across countries, areas of operations, etc. Today, as a response to this criticism, Nike's website provides a great deal of transparency about who its suppliers are, where they operate, how many employees they have in each facility, as well as the percentage of females and migrants in the work line (see: http://manufacturingmap.nikeinc.com/).

Not surprisingly, companies have become extremely careful and prudent about their sustainability efforts – and certainly with good reason. Implementing strategic CSR has been found to be very complex in practice. In the recent past, companies in the agricultural sector such as Dole and Del Monte have shown little interest in signing global union agreements to provide further protection to plantation workers because there are uncertainties around the business rewards from adopting more ethical practices, as has been shown by *The Economist* magazine (*The Economist*, 2012).

Large organisations have extended their social responsibilities to their supply chains to embrace critical links in the entire life cycle of their production process, i.e., processing of the raw material at the initial stage to the final delivery of the finished product. Assisting local communities and global philanthropy have also gained importance. Two frameworks can assist companies in planning these actions strategically. First, the Strategic CSR (Shared Valued) model by Porter and Kramer (2011) suggests that companies should assess their current socio-environmental impact and make a societal contribution in areas where they are most competent.

Second, Prahalad and Hart (2002) believe firms should adapt their products and technologies to serve the 'Bottom of the Pyramid'. There are between 2 and 4 billion people without proper means that spend USD 2 per day. They constitute a large business opportunity so if companies can innovate their products to serve them; they would improve lives where it is most needed while still making a profit – a strategy of *doing well by doing good*.

Towards a unifying theory of operations sustainability

As sustainability becomes a consolidated concept in the world of business, producers of goods and services must be able to identify sustainability demands, develop more sustainable processes, practices, and products, and finally build organisational structures to internalise sustainability values. While sustainability concepts, practices, and key performance indicators seem to work well at the operational and tactical levels, the literature still lacks a unifying operations sustainability theory and framework at the strategy level. This of course requires a change of paradigm.

In this chapter, the established theory in the area was presented. From a critique of this theory it becomes clear that a robust sustainability fitness requires consideration of the following elements:

- the needs (or survival) of the firm: financial health, customer relationships, technological capabilities, and organisation and development of new products;
- alignment with the needs of society (e.g. essentiality of products and processes at both global and local levels);
- respect for environmental limits, both local and global, in all aspects of the environment: air, water, land, biodiversity (including human health);
- time and space dimensions.

Within this sustainability fitness domain, the following model considers all the above elements (Figure 3.8).

By using the above model, companies minimise the risk of misrepresenting 'reality' by only considering the drivers presented in the previous section of this chapter. For instance, it is often expected that environmental legislation and its enforcement is a fair representation of environmental limits. Unfortunately, this is rarely the case for many locations, particularly in the least developed nations. Thus, companies need to monitor their environmental aspects and impacts and then build an operations strategy that

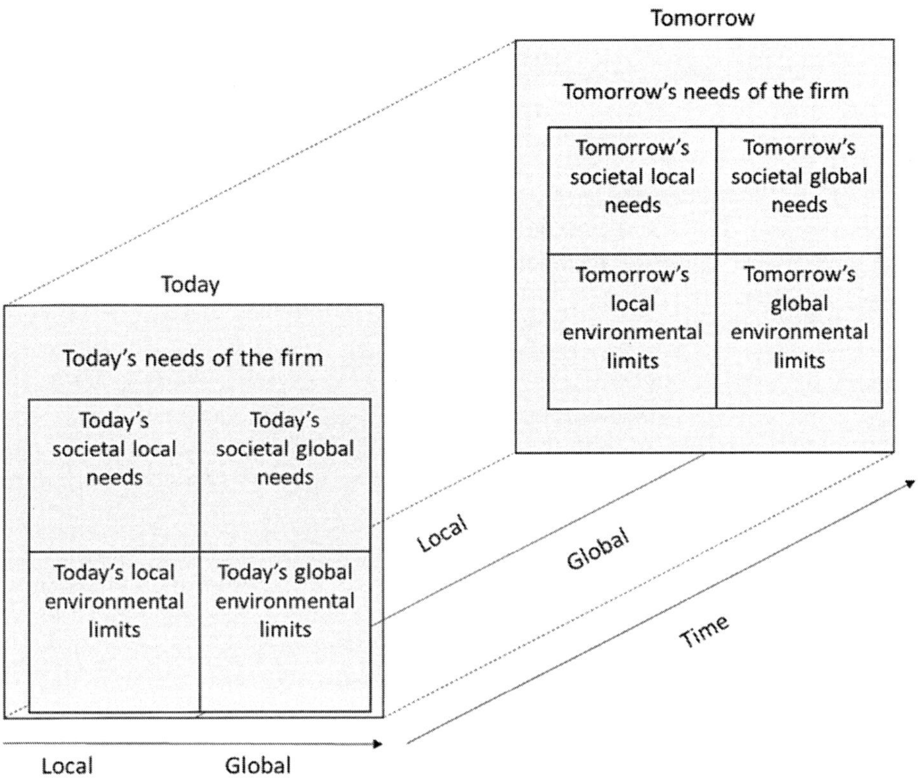

Figure 3.8 Unifying model for sustainability fitness

respects the local and global environmental limits while delivering socio-economic value to society in both the short and long term. This is no different in the other dimensions of sustainability (economic and social). The survival of the firm in the long term (in an economic sense) depends upon more variables besides short-term profit, namely: customer relationship, process technology and capabilities, and learning and development. Often, long-term goals may not be fully supported by shareholders and investors who might favour short-term results instead. In the social dimension, companies can also risk being a hostage of non-governmental organisations, or social movements that have little commitment in addressing essential societal needs. Hence, operations sustainability is of high strategic importance and needs to be planned and implemented accordingly. The traditional perspectives of operations strategy (operations resources and market requirements) should not be forgotten either (Figure 3.9).

The proposed unifying theory for operations sustainability follows an ecologically dominant perspective. It is recognised that the integration of the sustainability fitness elements is a complex and difficult task, which requires companies to monitor or collect information about the ecological (natural) environment when managing businesses operations. Nevertheless, the path to a robust and feasible sustainability strategy needs to address the two key concepts from the sustainable development definition: *essentiality* and *environmental impact*.

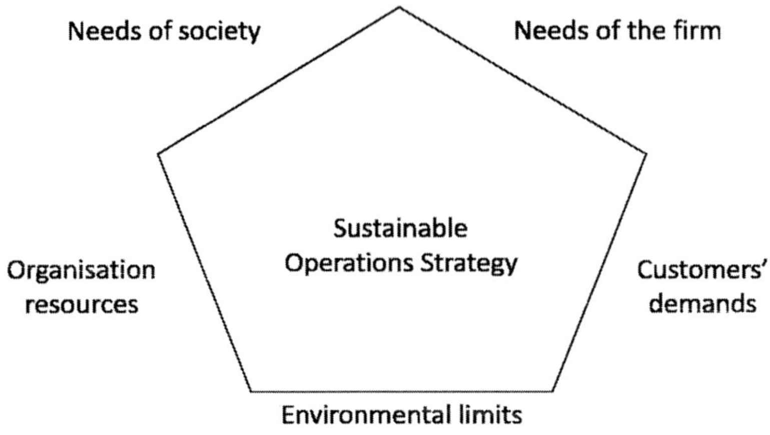

Figure 3.9 Reshaping operations strategy for sustainability

Essentiality is defined as a measure of how the consumption of a resource meets a societal need. Environmental impact is a measure that considers the consumption of resources of a given system (e.g. the absolute consumption of a renewable or non-renewable stock). When decomposing those concepts, the macro-objectives of a business sustainability strategy become clear, and from there they can be connected to the decision areas of operations strategy in order to be effectively implemented. Thus, essentiality can translate into the alignment of needs between the company and society, and environmental impact into the element 'respect for the environmental limits', which is inspired by new concepts such as Planetary Boundaries' (Rockström et al., 2009). These macro-elements emerged from the scientific literature but have never been fully used in management research.

Nunes (2016) states that the sustainability (fitness) of a system is a function of how it meets its own needs within the limits imposed by the environment at a certain point in time. Essentiality, however, needs to be converted in an Essentiality Balance to account for undesirable states, usually found on the extreme of a spectrum of essential and superfluous consumption (e.g. consumption is limited to essential items only or an unhealthy percentage of superfluous consumption. At the systems level, sustainability fitness can be seen as:

$$Sustainability\ Fitness = f\left(\begin{matrix} Essentiality\ Balance \star Respect\ for \\ Environmental\ Limits \end{matrix}\right)$$

Since the system of analysis here is the business operation (transforming inputs into outputs), operations sustainability fitness would be a function of how a company meets its own needs and the needs of society within the limits of its operating environment. It is key when decomposing the variables to understand what it means to implement a sustainable operations strategy. First, Figure 3.10 provides the decomposition at corporate level. Then, Figure 3.11 presents the decomposition into a unifying operations sustainability fitness model in a way it is aligned to the corporate sustainability fitness.

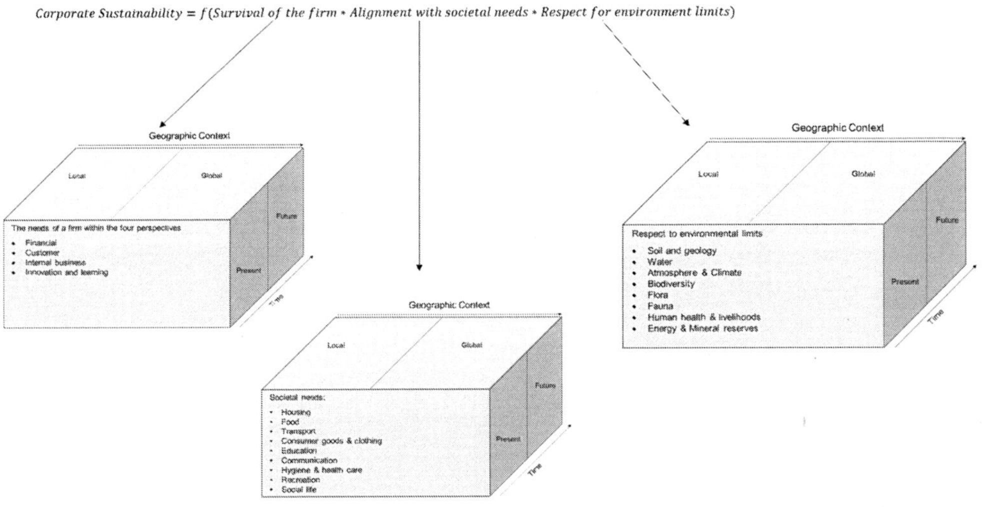

Figure 3.10 Corporate sustainability fitness in time and space

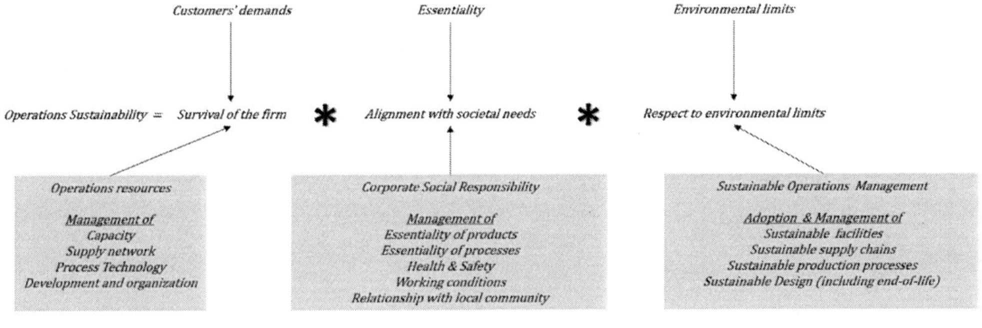

Figure 3.11 Decoupling the elements of operations sustainability fitness

In summary, the implementation of a 'sustainable operations strategy' will bring the corporate sustainability fitness logic into the scope of the operations function, which should contribute to pushing away the risk of collapse of the firm, the degradation of local and global communities who depend or interact with the firm, and the environmental limits of where the firm operates (Figure 3.11).

Table 3.4 provides a guide to formulate operations strategy aligned with sustainability values.

Summary of the chapter

Business strategies are plans that help firms to be fit and respond to events in the future. The organisation's vision of the future and of itself matter largely to formulate a strategy.

Table 3.4 Operations Strategy for sustainability

Decision area	*Capacity management*	*Supply network*	*Process technology*	*Development and organisation*
Key issues	Number and size of sites, location of sites, tasks, etc	Make or buy, customer relationship, supplier selection and relationship	Process type, types of technology, levels of automation, etc	New products (goods and services), organisational structures, product development strategy
Firm's needs	How do the decisions on capacity, location, and tasks impact on the needs of a firm today and tomorrow?	How do the decisions on supply network strategy impact on the needs of a firm today and tomorrow?	How do process technology strategy decisions impact on the needs of a firm today and tomorrow?	How do new product ideas and organisational structures impact on the needs of a firm today and tomorrow?
Alignment to local needs	How do the decisions on capacity, location, and tasks impact on the alignment with local societal needs today and tomorrow?	How do the decisions on supply network strategy impact on the alignment with local societal needs today and tomorrow?	How do process technology strategy decisions impact on the alignment with local societal needs today and tomorrow?	How do new product ideas and organisational structures impact on the needs of a firm today and tomorrow?
Alignment to global needs	How do the decisions on capacity, location, and tasks impact on the alignment with global societal needs today and tomorrow?	How do the decisions on supply network strategy impact on the alignment with global societal needs today and tomorrow?	How do process technology strategy decisions impact on the alignment with global societal needs today and tomorrow?	How do new product ideas and organisational structures impact on the needs of a firm today and tomorrow?
Respect to local environmental limits	How do the decisions on capacity, location, and tasks impact on the respect to local environmental limits today and tomorrow?	How do the decisions on supply network strategy impact on the respect to local environmental limits today and tomorrow?	How do process technology strategy decisions impact on the respect to local environmental limits today and tomorrow?	How do new product ideas and organisational structures impact on the respect to local environmental limits today and tomorrow?
Respect to global environmental limits	How do the decisions on capacity, location, and tasks impact on the respect to global environmental limits today and tomorrow?	How do the decisions on supply network strategy impact on the respect to global environmental limits today and tomorrow?	How do process technology strategy decisions impact on the respect to global environmental limits today and tomorrow?	How do new product ideas and organisational structures impact on the respect to global environmental limits today and tomorrow?

Some firms aim at 'building' the future, being leaders or pioneers. Others aim at growth or simply survival. A functional strategy, such as an operations strategy, should support and be aligned with the corporate strategy. For that, operations strategies not only set goals for the organisation's operations but are also concerned with the state of the operation (capabilities) when achieving those goals. Being able to meet market requirements and develop a minimum level of operations capabilities is part of the core agenda of an operations strategy and its economic sustainability.

Beyond economic sustainability, operations strategies need to better accommodate environmental and social demands in the decisions of capacity, supply network, process technology, and development and organisation. In the ecological domain, firms need to be aware and respond to changes in the natural world. From pollution prevention to being green leaders, several issues will play a role in the operations function, namely: resource allocation, timing, and transferring their philosophy to key stakeholders.

The social sphere of operations strategy highlights the importance of firms to offer a greater value to society, starting from mandatory and critical aspects such as decent working conditions towards more sophisticated ones such as addressing essential needs, social inequalities, etc. Several firms have found market niches in which they can say they do well by doing good.

Finally, this chapter proposes a unifying approach for operations sustainability in which the needs of the organisation, the needs of society, and the limits of the environment are taken into account in the strategy formulation process within the time and space context.

ECOEGG RESHORES PRODUCTION TO THE UK

Founded in 2008, Ecoegg has built its success on providing innovative and effective laundry and cleaning products to both the UK market and worldwide. Their key product is the Ecoegg Laundry Egg which is a complete replacement for laundry detergent and fabric conditioner but works without the use of harmful chemicals. Laundry Ecoegg contains mineral pellets that lift away dirt without fading colours or leaving chemical residue on clothing.

Both the Ecoegg Laundry Egg and Ecoegg Dryer Eggs have held Allergy UK's 'Allergy Friendly Product' award since 2011.

The company opened a factory in China, being seduced by low production costs. Ecoegg exports their products to over 30 countries worldwide including Italy, Germany, Brazil, and Australia. The company has also just started to break into the US market. This growth has enabled Ecoegg to expand its operations and open a new warehouse to hold stock. The company hits sales of approximately £1.5m per year.

Mr Knight said: "I always planned to bring manufacturing of the Ecoegg back to Great Britain, and after winning the Lakeland contract we've decided to do just that in 2012. We have spent a great deal of time researching the best manufacturers and I am thrilled that the final stage of production will take place right here in my home county of Kent".

The move will create a further eight jobs at their Maidstone warehouse. Ecoegg also have manufacturing warehouses in Wiltshire and South Wales, and an office in Bristol. Interestingly, the product itself has come full circle in that it now sells into China too.

The company received the Queen's Award for Enterprise for Innovation in 2016 plus New Product award from *The Grocer* in 2020.

Notes from:

www.ecoegg.com/our-story/
www.themanufacturer.com/articles/ecoegg-brings-production-back-to-the-uk/
www.themanufacturer.com/articles/a-return-to-british-soil-for-laundry-egg-company/
www.bbc.co.uk/news/av/uk-england-kent-19171127

What are the benefits of producing Ecoeggs in the United Kingdom as opposed to doing it in China?

References

Bowen, H. R. (1953). *Social Responsibility of the Businessman*. New York: Harpers and Brothers.

Hart, S. L., & Milstein, M. B. (2003). Creating sustainable value. *Academy of Management Executive*, *17*(2), 56–67.

Hill, T., & Hill, A. (2009). *Manufacturing Strategy: Text and Cases* (3rd ed.). London: Palgrave Macmillan; (10 Feb. 2009).

Nunes, B., Alamino, R. C., Shaw, D., & Bennett, D. (2016). Modelling sustainability performance to achieve absolute reductions in socio-ecological systems. *Journal of Cleaner Production*, *132*, 32–44.

Orsato, R. (2009). *Sustainable Strategies: When Does it Pay to be Green*. Hampshire: Palgrave Macmillan.

Platts, K. W., & Gregory, M. J. (1990). Manufacturing audit in the process of strategy formulation. *International Journal of Operations & Production Management*, *10*(9), 5–26.

Porter, M. E., & Kramer, M. R. (2011). The big idea: Creating shared value. How to reinvent capitalism—and unleash a wave of innovation and growth. *Harvard Business Review*, *89*, 1–2.

Prahalad, C. K., & Hart, S. L. (2002). The fortune at the bottom of the pyramid. *Strategy + Business*, *54*. https://www.strategy-business.com/article/11518

Rockström, J., Steffen, W., Noone, K., Persson, Å., Chapin, F. S., Lambin, E. F., ... & Foley, J. A., 2009. A safe operating space for humanity. *Nature*, *461*(7263), 472–475.

Slack, N. (1994). The importance-performance matrix as a determinant of improvement priority. *International Journal of Operations & Production Management*, *14*(5), 59–75.

Slack, N., & Lewis, M. (2020). *Operations Strategy* (6th ed.). Harlow, UK: Pearson.

The Economist. (2012). Going bananas, The economist – print edition, 31stMarch. Online version, available at: http://www.economist.com/node/21551500

Part 2

Sustainable operations management practices

4 Sustainable facilities

This chapter presents the topic of facilities management from a sustainable operations management perspective. Traditional operations management books will usually deal with this topic through their more mainstream 'capacity management' or 'facilities management' chapters and will usually have a focus solely on the economic dimension rather than considering sustainability per se. This chapter will consider all dimensions of sustainability in often neglected areas of facility and capacity management such as construction of buildings in addition to the traditional issues of size, location, and performance of manufacturing and non-manufacturing facilities.

The key learning outcomes of the chapter are:

- to develop an awareness of economic, environmental, and social issues surrounding the construction, operation, and end-of-life of buildings and physical facilities;
- to be able to identify problems and provide solutions to make facilities more sustainable in alignment with corporate strategy;
- to appreciate the value of sustainability certifications, their potential contribution and limitations to minimise negative social and environmental impacts in the entire life cycle of facilities.

We start this chapter with a case example about how neglecting the important matter of facilities management and sustainability can potentially lead to disastrous consequences that involve not only huge economic costs but also serious loss of public confidence and corporate image (Figure 4.1).

BRUMADINHO DAM COLLAPSE IN BRAZIL

People learn by making mistakes. The same is true for firms and society – success depends on being able to internalise lessons and behave differently in future, to avoid repeating the same errors. Firms tend to review their organisational structures and routine practices to flag problems before they occur, or respond quickly to unexpected problems to minimise their impact.

This is apparently not the case with Vale, however – the fifth largest mining company in the world. Vale is the world's biggest producer of iron ore and nickel and is also responsible for what may be the largest environmental disaster in Brazil's history, after one of its tailings dams – an embankment which is supposed to hold back a

DOI: 10.4324/9781003009375-6

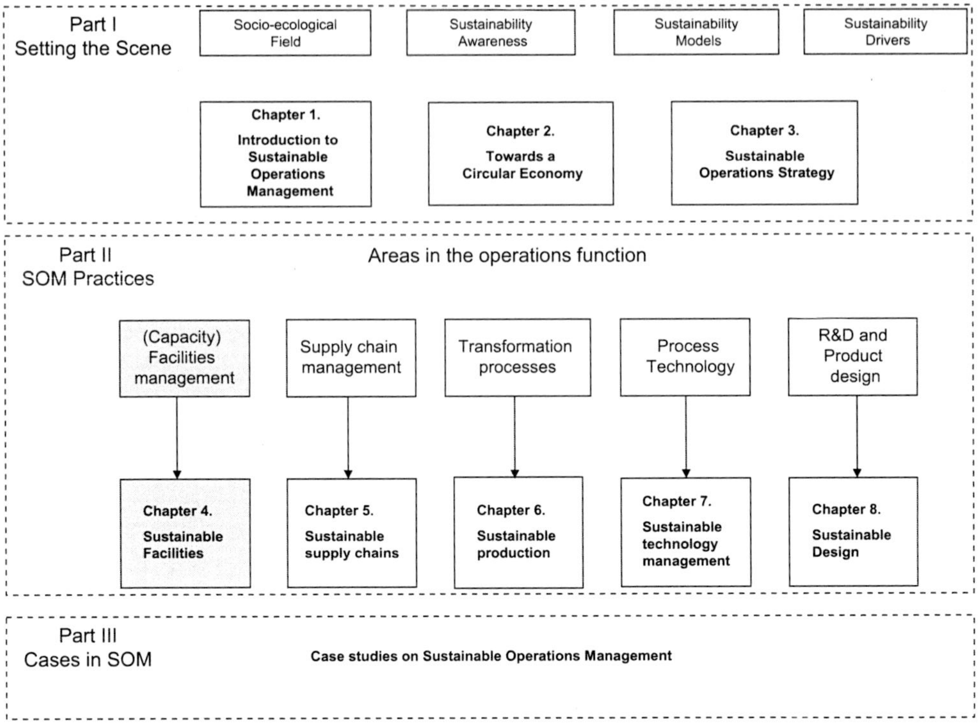

Figure 4.1 Chapter 4 within the book structure

vast reservoir of toxic mining by-products – collapsed on January 25, 2019 at the Corrego do Feijão mine in south-eastern Brazil.

Following the collapse, 186 people were confirmed dead and 122 are still missing. Official data from the Brazilian Environmental Agency says that the mudflow destroyed 270 hectares, of which more than half was native vegetation or protected forest. The swathe of natural habitat destroyed is equivalent to 300 football pitches. Tragically, this happened only three years after a similar accident on another ofVale's dams in the southern Brazilian state of Minas Gerais, near the city of Mariana, which killed 19 people.

By any measure of business sustainability, Brumadinho has been a heavy blow to Vale's performance and reputation. Since then, the company has had its credit rating downgraded, not to mention suffered crippling damage to its public image.

Vale appointed Fabio Schvartsman as CEO after the Mariana disaster in November 2015. Schvartsman took the job and announced to shareholders, employees and the Brazilian people a strong slogan: "Mariana, never again". He failed miserably.

Considering Vale's recent history and the magnitude of these disasters, the corporate response to Brumadinho's tragedy seems ludicrous. Schvartsman said to the Brazilian parliament, in a session which assessed the condition of other mining dams in Brazil after the collapse at Brumadinho:

> Vale is a Brazilian jewel that cannot be condemned for an accident that took place in one of their dams as much, as it was [considered] a tragedy.

Despite his confidence, questions remain unanswered. Why didn't the company move a canteen that was below the dam level and in a high-risk area, according to the assessment of reports dated October 3, 2018?

The precautionary principle states that *if an operation has a risk that might cause severe or irreversible harm to the public or to the environment, that operation must be stopped – even if the likelihood of it happening is low*. So why wasn't this applied?

Since standards clearly hadn't improved over the last three years, how can Brazilians now trust the safety of other dams? Considering the normal course of an accident, why did sirens allegedly fail to work when the dam collapsed to alert employees and the local community to evacuate?

Vale must account for its operational failure with the same gravity as is the standard in developed countries. The Canadian mining company Imperial Metals is still suffering from the environmental liabilities of the Mount Polley mine disaster in Canada.

There is precedent for CEOs and executives to be forced to resign after serious errors, such as the former CEO of BP, Tony Hayward, who resigned after the Deepwater Horizon disaster that killed 11 people in 2010. Schvartsman's temporary resignation sends an unclear message about the company's commitments to the lives of its employees and the communities it operates in.

Vale's next CEO will need to go beyond Schvartsman's rhetoric and consider what stricter operating procedures might be necessary. Otherwise, it could only be a matter of time before the next "accident". There are more than 50 similar dams still functioning under Vale's operations in Minas Gerais state alone that could be another tragedy waiting to happen.

Vale cannot operate at the expense of lives and environmental destruction. Brumadinho can still be a turning point in the history of the company and show it is able to learn to better avoid accidents and tragedies. It may still transform itself into a more responsible company. For that, however, it will need to urgently embrace change as never before.

Excerpt from "Brumadinho dam collapse: mining industry needs radical change to avoid future disasters" published in *The Conversation* by Breno Nunes and Flavio Hourneaux Jr. Source: https://theconversation.com/brumadinho-dam-collapse-mining-industry-needs-radical-change-to-avoid-future-disasters-112808

Questions:

What failures did Vale make when managing their facilities in Brazil? What can be done for tragedies such as Vale's in Mariana and Brumadinho not to happen so often again?

Introduction to facilities in operations and supply chain management

What is a facility?

According to the Cambridge dictionary: a facility is a place, especially including buildings, where a particular activity happens.

> In the field of operations and supply chain management, a facility is considered to be a physical asset (unit) where a business operation is carried out. The size, number and availability of facilities are the key determinants of production capacity. An operation's capacity dictates its potential level of productive activity.
>
> (Slack and Lewis, 2020)

What is capacity?

Capacity should be not confused with efficiency (ratio of outputs and inputs). Capacity is the maximum value of output for an operation in a given period of time. The concept may be very simple and easy to understand in several sectors but difficult to measure in others. For instance, in manufacturing it is fairly usual to identify key (bottleneck) equipment and from that to calculate the capacity of a whole facility in terms of products per day, week, month, or year. On the other hand, with a dental clinic or health centre, for example, it may not be possible to calculate overall capacity so accurately (e.g. using the number of patients they can treat per day or month) due to difficulties in predicting the time spent on each patient's treatment.

Take also, for example, sports events or the hospitality industries. It may often be heard that a football stadium or sports arena has a particular 'capacity' (e.g. 35,000 people). Or a theatre that says it has 348 seats capacity to watch a play. Although these numbers are theoretically correct and are easy to understand, they are not necessarily the operation's actual capacity. They are in fact just part of what needs to be considered to calculate the capacity over a given time period. For a football club, other factors need to be considered (e.g. conditions of the pitch, etc.) because in the end what matters for a football stadium is the maximum number of matches or events that can be held in the facility per month or year – and how many seats can be available for each of them (for example, under Covid-19 restrictions the number of available seats was greatly reduced). That more subtle calculation will therefore provide the overall capacity of a football stadium during the specified period of time.

Usually the decision on operations capacity (or capacity strategy) is taken based on market requirements (e.g. forecast level of demand) and operations resources (e.g. availability of capital, etc.). There are, however, more fundamental socio-ecological factors (in both space and time) that influence the capacity of an operation, particularly with regard to location and size. In practice, greenfield investments and plant expansions or repurposing need to go through regulatory approvals prior to construction and operation. The use of technology, which is primarily associated with enabling capacity change in the same site, also influences the level of environmental and social impact, as will be presented and discussed later in this chapter.

Before we actually move towards understanding the environmental and social impacts of construction, operation, and disposal of buildings and facilities, let us take a look at the types of physical 'buildings' that are currently listed in official classifications.

According to the American Environmental Protection Agency, US-EPA (www.epa.gov/watersense/types-facilities), there are various types of commercial buildings:

- office buildings
- hospitals
- hotels
- restaurants
- educational facilities
- industrial.

The above list in this US-EPA classification already gives us an idea that different buildings play different roles in determining the sustainability of the wider area or functional situation in which they operate. This is primarily because of their different inputs and outputs. For example, a primary or secondary school (educational facilities) can impact on the morning and afternoon road traffic during weekdays. This in turn can lead to higher levels of pollution during peak times. On the other hand, the waste from a school is a less serious hazard compared to that from hospitals or industrial facilities.

In order to better consider the areas of responsibility of operations and facility managers, buildings and physical facilities also need to be further characterised. So, they can be classified in various other forms, such as in terms of:

- size: small, medium, large
- location: urban/non-urban
- role: research and development, production, storage, service delivery
- purpose: focused or multi-purpose
- utilisation: capacity level
- industrial sector/category
- time: static/permanent or provisional/seasonal
- profit-orientation: For profit or non-profit/private, public, NGO property
- ownership: wholly owned, rented, shared.

All the above factors will influence how facilities should be managed. In this chapter, we often take a supply chain view of operations so we will make a clear distinction between manufacturing and non-manufacturing plants in both up-stream and down-stream sides of the supply chain. The management of sustainable operations also requires that suppliers' facilities and key distribution facilities such as warehouses are assessed for their environmental and social impacts, i.e.:

Manufacturing

- industrial plants (transformation processes)
- suppliers' industrial plants.

Non-manufacturing

- R&D centres
- warehouses
- sales stores
- customer services
- education (training), corporate entertainment and leisure centres.

BOX 4.3 TASK: NIKE'S GLOBAL FOOTPRINT

Go to http://manufacturingmap.nikeinc.com/

Choose a country and identify the number, the size, and the type of facility in Nike's manufacturing map.

What else did you learn from examining Nike's manufacturing footprint? Why do you think they provide detailed information about their facilities?

BOX 4.4 VOLKSWAGEN TRANSPARENT FACTORY

www.glaesernemanufaktur.de/en/about-us/our-sustainability.html

The Gläserne Manufaktur was not designed to stand in an industrial park but rather at the Großer Garten park in the heart of Dresden. For that reason alone, the planners assumed complete responsibility for the environment right from the start. When the complex was built around two decades ago, ponds, grass and hundreds of trees were laid out or planted on the 50,000 square meters of exterior grounds. Special sodium-vapor lamps that emit yellow light are used outdoors so as not to harm the insects from the nearby Botanical Garden. The foundations of the building were designed to maintain groundwater levels. And compared to the previous state of development on the site, the amount of impermeable surface area dropped from 6.7 to 4.8 hectares. Instead of fences or other barriers, passers by are now greeted by extensive greenery and a glass facade that allows them to look in and invites them to pay a visit. To prevent birds from flying into the glass facade, loudspeakers transmit bird calls of various species to encourage those types of birds to stay away and find somewhere else to settle.

The factory is the birthplace of VW e-Golf. Brightly lit, quiet, and clean – at Dresden's Gläserne Manufaktur, the zero-emissions future begins already with production. Workers in white overalls have been assembling the new e-Golf* here since 2017. They mount control units and install cockpits, seats and doors. The chassis, batteries and suspension components are delivered. Self-driving transport systems glide silently through the hall on the light beige parquet flooring. The plant uses 100 percent green power. From 2001 to 2016 the Volkswagen Phaeton was made here by hand, with about 56 cars produced every day. Now 74 all-electric Golfs* roll daily from the production line, made on two shifts a day from 6 a.m. to 10 p.m.

No combustion engine, exhaust, or particulate matter – the e-Golf* is climate neutral on the road. But at the Gläserne Manufaktur, the environment plays a role not only when the cars hit the road but also well before production starts.

To make work processes ergonomic for employees, ever more robots will be used to assemble vehicles in the future, doing tasks such as bolting on the safety belts. Whereas human assembly workers normally have to bend down and twist their bodies in order to reach the installation points, at the Gläserne Manufaktur they now simply put a robot into the car, and it does the rest.

At the test station located six kilometers away, experts are studying new functions for cars. Dresden has an advantageous location for developing mobility-on-demand solutions, because the results can also be tested across nearby international borders. A traffic-sign recognition system that works well on roads in Germany, for example, might initially mistake a vehicle weight limit posted on a bridge in Poland or the Czech Republic for the speed limit.

Volkswagen promotes digital transformation not only in its cars but also in its production and logistics facilities. In search of innovative software for digitalization in these areas, the Smart Production Lab at Group IT is developing its expertise at the Gläserne Manufaktur. While specialists in Wolfsburg work primarily on robotics and autonomous transport systems, the team in Dresden is conceiving and developing IoT software and putting it into practice.

This is not a new topic at the Gläserne Manufaktur. To make order picking more secure and efficient, specialists are implementing a Pick-by-Local-Light (PbLL) system following a successful test period in March 2018. The system uses multicolored LEDs to guide employees through the picking process. Complex procedural steps and scanning errors for barcodes and labels are now a thing of the past. That in turn frees up time for the work of the future.

The Gläserne Manufaktur also serves Volkswagen as a test lab for new production systems and technologies. Its specialists experiment with robots, test different processes and develop ways of integrating them into mass production at other plants. Assembly work at the Gläserne Manufaktur is thereby helping to advance automation. In the research center known as the Technikum, several robot stations are being installed as test fields on the Dresden site. The robots do jobs, such as installing ceilings and assembling and removing doors, that would be physically demanding for people. This forges closer ties between humans and machines.

Economic sustainability of buildings

According to the Bartlett School of Sustainable Construction at University College London,[1] a leading international centre for research on this subject, the economics and finance of the built environment (including individual buildings) involves macro-economics and micro-economics from institutional to firm and project levels.

First, a key aspect of a building is its location. Location choice has influences on construction costs, the sale price or rent of a facility, and its operating costs, and finally its residual value as well as demolition costs. From an economic perspective, organisations make careful and deliberate decisions in respect of location choice for their facilities. They usually consider macro-factors such as political and economic stability to reduce risks such as expropriation of business facilities or exposure to legal frameworks that may create disadvantageous ownership restrictions. Location can also impact on construction costs due to cost of land, labour, and capital (e.g. loans). In addition, some locations may create difficulties for accessing materials and consequently increase their cost, involve complex logistics, and cause precarious disturbances to infrastructure in their surroundings. Insurance premiums can also increase if construction and operation take place in sensitive locations.

Because location tends to be one of the key determinants of cost of land (GBP per m^2), it impacts the value of assets and their valorisation over time. When these are high, there will be greater pressure to increase the rate of asset utilisation (output/capacity). Finally, among other socio-economic factors that impact on the organisations' contributions to society, location can also influence how employees travel to work and their quality of life.

In addition to land and capital costs, the other key economic aspects in the design and construction phases of a building include:

- lead time and cost of design;
- cost of construction materials;

- labour cost;
- construction equipment: cranes, compressors, electrical, pumps, etc.;
- indirect construction costs such as contingency costs, freight, overtime, etc.;
- cost of energy and water for construction;
- sale or rental price.

In the operation phase, to maintain economic viability of any given facility, the following will need to be considered:

- energy and water costs in operation;
- maintenance cost;
- costs for refurbishment;
- facility depreciation and demolition costs;
- ratio between nominal and real capacity/utilisation (or output), etc.

Managing capacity levels

As mentioned earlier, capacity is the maximum value of output for an operation in a given period of time. And, as explained before, it is usually defined as a nominal capacity. So, to establish the 'real' capacity of a facility in a year, for example, consideration will need to be made concerning the necessary shutdowns due to maintenance and public holidays etc., among other factors that limit the facility when operating and producing outputs. Naturally, it is the job of facilities managers and operations managers to ensure that the operation runs smoothly and at the highest, or at the most desirable, utilisation rate.

The utilisation rate is the ratio between nominal capacity and output. Not surprisingly unscheduled maintenance, technical problems, shortage of inputs, lack of capital, and labour disputes can all reduce the utilisation rate of a facility and these reasons are different from any necessary stops to production that may be part of a long-term improvement plan.

Several issues will play a role in determining the utilisation rate. Some of them are under the control of the operations or facilities manager, notably: scheduled maintenance, production planning, and control. Other factors are under the control or responsibility of other departments in the same way as demand forecasting may be the marketing department's responsibility, and cash availability to pay suppliers is under the finance department. Finally, there is a group of factors which are not under the control of the organisation at all and can severely disrupt production. Unpredictable events such as natural disasters can impact on the utilisation of a facility and may need to be formally addressed within capacity management through contingency planning (Figure 4.2).

To have optimal capacity utilisation over a long period of time, companies will need to consider the demand variation and predictability to respond through a capacity change strategy. The reason capacity needs to be changed strategically is so the organisation can meet the demand requirements and seize upon higher revenues or adjust utilisation over time.

The timing of capacity change is a critical strategic decision. If there is a large gap between the demand level and the capacity of an operation, there will be unmet customer need or underutilisation of capacity and therefore poor economic performance because

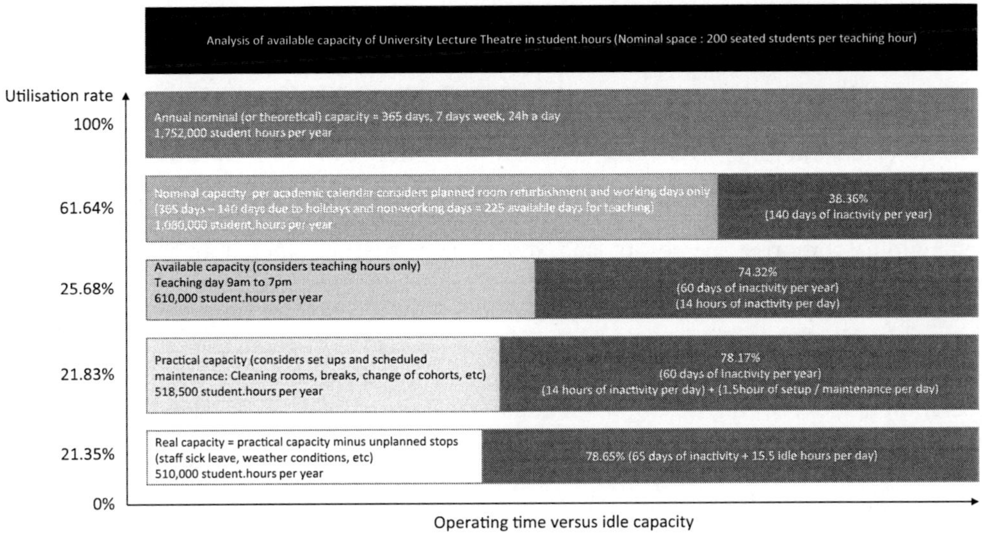

Figure 4.2 Analysis of a capacity utilisation of a university lecture theatre

of the prior capital investment required to build capacity. According to Slack and Lewis (2017), there are three main strategies for capacity change:

- capacity-leading demand;
- capacity-lagging demand;
- smoothing with inventories.

When capacity leads demand, the operation's capacity is always above average demand levels. Apart from extraordinary events and abnormal behaviour of demand, the operation should be able to meet all customer orders. Because demand naturally varies according to daily, weekly, or annual seasonality, there will be a higher probability of underutilisation. The capital investments on capacity expansion are also early and prior to demand surge.

When capacity lags demand, the organisation will take advantage of high plant utilisation but may not be able to meet all the demand requirements. Short-term increases in demand will be difficult to meet as capital investments are delayed until the average demand level has grown to the future capacity increment.

Many companies will not be comfortable with either capacity-leading or capacity-lagging strategies. For such companies a third strategy, smoothing-with-inventories may be more suitable. With a demand forecast available, the timing of capacity change will take place later than in the capacity-leading strategy but earlier than the capacity-lagging strategy. Inventories will then be built to accommodate the times when demand is above average capacity, including short-term demand increases. Utilisation rate can be kept high as inventories will be kept during periods when the demand level is lower than capacity. Of course, there is a cost associated with keeping inventories, and this is one of the disadvantages of the smoothing-with-inventories strategy. Nevertheless, capital spending can result in lower risk of shortages than in a capacity-leading strategy and high utilisation of the facility is still possible to achieve.

Environmental sustainability of buildings

According to the data of UNEP, the building sector consumes about 40% of global energy, 25% of global water, 40% of global resources and it emits one-third of GHG (global greenhouse gas) emissions. In this context, improving the environmental sustainability of buildings has become of significant importance. However, progress is slower than expected and requires the development of market-ready cost reduction solutions.

The first barrier to improving the environmental sustainability of buildings is economic. As seen in the previous section, taking into account its entire life cycle, the cost of a building comprises the cost of land, design, construction, operation, and recycling or final disposal (dismantling, land clean-up costs, etc.) – as well as capital costs (with consideration of any loan taken). The process of greening buildings may involve increased capital investment which in turn will result in overall cost reduction throughout the whole life cycle of a facility. Nevertheless, the main reduction is likely to happen in the operation phase. For this reason, owners and developers, who are involved in the capital investment and construction phases, have little economic incentive to use green buildings techniques if the building will eventually be sold or rented to a third party (unless the customers are willing to pay a premium for environmental performance). As green investment schemes become more popular, the incentives for owners and developers to adopt a green buildings approach tend to increase – when considering the economics of green buildings alone.

The most popular green buildings certifications advocate similar principles. The criteria for awarding a green building certificate can change according to the certifier and the industrial sector of applicants, but the principles are generally the same.

USGBC LEED

The US Green Buildings Council certification is called LEED (Leadership in Energy and Environmental Design).[2] The general rating criteria used by LEED certification will consider:

- location and transport (e.g. access to public transportation, etc.);
- sustainability of the site (e.g. optimised land use, erosion control, etc.);
- water efficiency (e.g. use of rainwater, water reuse systems, etc.);
- energy use (e.g. use of daylight, intelligent control systems, etc.);
- resources and materials (e.g. use of certified wood, construction waste management, etc.);
- indoor environmental quality (e.g. low emitting materials of volatile organic compounds, temperature, etc.);
- innovation and design process (e.g. use of innovative techniques, etc.).

BREEAM

The British BRE Group (formerly the Building Research Establishment) is the founder and owner of BREEAM (Building Research Establishment Environmental Assessment Method) certification. BREEAM is now internationally available and has become a popular certification for Green Buildings. BREEAM is an international scheme that provides independent third-party certification of the assessment of the sustainability performance of individual buildings, communities, and infrastructure projects. The first BREEAM scheme was launched in 1990 to help reduce the harmful impacts of building development on the environment.

Since that time the scheme has evolved and now takes wider sustainability measures beyond the environmental dimension. BREEAM's five principles are behind their approach to assess buildings and communities. They are: (1) delivery of sustainable solutions, (2) providing a framework to balance the dimensions of sustainability, (3) being based on sound science, (4) supporting change, and finally (5) delivering value to the occupants of the building.

BREEAM measures sustainable value of buildings in a series of categories. Each of these categories addresses the most influential factors, including low impact design and carbon emissions reduction; design durability and resilience; adaption to climate change; and ecological value and biodiversity protection.[3] The categories are:

- energy
- pollution
- ecology
- materials
- waste
- water
- transport
- land use.

BREEAM also recognises other issues such as health and wellbeing of building occupants, innovation, and management.

Nearly-Zero Energy Buildings (NZEB)

In the European Union, the concept of Nearly-Zero Energy Buildings (NZEB) is established in the Energy Performance of Buildings Directive, adopted originally in 2002 and subsequently revised. It required all new buildings to be at, or close to, zero-energy standards by the end of 2020. All new public buildings were to be nearly zero-energy by 2018.

A wide adoption of NZEB in the private sector is possible only with big reductions in initial expense, which have a significant influence on the end-user decision. Supporting NZEB market growth by different coordination and support actions will lead to reductions of cost when economies of scope will be reached. On the other hand, the initial expenses related to implementation of novel NZEB technologies can be reduced with a quality, integrated design.

Currently there are separate standards in different fields of the construction sphere which are directed to regulation of energy consumption, ecological performances, waste management, and economic efficiency of projects, structures, materials, and equipment. However, there is no unique instrument that could allow both producers and end-users to simultaneously apply all of the standards that are necessary for the design of affordable NZEB.

Currently almost every NZEB-related measure is directed towards reducing energy consumption. Such measures may play a significant cost reduction role but still do not seem enough to establish a common market practice. In recent years the implementation of different novel NZEB technologies and solutions resulted in a significant increase of NZEB costs and problematic and discontinuous dissemination of these technologies on the NZEB market – for example where subsidies are removed. To meet this challenge a conceptual model will be prepared by each EU nation aimed at supporting NZEB market growth by raising awareness of NZEB economic viability and promoting dissemination of cost-effective NZEB solutions.

The impact of NZEB solutions goes beyond the construction sector. They are an important milestone of the process towards sustainable facilities more generally and must be addressed in a broader context. For example, companies in the energy sector plan an integration for production and use of renewable energy sources which are now available for sale by energy utility companies – namely solar thermal, wind, geothermal, hydrothermal, and biomass energy.

As in the green building certifications, NZEB buildings are going to be more expensive than traditional ones if considering investment costs only. It is also well known that there are difficulties with implementation (design and construction) of many of the necessary solutions including renewable energy generation, and that we are facing many unknowns with regard to the operation, maintenance, retrofitting, and also end-of-life process of these buildings. With these barriers the market growth cannot be as planned by energy efficiency/NZEB policy makers in EU and on national levels.

Below is provided a detailed list of actions for each phase of a building life cycle to make it more sustainable:

Investment planning and design

- use of local materials (soil-concrete, wood, organic insulation plant, etc.);
- minimising the consumption of materials by separating the functions of structures (load-bearing);
- rational shaping to maximise space while minimising the area of enclosing structures (for example, the dome building, round in plan buildings, etc.);
- consideration of local natural climatic factors in building design (orientation, green spaces, keeping the terrain, accommodation, natural ventilation, etc.);
- use of simple engineering systems (for example, Trombe wall, individual air recuperation, air collectors, ground air collectors, etc.);
- application of combined engineering systems for different year seasons and climatic factors – based on external weather conditions and occupancy schedules continuous online regulation of the active elements usage level;
- design solutions adapted for low-cost reconstruction and recycling;
- justification of the renewable energy sources use (solar collectors, solar electric (PV) panels, heat pumps, wind turbines) – efficient utilisation of RES to reduce energy consumption from the grid according to each RES generation availability and battery stored energy;
- integration of engineering systems in the construction of buildings;
- application of rainwater harvesting system and reuse of water for sewage systems (e.g., after washing);
- common use of special places and equipment (laundry, swimming pool, lounge, fitness room, guest rooms, etc.) – based on user defined occupancy schedules regulation of active elements.

Production level, construction works

- application of mass-industrial prefabricated structures (prefabricated on the principles of typing, unification, standardisation);
- industrial building construction methods (for example 3-D printing).

Operations level

- indoor-climatising management affecting the internal microclimate of the individual should be able to regulate in order to meet the subjective feeling of comfort and well-founded consumer health and safety standards (for example, the content of CO and CO_2) – regulation of active elements so as to minimise energy consumption and cost while preserving user comfort levels. To this end specially tailored tools for automatised intelligent energy management and human behavioural analysis, monitoring, and profiling will be considered within the overall framework to assess the operational stage NZEB benefits and increase market awareness in a more comprehensive manner;
- use of systems of registration and regulation of microclimate parameters ('smart-house') – real-time control and management of active elements within the subject building so as to preserve comfort while minimising energy usage and utilising available RES able to fulfil the remaining net-energy demand.

Recycling, end of life level

- the use of local ecological materials without the deep treatment and with easy return into the environment (soil-concrete, timber, organic plant insulation, etc.);
- the use of structures and structural systems suitable for recycling (e.g., separable compound);
- the use of technologies of materials recycling after building deconstruction (concrete, glass, etc. as building materials; timber, organic insulation as energy raw materials).

Social sustainability of buildings

As advocated in BREEAM certification standards, the health, productivity, safety, and happiness of occupants in a building as well as their needs are crucial issues for sustainable facilities management. Sustainable facilities must address tangible aspects such as occupational health and safety, and also intangible issues such as collaboration and creativity in teams. In addition to indoor environmental quality, choice of materials, natural illumination, and access to key amenities (e.g. washrooms and toilets), the layout of facilities is one of the most important determinants to make a facility more socially sustainable. The balance between communal and private areas can enhance levels of workforce collaboration, creativity, and commitment. Having a layout that provides spaces which increase the opportunity for interactions among people from different work teams is also considered an approach that increases improved communication and cross-fertilisation of ideas. Various features of physical space influence creativity and the generation of novel ideas within organisations, among them accessibility, density, proximity, but also distance to others, layout, design, and visual cues (Sailer, 2011).

Barrett (2016) states that research on the effect of the work environment on individual perceptions of creativity has been reported through a variety of different elements, such as interior design (aesthetic objects); interior architectural surroundings (arrangement of workspace areas); and ambient conditions (light, sound, temperature). According to Kallio et al. (2015), three specific functions for physical space can be distinguished: instrumental, symbolic, and aesthetic. Instrumentality refers to how the physical environment and its features support or impede specific activities (Rafaeli and Vilnai-Yavetz, 2004). Examples include lighting and noise control, which can impact upon the ergonomics of workspace and positively affect worker productivity.

From the symbolic perspective, an organisational environment can be regarded as a set of organisational symbols, which have an important role in the formation of organisational culture, identities, and meanings (Kallio et al., 2015).

The aesthetic perspective refers to sensory reactions to a physical space and its artefacts, but it has been much less explored compared to the instrumental and symbolic perspectives (Kallio et al., 2015). The work in psychology shows that people will react and behave differently when facing 'beauty' or 'ugliness' according to their own notion of what is beautiful or ugly. Accordingly, 'exciting' and 'stimulating' brainstorming facilities, in contrast to 'calming' and 'pleasant' break rooms, may be used as supplementary work environments – adds (Kallio et al., 2015).

Mapping the health and safety risks and requiring the appropriate use of personal protective equipment (PPE) can not only save lives but also reduces the risk of unintended closure of a facility or shutdown of production due to work accidents. Adequate signalling and personnel training in the work environment is a basic and essential step towards sustainable facilities management.

Service providers also need to ensure their customers have access to suitable PPE in order to keep their facilities safe. Consider an entertainment facility that has a paint-ball arena. Staff and players need to wear PPE when entering the shooting zone to avoid accidents. This may include special clothes, gloves, and eye protection (Figures 4.3 and 4.4).

MAKING FACEBOOK'S HEADQUARTERS A MORE ENVIRONMENTAL WORKPLACE

The company OfficeSpace helped Facebook to design the interior of its offices. Among the features are:

1. **A workplace in an urban environment:** Their integration of urban elements into its overall design, creating a community rather than just a workplace. Facebook's new office includes two cafes, a burrito bar, a pizza window, a sit-down restaurant and several kitchens. It even has its own coffee shop. This helps to cultivate an environment of collaboration and comfort that extends well beyond the individual workplace.
2. **Balance between openness and focus:** Facebook's new campus spans 40,000 square meters and is one of the largest open office settings in the world. Even CEO Mark Zuckerberg sits at one of the plain white desks on the office floor. This collaborative atmosphere helps to foster creativity and camaraderie because no one feels like another employee is receiving special treatment. The

Figure 4.3 A paintball player wearing appropriate PPE. Source: https://upload.wikimedia.org/wikipedia/commons/thumb/0/08/JTF3_wood-simulation.JPG/2048px-JTF3_wood-simulation.JPGHERE]–Photoauthor/user:Nado24

site also offers a number of conference and private rooms to help employees to focus when needed. This unique blend offers the best of both worlds and helps to cater to every style of worker.

3. **Art incorporated into workplace culture:** Facebook lives and breathes creativity, but this can be hard to recognize since most of the company's activities are online. To showcase physical manifestations of creativity, there is an artist-in-residence programme. Works by local artists provide visual inspiration throughout the office setting. Employees can also contribute their own art. This personal touch cultivates a community of self-expression.
4. **Design with a purpose:** Every aspect of Facebook's office design is intentional. For example, there are large windows that flood the entire office with natural light, which is one of the many things that improve worker happiness.

   The open office setting keeps a fluid and informal design. Senior management sits side-by-side with the other staff, which contrasts with the idea of a 'corner office', and encourages everyone to voice their opinions.
5. **Health as a priority:** The office features a rooftop garden where the workday can be forgotten, employees can get some fresh air, or be used for walking meetings. With focus on health and movement, Facebook offers its employees

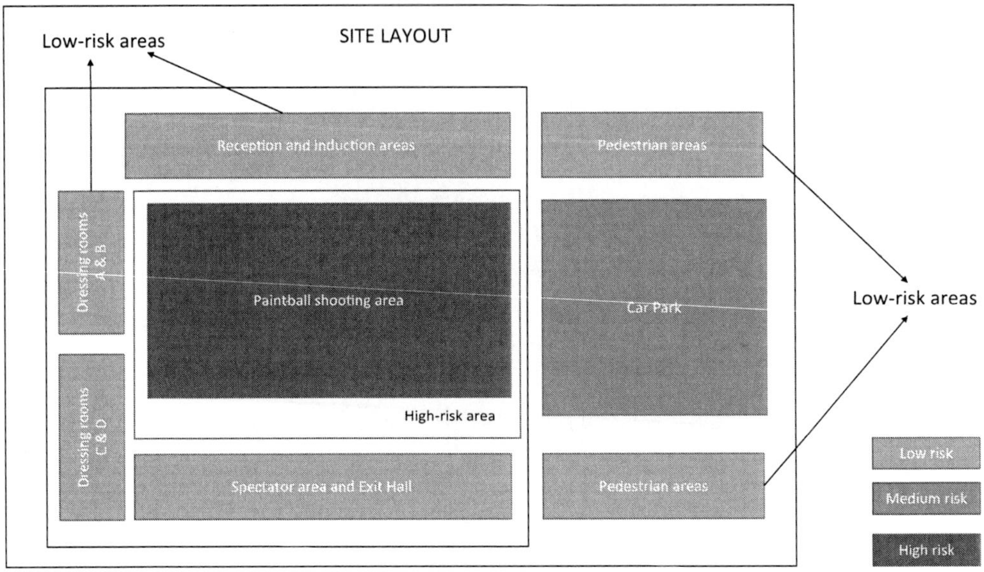

Figure 4.4 Risk map presented in a site layout of a paint-ball club

adjustable desks so they can stand while working. The office even has showers for those who decide to ride their bikes to work. Their new building truly infuses health and wellness into the workplace.

This text was adapted from OfficeSpace's article. See original source at: www.officespacesoftware.com/blog/heres-what-makes-facebooks-hq-design-and-workplace-so-attractive/

Question:

For a facility manager, it can be helpful to take notes from companies that are revolutionising the traditional office setting. Facebook combines urban inspiration, creative artwork, intentional design as well as a focus on health to create an innovative, open office. How can these ideas be applied in any office?

Summary of the chapter

Climate adaptation, energy efficiency, sustainable development, and green growth are societal challenges for which the facilities management (FM) profession can develop solutions and make positive contributions at the organisational level and also have societal-level effects. Learning, creativity, and innovation are crucial to overcome those challenges.

The operating phase of a building is important not only for energy use but with respect to other dimensions of sustainability such as food consumption, biological diversity in the built environment, health, poverty, and the use of non-renewable resources. Therefore, the ways we use, operate, and manage buildings and facilities will have a substantial influence on the entire sector, as well as accelerating advances in the sustainability sphere.

Sustainability in facilities management requires consideration of environmental, economic, and social sustainability in existing facilities management functions. The key aspects that facilities managers could harness to deliver sustainable FM functions within an organisation are: energy management, water management, waste management, air and environmental quality management, reducing vehicle use, sustainable maintenance, sustainable purchasing, environmental or ecological management, and health and safety. Location of facilities is a key determinant that may impact on all these aspects.

Notes

1 Please visit: www.ucl.ac.uk/bartlett/construction/research/economics-and-finance-built-environment
2 Please visit: www.usgbc.org/leed
3 www.breeam.com/discover/how-breeam-certification-works/

References

Barrett, L. E. (2016). *The effect of workspace layout on individual perceptions of creativity across generational cohorts* (Doctoral thesis, Walden University. College of Social and Behavioral Sciences).

Kallio, T. J., Kallio, K. M., & Blomberg, A. J. (2015). Physical space, culture and organisational creativity: A longitudinal study. *Facilities*, 33, 389–411.

Rafaeli, A., & Vilnai-Yavetz, I. (2004). Emotion as a connection of physical artifacts and organizations. *Organization Science*, *15*(6), 671–686.

Sailer, K. (2011). Creativity as social and spatial process. *Facilities*, *29*(1–2), 6–18.

Slack, N., & Lewis, M. (2020). *Operations Strategy* (6th ed.). Harlow, UK: Pearson.

5 Sustainable supply chains

A supply chain is the totality of actors, activities, and processes required by organisations to deliver goods or services to the end-customer (purchaser) and final consumer (user). In a traditional manufacturing environment and in its simplest form, the typical activities within a supply chain include the supply of raw materials and components coordinated by the procurement function, the temporary storage of these materials within warehouses, coordinated by the logistics function, the transformation of raw materials and components within the manufacturing site, coordinated by the manufacturing function, and finally the distribution of finished products to the retailers or the final consumers, again coordinated by the logistics function. Sustainability in supply chain management concerns not only environmental and ecological considerations but also issues relating to human rights, labour practices, and ethical and anti-corruption practices.

The key learning outcomes of the chapter are:

- to define sustainable supply chain management;
- to discuss the main principles and approaches of socially sustainable planning, sourcing, making, and delivering;
- to discuss the features and the value drivers of a closed-loop supply chain.

Introduction to supply chain concepts and principles

The accomplishment of supply chain activities requires the coordination of three different flows: materials, information, and money. Materials move from the upstream to the downstream side of the supply chains, namely from the suppliers down to the manufacturers and retailers. Information moves throughout the entire supply chain, downstream from suppliers to manufacturers as well as upstream from consumers and retailers to manufacturers and suppliers. Money (through financial transactions) typically moves upstream, from the final consumers up to manufacturers and suppliers.

A supply chain can deliver to the final consumers' products, services, or a combination of the two. Examples of service supply chains are the supply chains that enable, for example, airline firms to offer transportation services or hotels to offer hospitality services. Examples of mixed supply chains, offering what is called a product–service system, are the supply chains that offer the temporary use of a product in exchange for a fee.

If we consider the number of components and materials that are embedded in a single product, it is easy to understand how complex supply chains can become. If we look at the upstream side of the supply chain for an automotive manufacturer, the first

DOI: 10.4324/9781003009375-7

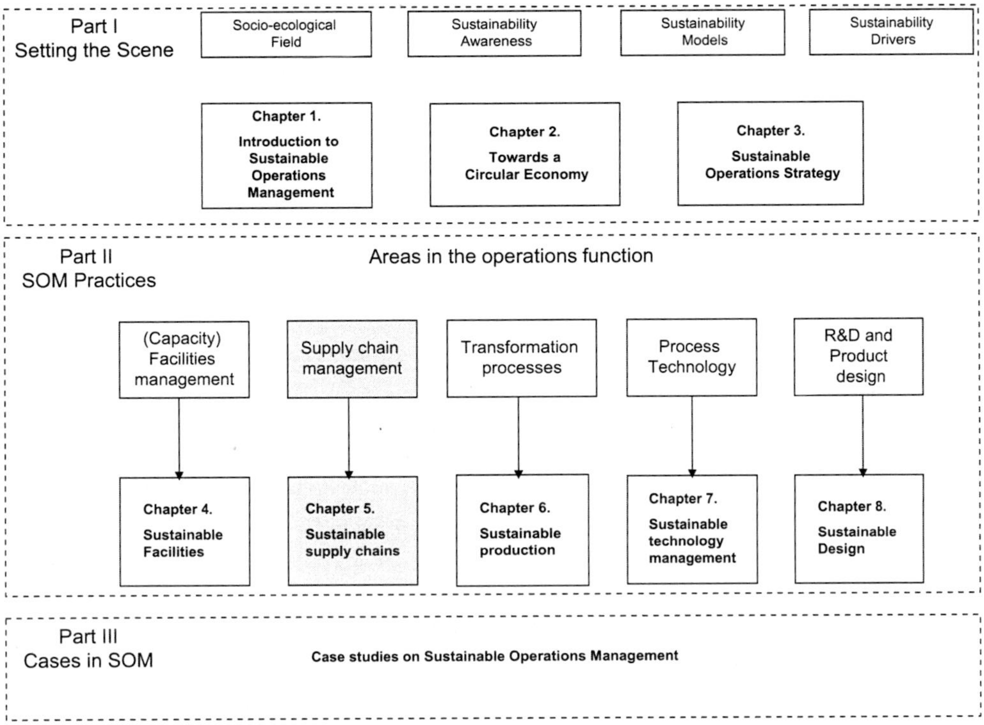

Figure 5.1 Chapter 5 within the book structure

tier of supplier can include hundreds of different firms. These firms will, in turn, purchase products and services from other suppliers, the second tier, and so on. If we look at the downstream side of the supply chain, the manufacturers can use different channels to provide the product to the final consumers, using the mediating role of logistics service providers, retailers, warehouses, and so on. In view of this complexity, there is a broad range of different activities that enable the correct running of a supply chain.

The supply chain operations reference model (or SCOR, see Poluha, 2007) classifies the activities used to address, improve, and communicate supply chain management decisions within a company and with suppliers and customers of a company. It identifies five areas of the supply chain: plan, source, make, deliver, and return. These are described below:

Plan: The key planning activity within a supply chain aims at balancing supply and demand, and it is often identified by the specific term "Sales and operation planning". This main activity is supported by other secondary activities that plan and coordinate specific processes, such as the information flow along the supply chain, inventory, transportation, and regulatory compliance. The planning activities are at the core of the supply chain and determine its performance and its results. Therefore, planning also has to take into account the financial plan of the company.

Source: The sourcing activities include sourcing infrastructure as well as materials acquisition. The main objective of the sourcing activities is the effective management of inventory. Effective inventory management processes should consider the nature of the supplier network and the supplier agreements, as well as of supplier performance.

Make: This step focuses on manufacturing and production, including production activities, packaging, staging the product (preparing for sale), and releasing. The production activities should be carefully planned in order to maximise efficient use of the machines and of the input materials. The maximising machine efficiency and use of the input materials is enabled by production planning and control techniques. Also, the maintenance of the machines is ensured by techniques such as condition monitoring and preventive maintenance. Other specific techniques used to manage the production-related activities should also include internal logistics and facilities management.

Deliver: Delivery refers largely to the logistics-related activities, such as order management, warehousing, and transportation. When an order is received, an invoice will be sent to the customer, existing inventory will be used to fulfil the order, and a transportation process will be used to deliver the finished product to the end-customer, and ultimately the final consumer.

Return: Because of the growing importance of a circular economy, activities related to returning products have more recently been added to the core activities that characterise a supply chain. The idea is that companies should be able to efficiently manage different types of product returns. These may include both defective or unwanted products and products at the end of their life cycle, which should be managed properly to minimise their environmental footprint. The activities related to properly managing product returns are diverse and they include the handling of returned products, reverse logistics activities, as well as remanufacturing and reselling the product returns to recover their residual value.

The SCOR reference model can be used to describe the implications of the different activities in terms of sustainability, as well as the approaches commonly used to guarantee results that are both environmentally and socially sustainable.

Sustainability in planning

As briefly discussed in the introductory section of the chapter, the planning activities of a supply chain essentially deal with balancing supply and demand. The planning activities can have different time horizons, and they are typically classified as long-term or strategic planning, medium-term or tactical planning, and short-term or operational planning.

To understand the sustainability-related implications of planning activities, the long-term decisions have a considerable relevance, since they determine the shape of the supply chain and therefore its environmental and social footprint. Among the long-term decisions, supply chain design is essential for its sustainability performance. Designing a supply chain implies making decisions regarding the design and location of the facilities, namely the placement, size, and capacity of buildings such as production and manufacturing plants, distribution centres, and retail outlets.

The criteria adopted in supply chain design include economic, environmental, and social dimensions of sustainability. The economic criteria include cost or profit, and competitiveness criteria such as market responsiveness, or service level. The best configuration of the supply chain from an economic point of view will depend on the competitive strategy of the firm. A firm that is competing through cost leadership will try to minimise the supply chain-related costs, for instance by locating its production plants in countries characterised by lower labour costs. The reduction of labour-related costs is often the reason for locating production plants in developing countries, such as those of firms operating in the apparel, fast-moving consumer goods, and information and communication technologies industries. A firm that is competing through differentiation will try to maximise its performance with regard to the factors that differentiate the company in respect of its competitors in the market. A typical differentiating factor that companies try to optimise is responsiveness. The achievement of higher levels of responsiveness is the reason for the location in Europe of the production plants of some apparel producers such as the giant Spanish fashion company, Zara.

The economic factors discussed above only represent the first of the pillars of sustainability. The environmental and social criteria will now be considered.

Examples of environmental criteria considered in the design of a supply chain are carbon emissions, waste generation, energy consumption, and water usage. There are multiple considerations that should be taken into account to identify the optimal configuration of a supply chain from an environmental point of view. The different environmental criteria often imply uniquely optimal supply chain configurations, and a trade-off may be needed. For instance, splitting production among several plants closer to the different markets will reduce the carbon footprint from finished goods transportation, but at the same time could imply the loss of economies of scale and therefore the consumption of more natural resources for the realisation of multiple production plants.

Moreover, a supply chain configuration should consider together both environmental and economic criteria, thus further complicating the identification of the optimal supply chain configuration. Environmental and economic criteria could operate in synergy or require a trade-off. Synergies between environmental and economic criteria are often possible, because the optimisation of economic criteria may imply reducing the consumption of resources, while cutting the corresponding costs. For instance, a more environmentally efficient solution could reduce the consumption of water by 20%, while also cutting the corresponding costs by 20%. However, in other cases, a trade-off between environmental and economic criteria is needed. A typical example concerns the management of waste. For example, with several classes of materials, landfilling is the cheapest disposal alternative when compared with other solutions such as recycling or remanufacturing. But at the same time landfilling has the worse consequences in terms of the environment. The optimal supply chain configuration is identified through optimisation models, and such models generally help decision makers to examine trade-offs between the environmental and economic objectives.

Examples of criteria fostering the social sustainability of supply chains include decent work conditions, human rights, impact on local societies, and product safety. Neglecting these criteria can have catastrophic consequences from an ethical perspective as well as from a business perspective. Boxes 5.1 and 5.2 present the consequences of a low consideration of social sustainability criteria while designing a supply chain.

BOX 5.1 THE RANA PLAZA DISASTER

In April 2013 an eight-storey clothing factory building in Rana Plaza (Bangladesh) collapsed killing at least 1,134 people and injuring more than 2,500. The building housed five garment factories supplying products for several companies and brands such as Zara, Mango, Benetton, and Walmart.

The scale of this tragedy increased awareness of the risks and costs of sourcing from low-cost countries, although the reaction of the financial markets was unexpectedly of low significance. Western brands and retailers realised the need to improve supply chain governance mechanisms for working conditions and safety in the global garment industry. After the disaster, about 250 companies signed two initiatives, the Accord on Fire and Building Safety in Bangladesh, and the Alliance for Bangladesh Worker Safety, with the objective of improving safety in the 2,300 factories supplying Western brands. The Accord and Alliance had positive results for the factories supplying major Western brands, but progress seems to be more difficult for the companies that do not supply major Western brands.

Sources:

[1] www.ilo.org/global/topics/geip/WCMS_614394/lang--en/index.htm
[2] www.theguardian.com/global-development/2018/apr/24/bangladeshi-police-target-garment-workers-union-rana-plaza-five-years-on
[3] https://fashionunited.uk/news/fashion/5-years-on-what-effect-has-rana-plaza-had-on-garment-workers-lives/2018041629133
[4] www.sciencedirect.com/science/article/pii/S0272696317300098?casa_token=pDvAogPf4oAAAAAA:kjLg19X4d4sMhyzjVIs7B_CIcaX_5Arw7RDEsq2Fj0NH3zlMasf0F5eSY-VEQP560T9S-qIEIEQ
www.sciencedirect.com/science/article/pii/S0272696317300098?casa_token=pDvAogPf4oAAAAAA:kjLg19X4d4sMhyzjVIs7B_CIcaX_5Arw7RDEsq2Fj0NH3zlMasf0F5eSY-VEQP560T9S-qIEIEQ

The difficulty of considering social sustainability-related criteria in the design of a supply chain is greater compared to environmental sustainability because social performance is more difficult to capture, measure, and embed into an optimisation model.

In the same way as for environmental sustainability, a supply chain configuration should consider both social and economic criteria, and social and economic criteria can operate in synergy or require a trade-off. So, synergies between social and economic criteria are also possible. For instance, better working conditions imply a more productive workforce as well as a more resilient supply chain. In other cases, however, a trade-off between social and economic criteria is needed. A typical example concerns the purchase of products from suppliers operating in developing countries, where lower labour costs often come together with a higher risk of social malpractice.

Sustainability in sourcing

Procurement is a key process in supply chain management and comprises the identification, evaluation, and selection of the most suitable supplier, as well as the acquisition of goods and services, often via a tendering or competitive bidding process. It is an activity of strategic importance for a supply chain, because if the selected suppliers cannot deliver the products, the supply chain is disrupted and must face significant tangible and intangible losses, as well as procedural, financial, and relational costs. The procurement process can be complex, especially for critical supplies, and it can include different steps that include devising a procurement strategy together with identifying, qualifying, selecting, and managing the relationship with suppliers. All these different steps must be managed carefully to ensure that environmental and social sustainability are considered.

Devising a procurement strategy is a pivotal step for the characterisation of the procurement process itself, since the procurement strategy will determine the size of the supply base for a specific item or service, the type of relationship with the different suppliers, as well as the nature of the agreements that the company will try to make with the suppliers. Embedding environmental or social sustainability within a procurement strategy implies the consideration of environmental and social criteria while making the strategic decisions. For instance, while deciding whether to engage with a specific supplier in the short or long term, the company should consider what are the implications in terms of environmental or social sustainability. Generally, only a long-term engagement with a supplier can engender a change of the suppliers' culture towards more sustainable behaviour. Similarly, when determining the nature of contractual agreements with suppliers, specific clauses related to environmental and social sustainability can be considered. Having finalised its overall procurement strategy, a company can move to the next step, which consists of the identification and qualification of the suppliers.

Supplier identification, qualification, and selection are an important step for the economic, environmental, and social performance of the supply chain. Choosing a supplier usually involves starting from a long list of bidders and reducing this initial long list to the final number that the company wants to include in its supplier pool for the specific item. This selection happens through several steps and by applying different selection criteria. In the very first selection, when the company reduces the initial long list to a small number of suppliers that are potentially qualifiable, the criteria that drive the selection are very general, involving checking the basic requirements of a supplier to establish whether they are a "qualifier". Sustainability-related criteria should start playing a role in these preliminary steps to verify some basic sustainability-related performance indicators of the suppliers, such as for occupational health and safety in construction firms or hazardous chemicals management policies in chemical firms. Business-related selection criteria are also very general at this stage, being aimed at assessing the financial stability of the suppliers and their performance as summarised in their company accounts and balance sheets. These criteria can be easily verified with simple documentary checks or through the analysis of the certification schemes adopted by the suppliers. In the succeeding steps of the selection, the criteria become increasingly stringent and detailed in terms of business and sustainability performance. Examples of business-related criteria used in the final steps include the total cost of ownership for a specific supplier or the quality that the supplier can deliver. Examples of sustainability-related criteria used in the final steps of the selection include the adoption of sustainability-related management systems, such as ISO 45001 for occupational health and safety management, or the alignment between the sustainability strategy of the supplier and that of the firm, hence being able to maximise the generation of environmental and social value. The assessment of these criteria is relatively complex and expensive, and generally goes beyond simple documentary checks or an analysis of the certification schemes. The managerial complexity and the costs related to the assessment of these criteria explain why the company can make this type of assessment only for strategic items and only for a very small number of suppliers.

The concluding important step of the procurement process consists of establishing and maintaining relationships with the selected suppliers, usually regulated by a contract. To ensure effective management of the relationship between the sourcing company and its suppliers, the sourcing company should firstly segment the supply base. Segmentation involves separating the suppliers into a small number of groups or segments and formulating different and appropriate strategies for each segment. By adopting segmentation, the company can allocate more effectively the available resources to manage the relationship with its suppliers. For suppliers that are classified as "strategic", the company should carefully assess the fit between its sustainability strategies and the suppliers' strategy, as well as a long-term collaboration and integration for the achievement of long-term sustainability-related goals. For suppliers classified as "non-strategic", the company can check their credentials in terms of sustainability by assessing the certifications or their general supplier performance. The sourcing company might recognise that some of its suppliers need development and support for their sustainability-related activities; in such cases, appropriate development strategies should be formulated, taking into account the power balance between buyer and supplier.

BOX 5.2 SUBSTANDARD SURGICAL TOOLS IN NHS SUPPLY CHAIN

In an article on "Surgery's Dirty Secrets" published by *Panorama* it was highlighted that substandard surgical tools from Pakistan have been putting UK patients at risk of potentially deadly injury and infection.

Faults include rough edges, steel burrs that can splinter during operations, and corroded metals. All surgical instruments have to meet regulatory standards but only one of the more than 180 NHS trusts and boards conducts rigorous tests on every tool. Barts and the London NHS Trust reject almost 20% of tools as unsafe for use. Tom Brophy, the dedicated technologist at Barts, said the prevalence of faulty equipment that could endanger patients' lives or cause serious injuries is so worrying that he has started documenting the faults. While he is able to return unsuitable or faulty tools to suppliers, he said there is nothing to stop those same instruments from being sold on to another UK hospital, either within the NHS or private. "On more than one occasion a supplier has rung me up and said that the instrument you rejected, I passed it onto another hospital, and they accepted it", he said. "Of course, they're going to accept it, because they haven't checked it". While most hospitals carry out some degree of visual checks on instruments, only Barts employs a dedicated technologist.

Poor quality surgical implements have been identified as a likely cause of MRSA infections because shards of steel have caused microscopic holes in surgical gloves. Badly made instruments that have unwanted grooves or trenches can trap body tissue and fluids – another possible source of infection. All of the 916 companies making or supplying surgical instruments in the United Kingdom must be registered with the Medicines and Health Care Products Regulatory Agency

(MHRA), but responsibility for quality rests with suppliers and manufacturers. Neither the NHS nor the MHRA requires suppliers to inspect manufacturers. In a statement, the MHRA said "it has no evidence that non-compliant instruments are being supplied to the NHS", but added that if there were such evidence, it had "a range of powers and sanctions available to deal with the problem". In addition to rejecting poor quality equipment that is sold to Barts, Mr Brophy said he has been sent used equipment – with traces of blood still on the instruments – being passed off as new.

Two-thirds of the world's surgical instruments are made in the city of Sialkot in northern Pakistan and 70% of the UK's registered manufacturers are based in the city. While some of the larger companies operate state-of-the art facilities and have rigorous quality-control procedures in place, *Panorama* found evidence of smaller firms that do not use magnifying glasses to inspect finished instruments before putting the required quality stamp on them. Others outsourced manufacturing to some of the 3,000 back-street workshops in the city where undercover filming revealed a complete lack of hygiene or quality control. Professor Brian Toft, a government adviser on patient safety, said if procurement officers in both the NHS and private hospitals in the United Kingdom knew of the conditions in which the surgical instruments were being made, they would "faint at the thought of it". "I cannot believe that anybody in the NHS knows this is going on", he said.

The governments in Northern Ireland, Wales, and Scotland gave the following responses to "Panorama: Surgery's Dirty Secrets".

The procurement process for surgical equipment in Northern Ireland Business Services Organisation, Procurement and Logistics Service, carries out the procurement activity for all Health and Social Care organisations in NI. Surgical instruments are in the main used by the five acute hospital HSC Trusts and are procured for them by the BSO PaLS. Procurement of all equipment is governed according to the various levels of expenditure. The DHSSPS mini-code allows for local competition at the lower level spend moving to EU competition on the appropriate higher level spend. In some cases, Northern Ireland has scope to utilise a range of existing UK-based contract arrangements and/or conduct its own competitions as is appropriate. Products of British Standard and source of production/child labour BSO, Procurement and Logistics Service will purchase goods to EU/British Standards. In terms of the source of production, BSO, Procurement and Logistics Service has for some years been attentive to the issues of 'ethical procurement' which covers the issues associated with child labour.

Discussion questions

- Can you identify the main stakeholders and draw a supply chain map for NHS surgical tools?
- Why is the NHS procuring surgical tools from Pakistan? What are the main implications for the NHS to manage Pakistani suppliers?
- What were the main issues the NHS faced with the purchased materials?
- What are the likely causes of the problems faced by NHS hospitals?
- What were the options for the NHS's procurement policy after these issues?

Sources:

[1] BBC Panorama: Surgery's Dirty Secrets
URL: www.bbc.co.uk/programmes/b012b0v5
[2] NHS responses to Panorama. Available at:
http://news.bbc.co.uk/panorama/hi/front_page/newsid_9524000/9524136.stm
[3] *The Guardian* article: "New guidelines to improve healthcare's 'horrendous' supply chain record", available at:
www.theguardian.com/sustainable-business/nhs-healthcare-supply-chain-guidelines

Sustainability in making

Sustainable in making, or manufacturing, involves designing and managing manufacturing processes while concurrently considering the three pillars of sustainability: economic, environmental, and social. This is a key aspect for the achievement of sustainability-related goals, and therefore this topic will be discussed in more detail in Chapter 6. This section provides an overview of the key concepts and approaches related to sustainable manufacturing and will discuss these concepts and approaches within the broader context of supply chain management.

There are different tools adopted for the achievement of environmentally sustainable manufacturing, such as the Environmental Impact Assessment (EIA), the Life Cycle Assessment (LCA), or the ISO 14000 standards. Similarly, there are different tools adopted for the achievement of socially sustainable manufacturing, such as the Risk Assessment matrix for Occupational Health and Safety. These approaches will be discussed in more detail in Chapter 6.

The different levels at which energy efficiency interventions can be implemented suggest that the selection of the appropriate intervention is not easy. A guiding principle for the selection of the best intervention can be the alignment between the environmental, social, and business value that the intervention can generate and the value streams that the firm is trying to identify and capture.

Sustainability in delivery: sustainable logistics

Logistics ensures the smooth flow of materials along the supply chain, connecting the point of origin for raw materials and the point of consumption to meet customers' requirements. The activities typically classified under the umbrella of logistics include transportation, inventory management, and warehousing. All these activities have profound implications in terms of sustainability. Transport activities use fuel and generate emissions, usually consuming non-renewable resources and polluting air, water, and land. Warehousing activities use energy for lighting, refrigeration, and air conditioning, consume land, and can potentially contaminate soil though chemical or waste spillage. To understand the magnitude of the environmental impact of logistics activities on a global scale, we can consider the assessment of the Energy Information Administration, which estimated that the transportation of people and goods accounts for about 25% of all energy consumption in the world (maritime–executive). This section will present some potential approaches to enhance the sustainability implications of the three main logistics-related activities: inventory management, transportation, and warehousing.

Sustainability implications of inventory management

The inventory policy essentially deals with deciding the level of inventory kept in the company or, in more general terms, along the supply chain. The target level of inventory has implications in terms of number of orders, quantity ordered, sourcing location, and average level of inventory. All these decisions have different implications in terms of environmental sustainability. For instance, a big number of orders implies higher environmental costs related to the transportation. Therefore, local sourcing is generally more environmentally sustainable than international sourcing, at least from the perspective of the transportation-related costs. Similarly, a high average level of inventory implies higher environmental costs because of the emissions generated by the warehousing-related activities. There are different models that support decision makers in assessing the right level of inventory, such as the economic order quantity (EOQ), or the more general lean management principles. These models can also consider sustainability-related criteria, thus generating approaches like the EOQ revisited with sustainability considerations (Arslan and Turkay, 2013) or the Green Lean (Mollenkopf et al., 2010). These models represent an attempt at introducing some structured approaches for sustainable inventory management. However, environmental sustainability is so complex and it implies the consideration of so many variables that the sensitivity of the manager should always oversee the process and should understand the output of the mentioned models within the broader context of the sustainability strategy that the company is implementing. For instance, if we think of an example from the food industry, a company could have to decide between sourcing apples locally, with lower transportation costs but also higher levels of fertiliser, or internationally, with more transportation resources but also less fertiliser. It is ultimately the sensitivity of the manager rather than a specific model that will drive the choice towards the priorities of the firm and the highest environmental and economic value.

Sustainability implications of transportation

Transportation moves inventory along the supply chain. The decisions involved in transportation include the design of the transportation network and the choice of the transportation mode (Chopra and Meindl, 2007). Both these decisions have implications in terms of sustainability. The design of the transportation network sets the routes to move the products. Decision makers can use models like linear programming to identify the best transportation route that minimises the economic and environmental costs. Generally, there is a synergy between the reduction of the economic and environmental costs, but this is not always the case because different routes could imply different transportation modes. While designing the transportation mode, the company selects the modes of transport for products between air, rail, road, or water. The different transportation modes have different implications in terms of sustainability. It is, however, difficult to assess the environmental costs of the different alternatives, especially if the costs incurred over the entire life cycle are considered. For instance, air transportation is highly intensive in terms of CO_2 emissions per transported ton, but it is less intensive in terms of infrastructure needed for the transportation.

Sustainability implications of warehousing

Warehousing involves the activities of storage, materials handling, unpacking, and packing of different types of inventory (materials, parts, and goods), including order picking. The different warehousing choices have several sustainability implications. An increasingly stringent environmental regulation, as well as the attempt to reduce the costs, has triggered several efforts on the improvement of sustainability in warehousing.

A first example of these efforts is the energy use. A typical non-refrigerated warehouse or distribution centre will need lighting and heating, with considerable potential savings related to the introduction of insulation and energy efficient lighting. Progress has been made in the last decades, although several if not most of the warehouses are still energy inefficient and poorly insulated (Building Energy Efficiency Survey, 2014).

A second example of sustainability-related effort in warehousing regards packaging.

There are different types of packaging, generally classified as primary, secondary, and tertiary, and addressing different functions in the supply chain, from handling materials throughout the logistic system to presenting to consumers. The choices related to these different types of packaging have considerable environmental implications: the packaging materials can be disposable or reusable and an appropriate use of packaging can reduce the transport and storage space, by affecting the size of the lot. As for energy efficiency, progress has been made in the last decades, including the introduction of novel packaging processes that minimise the transport of empty space, the use of reusable packaging, as well as labelling that clearly identifies reuse, recycling, and composting options.

BOX 5.3 COVID-19 PANDEMIC BOOMS ONLINE SHOPPING AND CREATES SHORTAGES OF CARDBOARD

www.bbc.co.uk/news/business-55878062

The boom in online ordering during the pandemic has also meant rocketing demand for cardboard, as consumers have started taking delivery of everything from bicycles to houseplants.

The Confederation of Paper Industries (CPI) says while there is always a peak in demand in the run up to Christmas, stockpiling around the Brexit deadline exacerbated the problem. Covid-19 also led to complications with shipping and staffing challenges, which affected the industry on a global basis. The CPI described it as a "perfect storm" but said new capacity coming on stream would help ease the pressure.

Multinational packaging firm, DS Smith, said the problem lies partly in the recycling chain. Pre-pandemic when most deliveries were made in bulk to high street shops and restaurants, packaging found its way quickly back into the system via recycling firms.

Disappointed customers

"All our boxes are made from recycled material", said group chief executive Miles Roberts.

"One of the challenges for us is that, with so much packaging now in people's homes or in their garages, how do we get that paper back into the recycled network, how we can get it back into our mills so we can convert it into paper and reuse it again?"

Richard Ellison had to explain the problems to some disappointed customers. About 100 customers, expecting a next-day delivery of organic wine from Wanderlust Wine, saw their orders slip by a day or two.

"We were warned there was a shortage of raw materials", says Mr Ellison. Prices jumped and the lead time on orders went from a week to three months.

"That's a huge lead time to get boxes made", he says. He ended up buying 3,000 boxes at double the cost, he says. And now he's switched to using non-branded standard boxes rather than the bespoke ones designed for Wanderlust.

Even supermarkets are feeling the pinch with Asda, Lidl, and the Co-op finding they had to switch to plastic boxes for their eggs for the same reason, prompting criticism on social media.

"There is a shortage of the pulp used to make the cardboard boxes that is affecting all retailers. These plastic ones are 100% recyclable but we hope to go back to the cardboard ones as soon as we can", Asda responded on Twitter.

Axl Barber, boss of packaging firm Rightbox, says the problems started back in October but now "it's really crazy". "A standard box with flaps at top and bottom can get made up in days and delivered in a week in normal times", he says. "At the moment it's two months, three months".

He's helping small firms find solutions on a case-by-case basis, using whatever boxes can be found. One firm selling PPE resorted to using boxes without lids by wrapping them thoroughly.

Some firms are blaming the suppliers of raw materials themselves, others point the finger at the retail behemoths, like Amazon, for taking more than their fair share. Amazon said it has been reducing the amount of packaging it uses in recent years, including sometimes shipping products in their own packages without additional "shipping boxes".

Sustainability in returning: closed-loop supply chains

Closed-loop supply chains are those where the traditional flow of materials and goods from suppliers to consumers is complemented by a reverse flow of product returns from the consumers to manufacturers, with the objective of recovering residual value as well as limiting the production of waste and the consumption of virgin (original) raw materials.

There are different types of product returns. Flapper et al. (2005) classify product returns into three types, i.e. commercial returns, end-of-use returns, and end-of-life returns. Commercial returns are the products that consumers return within a few days after purchase, according to the return policy of a particular country. These product returns are particularly important because they are often fully functional and may be part of new or recent product lines. Therefore, their residual value after the return is very high. The importance of these products is growing increasingly with the development of e-commerce, and in some industries such as fashion commercial returns can be worth up to 70% of the turnover (Flapper et al., 2005). End-of-use returns are products that are still functional but have been replaced by the customer with a newer version of the same product. The residual value of these returns is probably not as high as the previous case but can still be considerable. A typical example of these products returns are mobile phones or fashion apparel. End-of-life returns are products that are no longer used or needed or are broken beyond repair. The residual value is very low and often limited to the value of the materials embedded in the product.

There are different alternative processes that can be used to process product returns. These include re-selling, refurbishing, remanufacturing, recycling, or sending for disposal when no residual value can be recovered. From an environmental point of view, there is a hierarchy among these methods of processing returns, since re-selling consumes the least amount of energy, followed by refurbishing, remanufacturing, and recycling. Disposal by incineration or sending to landfill is at the bottom of the hierarchy.

It is clear how significant the environmental savings can be for the different methods of processing returns. However, the business-related advantages can also be considerable. An important advantage concerns the reduction of production costs. Taking the case of re-manufacturing, it has been estimated that a re-manufactured product can be from 30% to 90% cheaper than producing a new product from virgin materials. A second advantage concerns the image of the firm, since it can brand itself as a "green" company by being involved in a closed-loop supply chain. A third benefit concerns the knowledge about product performance that a company can gain from collecting returned products and understanding the causes for their return. Other benefits include increased customer loyalty and increased supply chain resilience because of the control of closed-loop flows of material, thus reducing the dependency on materials suppliers.

Because of these advantages, closed-loop supply chains are being increasingly implemented by companies, in line with the development of the circular economy concept described in Chapter 2. The transition from a linear to a circular economy is, however, still ongoing and therefore there continue to be many barriers to the implementation of closed-loop supply chains, such as the lack of infrastructure for the reverse logistics processes or the attitude of consumers towards the purchase of used or refurbished products.

Conclusions

The key activities of a supply chain include the planning, sourcing, making, and delivering of products and services. The way in which these activities are implemented had profound implications in terms of sustainability. Being sustainable when designing and operating supply chains often means adding environmental and social criteria to the more traditional criteria used in the decision-making processes. While the sustainability-related and environmental criteria often operate in synergy, in some cases a trade-off is needed. The ability of the supply chain manager, or the decision maker more generally, will suggest the best trade-off between the different criteria, and therefore the optimal intervention. A guiding principle for the selection of the best intervention can be the alignment between the environmental, social, and business values that the intervention can generate and the value streams that the firm is trying to identify and capture.

References

Arslan, M. C., & Turkay, M. (2013). EOQ revisited with sustainability considerations. *Foundations of Computing and Decision Sciences*, *38*(4), 223–249.

Chopra, S., & Meindl, P. (2007). Supply chain management. Strategy, planning & operation. In *Das summa summarum des management* (pp. 265–275). Gabler.

https://www.maritime-executive.com/article/transport-uses-25-percent-of-world-energy. (n.d.). Building Energy Efficiency Survey, 2014. Accessed at: https://assets.publishing.service.gov.uk/government/uploads/system/uploads/attachment_data/file/565748/BEES_overarching_report_FINAL.pdf on 22 July 2021

Mollenkopf, D., Stolze, H., Tate, W. L., & Ueltschy, M. (2010). Green, lean, and global supply chains. *International Journal of Physical Distribution & Logistics Management*, *40*(1–2), 14–41.

Poluha, R. G. (2007). *Application of the SCOR Model in Supply Chain Management*. Youngstown, New York: Cambria Press.

Flapper, S. D., van Nunen, J., & Van Wassenhove, L. N. (Eds.). (2005). *Managing Closed-loop Supply Chains*. New York: Springer Science & Business Media.

6 Sustainable production

In this chapter we consider the production function of an organisation, which is core to operations management and can involve the production of manufactured goods or services. The production function, sometimes referred to generally as a production system (and more specifically as a manufacturing system or service delivery system, depending on the context), comprises inputs, transformation processes, and outputs. This chapter therefore has close connections with supply chains, which provide the flow of inputs and outputs (see Chapter 5), and process technologies, which enable transformation of the inputs into outputs (see Chapter 7). The main difference between production systems for manufactured goods and services is that with manufacturing the customer is external to the system, whereas in services the customer (or something belonging to the customer) is internal to the system and part of the objects being processed. Here, we consider the sustainability aspects of production with the main focus on manufacturing. Where relevant, consideration is also given to the unique sustainability perspectives regarding service production.

The key learning outcomes of the chapter are:

- to define sustainable production;
- to discuss the main principles and approaches of green production;
- to discuss the main principles and approaches of socially sustainable production.

Introduction: what is sustainable production?

Nowadays sustainability is closer to the core competitive priorities of a firm. In addition to the ethical relevance of sustainability, ignoring sustainability-related principles implies costs in the form of fines, penalties, local unrest, and loss of customers. On the other hand, the management of production based on good environmental and social practices can enable money savings, build an attractive brand, attract investment, spur innovation, and secure loyal customers. These benefits can interest both large and small and medium-sized enterprises (SMEs), despite the latter often having more flexible business models and less established ways of working. There are different definitions for sustainable production, and in particular sustainable manufacturing. The US Department of Commerce's Sustainable Manufacturing Initiative refers to: "Manufacturing processes that minimize negative environmental impacts, conserve energy and natural resources, are safe for employees, communities and consumers and are economically sound". Simply put, sustainable manufacturing is about designing and managing the manufacturing processes while considering the three pillars of sustainability: economic, environmental, and

DOI: 10.4324/9781003009375-8

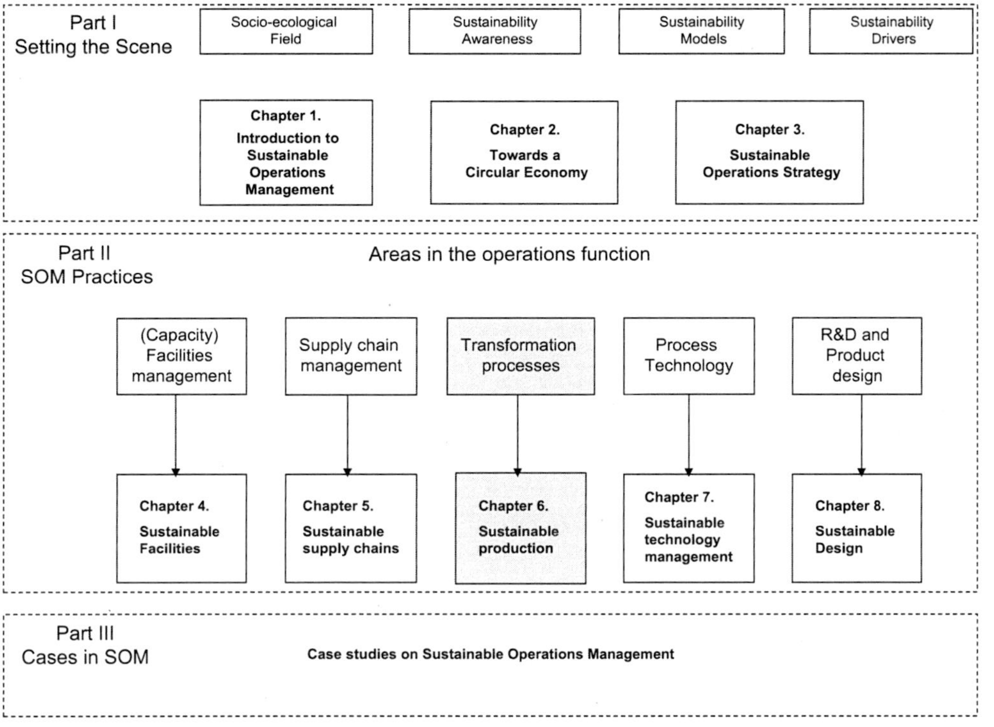

Figure 6.1 Chapter 6 within the book structure

social. This chapter presents the key concepts of sustainable manufacturing as well as their relevance to the delivery of services, together with the main industrial approaches used to translate these concepts into practice. The chapter is structured as follows. The following section will briefly discuss the relevance of production, both from a macro-economic perspective and from a company perspective. Then the next section will focus on the environmental side of sustainable production, focusing on manufacturing, introducing some of the most often used tools for improving sustainability. After that is a section focusing on the social aspects of sustainable production, and in particular on Occupational Health and Safety (OHS), which is a key area of sustainability focus within production. The final section will present the chapter's conclusions.

The importance of production

Producing manufactured goods generates 14% of the gross domestic product (GDP) of OECD countries and of Europe (OECD, 2016), and 31% of the world GDP (US Central Intelligence Agency, 2017). The production of manufactured goods also has a profound impact on the development of other related sectors, and it is therefore considered an enabler for the development of modern economies. Service production on the other hand, when measured by GDP, has overtaken manufacturing in most industrialised economies, being 70.9% of GDP in the European Union and 80.0% of GDP in the USA (US Central Intelligence Agency, 2017).

In the light of the importance of production for the wealth and the growth of a country, it is easy to understand that manufacturing and service production as an industrial sector has a considerable impact on sustainability. Indeed, manufacturing alone directly contributes to the extraction and transformation of materials, since it acquires materials in input and produces outputs. The outputs of manufacturing include both the products and by-products of the manufacturing processes, with different degrees of residual value and recyclability at the end of the manufacturing processes.

Considering manufacturing in particular, some figures on the entity of its inputs and outputs help to understand its sustainability impact. Manufacturing accounts for 26% of the final energy consumption and 28.5% of the greenhouse gases in the EU 27 (Lapillonne et al., 2016, data from 2013). The impact of the manufacturing sector is also very high if we consider the environmental impact of its products over their life cycle. This aspect is increasingly relevant because of the increasingly high number of products and appliances that consumers currently purchase compared to a few decades ago (Energy Saving Trust, 2016).

Manufacturing also has profound implications in terms of social sustainability. It employs 17% of the European workforce (Eurofound, 2012) and represents more than 23% of worldwide total employment (International Labour Organization, 2014). A critical aspect determining the social sustainability of manufacturing activity is the Occupational Health and Safety conditions within manufacturing firms. While the Occupational Health and Safety conditions within manufacturing firms have considerably improved over the last decades (World Health Organization, 2013), problems still persist and they result in an unacceptable number of work-related deaths and injuries, both in developed and in developing countries. The economic losses related to these accidents can account for 4% of the gross domestic product of a European country (Loke et al., 2013).

Environmentally sustainable manufacturing

This section specifically focuses on manufacturing within the overall scope of production in countries' economies. The benefits generated by green manufacturing can be understood by considering the different types of value they are able to create. Schenkel et al. (2015) define four types of value: economic, environmental, information, and customer related. The mechanisms behind the generation of economic value include cost reduction from the optimisation of the manufacturing processes related to green interventions, from the reduction of raw material consumption or from the reduction of disposal costs. The mechanisms behind the generation of environmental value include waste reduction and pollution prevention related to green interventions, as well as the reduction in consumption of scarce virgin materials. Mechanisms behind the generation of information value include life cycle information on product performance from life cycle assessments or information on the performance of the product taken from collecting product returns. Mechanisms behind the generation of customer-related value include the increased customer satisfaction and loyalty that increasingly follows the implementation of green manufacturing.

There are many interventions that manufacturers can implement to achieve the above-mentioned benefits. Providing a comprehensive description of all these interventions goes beyond the purpose of the chapter but described here are the most common and impactful interventions used for the achievement of environmentally sustainable manufacturing. These are Life Cycle Assessment, Energy Efficiency, and Waste Reduction.

ISO 14000

ISO 14000 (ISO 14000, n.d.) is a set of rules and standards used in the context of green manufacturing. It is a voluntary approach and its purpose is to guide companies in the minimisation of the environmental impact of their operations as well as in the achievement of the compliance with the compulsory environmental laws and requirements. Being a standard, the certification process implies the involvement of a third-party organisation that performs the certification.

Among the standards included in the ISO 14000 family, ISO 14001 is the pivotal one and it guides companies in the design and implementation of an effective environmental management system (EMS). Other standards have a more specific focus and purpose; for instance, ISO 14064 focuses on measuring, quantifying, and reducing greenhouse gas emissions, while ISO 14090 focuses on the principles and guidelines for the adaptation to climate change.

The basic approach of ISO 14000 is the Plan–Do–Check–Act (PDCA) cycle, which iteratively applies the steps of establishing the objectives and processes required (Plan), implements the processes (Do), measures and monitors the processes and reports the results (Check), taking action to improve the performance of the environmental management system based on the results (Act). A look at a section of the ISO standard will show how simple but detailed are the recommendations that it includes. For instance, the standard might suggest that while planning for the environmental management system, the organisation shall consider the issues, requirements, and scope of the system itself, while providing a checklist for issues and requirements. Similarly, while discussing the compliance with obligations, the guidelines suggest that the organisation shall have access to obligations, understand how they apply to the organisation, as well as take them into account while implementing the systems.

There are advantages and disadvantages in using a standard for the implementation of green manufacturing within a production plant. The first main advantage is that a standard is relatively simple to understand and to implement. Moreover, a third-party company will perform the certification, thus giving the possibility of outsourcing part of the assessment work. However, the negative side of this simplicity, and more in general the negative side of adopting a standard, is that a standard does not necessarily match the specific needs and requirements of a specific firm, and specific skills are needed to adapt the requirements of the standard to the specific context of the firm. Another consideration regards the costs involved in the implementation of a standard. The costs related to the implementation of an ISO standard would be not affordable for a small or micro enterprise, especially if it operates in a developing country. Unfortunately, these companies are the ones that often need more support in terms of environmental management. A third consideration regards the possibility of innovating and introducing state-of-the-art interventions. A standard is by definition based on practices whose effectiveness has been tested and validated by several previous implementations. Therefore, these practices are not necessarily aligned with the most recent innovations in the sector.

Energy efficiency

Manufacturing processes use one or more physical methods to transform a material's form or shape. The energy required for such operations is considered as an input of the process, which is partially transformed into useful work, embodied into the form and composition of the products and unused (waste) material while the rest is transformed into lost heat. Manufacturing processes utilises only a fraction of the consumed energy for the actual value adding process, while the majority of the energy is used for creating stable process conditions and peripheral functions. Energy efficiency becomes a driver for the manufacturing industry, since it is historically one of the greatest energy consumers and carbon emitters among all industries. The manufacturing sector is responsible for about 33% of the primary energy use and for 38% of the CO_2 emissions globally (Fysikopoulos et al., 2013). Moreover, the increasing price of energy and the current trend of sustainability have exerted new pressures on manufacturing enterprises that have to reduce energy consumption for both cost saving and in response to environmental pressures, as well as Life Cycle Inventories initiatives. During the last 20 years, there has been an increase in energy prices of up to 100%. Energy savings are expected to be achievable by increasing both the energy efficiency of production and the logistics processes, as well as in innovative energy monitoring and management approaches, leading industries to a way of producing "more with less".

The challenge for manufacturing companies is to tackle the apparent dichotomy between competitive and environmentally friendly operations. Increasing demand for energy, coupled with a restricted supply on world markets, has resulted in prices of energy continuously increasing. This general development, as well as the dynamics in price setting, generates uncertainties for organisations with respect to accurately predicting energy costs. The situation becomes even more complex since proper improvements in energy efficiency may be achieved by an approach that considers multiple actions and the involvement of relevant third parties.

Production planning plays a significant role in achieving energy efficiency. Load management of the production facilities can offer great savings from an energy point of view. Moving towards energy efficient production planning requires the inclusion of energy efficiency within the goals of production systems design and control at all levels, together with time cost and flexibility. The reduction of idle time through energy efficient process planning, with a combination of better batch scheduling and organising the customer will lead to a better prediction of workflow. Order distribution combined with planned "machine shut down" can reduce significantly unplanned idle time, which is the most inefficient state of the systems. Managers and production controllers should be able to plan production not only by considering the costs, but also by considering energy efficiency. The need to have indicators for the integration of energy efficiency, systematically within planning processes, is now greater than ever before.

Energy efficiency indicators, or more generally energy performance indicators, provide the links between energy use and relevant monetary or physical indicators measuring the demand for energy services. They may be defined at different levels of aggregation in terms of energy demand, e.g. economy-wide, sector, sub-sector, end use, technology, process, and device. Energy performance indicators can be used to quantify improvements in energy efficiency, use, and consumption at the organisation, facility, system, and process or equipment level. Energy performance indicators are a measure of energy intensity used to gauge effectiveness of energy management efforts. These indicators, previously defined during the preparation of the company's energy policy, express a quantitative value of energy performance measurement. The value of energy consumption should be related to a reference variable that allows it to be correctly interpreted. For example: kWh/m^2, kWh/m^3, etc. Responsibility for determining the energy performance indicators typically rests with the energy management representative and may involve other members of the energy control team, as well as general management. Resources to complete the energy performance indicators determination process are allocated by senior management. The concept of energy performance includes energy use, energy efficiency, and energy consumption. The organisation can choose between a wide range of energy performance activities. For example, the organisation could reduce peak demand, utilise surplus or waste energy or improve the operations of its systems, processes, or equipment. Energy savings and reducing energy waste are often subservient to production targets, and decisions about changing machine states involve weighing up a complex set of goals and constraints. These include constraints such as production capacity, predicted inventory, and product priorities as well as soft constraints as technician skill level, engineering requests, and autonomous maintenance.

METAL ASSEMBLIES LTD

Metal Assemblies Ltd (MAL) produces press metal parts, machined components and welded assemblies for the automotive supply chain (accredited TS-16949:2016) with over 60 years' experience in the sector. Its customers are first-tier suppliers to OEMs, e.g. Toyota, BMW, and Nissan. Turnover is split between the United Kingdom (80%) and the European Union (20%), based on 2018 Accounts. MAL works with clients using its technical competency to offer design review and feasibility advice across the range of processes available to reduce product complexity and lower production costs. It is accredited to ISO 9000, Automotive Quality, and Environmental Management Standards. The main requirements in obtaining a contract are rapid delivery time and low cost, given the low margins with which the company operates. MAL runs a core staff of 87 permanent employees supplemented by agency staff (approx. 30% of workforce) at a premium cost.

The new contract

Metal Assemblies Ltd (MAL) has won a large contract to supply components (steel pressings) to Calsonic, a Tier 1 Automotive supplier, for Nissan Qashqai vehicles worth GBP17.5M over 5 years. There is potential for more contracts to Russian and French plants, building its relationship with customers to be seen as a supply partner.

The press shop facilities

MAL has invested in press shop machinery but it still faces capacity constraints. The Overall Equipment Efficiency (OEE) for the press shop facilities is 30%, compared to 75% in other production areas. The press machines are characterised by low utilisation and high setup times. The company wants to analyse the current operational equipment effectiveness (OEE) of the machines and apply a production flow analysis technique to minimise the setup times, by improving the daily production plan and aggregating the production lots. The correct execution of this analysis will require a proper understanding of the people and procedures currently operating in the company. Improvements in OEE by implementing dynamic Operations & Process Management techniques will increase press shop productivity without major capital investment and will reduce the expensive temporary labour.

Digitalisation of operations

The company currently collects data useful for production planning and control through several white boards, one per critical machine. In order to implement dynamic Operations & Process Management techniques, MAL will implement digitalisation, and leverage real-time data collection and digital technologies to deliver productivity improvements and growth, establishing MAL as an exemplar Tier 2 supplier deploying a data-driven management strategy. Key steps for the implementation of a digitalisation strategy include:

- streamlining processes for operational improvements;
- using accurate, real-time data to review performance and efficiency;
- continuous review of performance measures to identify issues, e.g. unplanned downtime due to equipment failure;
- accurately scheduling and predicting how jobs will run to streamline storage and delivery of raw materials;
- identifying trends in tooling/set-up and press tool performance that will feed into improved tooling design, construction, and change times;
- expand management/leadership capabilities using KPIs to increase autonomy for shop floor staff.

Questions

1. Comment on the impact of MAL's initiatives on its manufacturing performance considering all three dimensions of sustainability (economic, environmental, and social).
2. What approaches would you adopt to gain a proper understanding of the people and procedures currently operating in the company?
3. What measures would you use to analyse their operational equipment effectiveness of the press machines? How does OEE impact on their environmental sustainability performance?
4. What approaches would you adopt to expand the management and leadership capabilities of the staff and increase the autonomy for shop floor staff? What sustainability benefits can MAL obtain by increasing shop floor staff autonomy?

Waste reduction

Manufacturing waste is generated in almost every manufacturing plant, so it is important to establish practices for its minimisation. Some types of commonly observed wastes in manufacturing facilities include overproduction, defects, unnecessary inventory, motion, and transportation, as well as waiting times, over-processing, and unused time and creativity of employees.

Manufacturing waste can be reduced by controlling the materials being used in the manufacturing process. This implies reducing the amount of excess raw materials in stock and the quantity of hazardous materials by ordering only the necessary quantities and in only the amount needed for a specific period of time.

As mentioned in Chapter 5, another key source of waste is packaging, which can be reduced by redesigning it to ensure it uses the minimum amount of materials. Reusable or recyclable packaging materials should also be used and for internal protection air packs or, for example, biodegradable vegetable-based materials should be used when possible. Packaging can also be reduced by purchasing products in bulk. Recover, reuse, and recycle are other key strategies for the reduction of waste, as part of creating the circular economy described in Chapter 2. Manufacturers can recover waste from onsite and offsite locations by employing different techniques like electrolysis, filtration, reverse osmosis, centrifugation, etc. Recycling is another popular choice, which can be done for most materials such as paper, thermoplastics, and metal. Recycling of hazardous materials should be avoided as it rarely has any environmental benefits. Industrial shredders are helpful because they can reduce waste to a fraction of its original size. They can be used for shredding asphalt, wood, rubber, and plastics. Sorting of waste ensures that the recyclable items are going to the right place. There should be a means of monitoring waste bins, and a viable solution for eliminating, reducing, or reusing the generated waste should be introduced.

Although wear and tear is a normal occurrence in any production process, a business will end up wasting a lot of time and money on seriously damaged equipment if regular maintenance is not performed. It would be better to anticipate and prevent a failure instead of reacting to a breakdown later, which results in unnecessary overtime and increased shipping costs to expedite delivery. Finally, companies should ensure that warehouses are organised and well marked with clearly defined areas and signage. All the locations of inventory, tools, supplies, and assets necessary for the production processes must be clearly marked throughout the warehouse. Over time, the markings may become faded, erased, or outdated. While this may not be a hindrance for experienced employees, any new or temporary workers may have difficulty navigating through a warehouse that is not organised or marked properly.

A closed loop manufacturing system or "green chemistry" in process industries can keep track of inventory and utilise recycled materials in production. Moreover, closed loop systems help in extending the lifespan of lubricants, cleaning materials, or chemicals etc. by maximising how efficiently they are used. This helps in reducing the amount of contamination being produced and minimises the number of new materials or chemicals that need to be purchased.

Industrial sludge and wastewater make up a significant portion of manufacturing waste streams. These elements can be reduced by minimising water usage in the operations. This can be achieved by using chemical drying agents, reverse osmosis, dry machining, or membrane biological reactors. And finally, even employees can contribute by reducing the number of disposable containers they use, such as plastic cups or polystyrene food boxes.

Socially sustainable production: Occupational Health and Safety

In addition to its impact on the environment, production also has a considerable impact in terms of social sustainability. A key aspect of this is the Occupational Health and Safety (OHS) conditions within the manufacturing plant. Although this has often been neglected because of the improvements to conditions in industrialised countries, the Covid-19 pandemic and its impact on workers' safety has highlighted again the pivotal importance of OHS. Moreover, while in most industrialised countries there has been an improvement, good OHS conditions are still often lacking in many developed and emerging countries.

Overall, the numbers of occupational accidents and work-related diseases are still high globally. According to a recent report by the International Labour Organization (ILO), on average 6,300 people die every day as a result of occupational accidents or work-related diseases, accounting for more than 2.3 million deaths per year (ILO, online). The US Bureau of Labour Statistics has recorded a total of 4,679 fatal work injuries in 2014 (2015a), with an increase of 2% over the previous year, and nearly 3.0 million nonfatal workplace injuries and illnesses, a rate of 3.2 cases per 100 equivalent full-time workers (2015b).

Moreover, work morbidity and mortality has resulted in increasing the overall cost to society due to productivity loss and additional costs for medical care. According to the WSH Institute (2015), based on country estimates, the economic costs of work-related injury and illness vary between 1.8% and 6% of GDP, with an average of 4%. In previous similar studies, other authors have estimated the total cost to society of diseases and injuries due to occupational factors to be in the range of 2% to 14% of the GNP (Leigh et al., 1999).

The International Labour Organization (ILO, 2014) highlighted the potential negative influence of the recent global financial crisis and economic recession (2007–09) on occupational safety and health. The chronic worrying figures of fatal and nonfatal accidents are strongly influenced by the concurrent effects of more structural factors. Among others, it is recognised that the diffusion of Occupational Health and Safety Management Systems has not yet yielded the benefits that were expected by managers and policy makers (da Silva and Amarala, 2019). Similarly, the negative effects of rapid technological or organisational changes have many times outweighed the development of safe work standards and the implementation of safety improvement programmes. Nevertheless, the urgency of intervening on Occupational Health and Safety (OHS) is widely acknowledged (see e.g. WSH Institute, 2015).

Managing OHS from the point of view of a manufacturing plant includes several activities. The activities focused on OHS have become increasingly complex, and they can include installing sensors monitoring the working conditions within the plant, or establishing an OHS management system, like the ISO 45001:2018 (ISO 45001, 2018). All approaches to the improvement of OHS share three key activities: the identification of the hazards, risk assessment, and design of interventions for the mitigation of risks.

The identification of the hazards consists of identifying and describing all the potential sources of risk for the safety or health of workers. The main sources of risk include biological, chemical, physical, ergonomic, and psychosocial hazards. Biological hazards include viruses, bacteria, and similar agents that can cause adverse health impacts. Those most at risk from these hazards are the workers in the healthcare sector, or cleaners, waste and refuse collectors. Chemical hazards are those originating from hazardous substances that can cause health and physical impacts, such as irritations, or explosions. Hazardous substances include such things as cleaning chemicals or welding fumes, and these can be potentially more dangerous because they might not always be immediately identifiable in the workplace. Many categories of workers are potentially at risk from these hazards, given the wide use of chemicals in many industries. Physical and ergonomic hazards are environmental factors that can harm an employee or result in musculoskeletal injuries. These hazards including heights, noise, radiation, and pressure, exposed wires, or a damaged floor that might cause a tripping hazard. Finally, psychosocial hazards include those that can have an adverse effect on an employee's mental health or well-being. For example, sexual harassment, victimisation, stress, and workplace violence.

Having identified the hazards that are relevant for the production plant, the next step in ensuring appropriate OHS conditions will consist in carrying out an appropriate risk assessment for the nature of the work and hazards. Risk is typically assessed by measuring the probability of occurrence and the impacts of the risk. By combining probability and impact, the overall level of risk can be determined. Based on this, decision makers can decide what are the priorities of intervention within their production plant. The risks are typically classified into three categories: low, medium, and high. It is important to note that a risk classified as high can be created both by a very high probability and a moderate impact, or by a very high impact and a moderate probability. Events like a fire (very high impact and a moderate probability) or fall from height (very high probability and a moderate impact) would therefore carry the same level of risk. The aggregated level of risk will determine the priority of intervention and the allocation of resources. However, while managing a production plant, it is important to consider both the aggregated level of risk and its components in terms of probability and impact. Indeed, these components will suggest the nature of the related interventions, that could reduce either the probability or the impact. A good tool to keep track of both the aggregated level of risk and its components in terms of probability and impact is the risk matrix shown in Figure 6.2.

Having assessed the risks, the last step consists of designing the interventions for mitigating risks that cannot be tolerated.

OHS interventions can take many forms, including work redesign, training, ergonomic programmes, adoption of personal protective equipment, or implementation of an OHS management system. There are several tools that support the decision maker in the design of the most appropriate OHS interventions. The literature offers general recommendations for implementing interventions (e.g., Fixsen et al., 2005; Meyers et al., 2012); practical guidelines for conducting interventions aimed at improving employee health and well-being at work (e.g., Nytrø et al., 2000; Sheldon, 2007; Weiner et al., 2009; Nielsen et al., 2010); and even more specific guidelines for implementing certain interventions in organisational contexts, such as those dealing with workplace stress management (Health and Safety Executive, 2007).

		Impact				
		Trivial	Minor	Moderate	Major	Extreme
Probability	Rare	Low	Low	Low	Medium	Medium
	Unlikely	Low	Low	Medium	Medium	Medium
	Moderate	Low	Medium	Medium	Medium	High
	Likely	Medium	Medium	Medium	High	High
	Very Likely	Medium	Medium	High	High	High

Figure 6.2 Risk matrix

CASE STUDY: SLIPPING ON DUST IN A PRODUCTION WORKSHOP

Source: www.hse.gov.uk/slips/experience/dust.htm

Statistics show that slipping and tripping are the most common causes of injuries. They can occur in all work-related activities, regardless of whether these are in manufacturing or service delivery settings.

The slip risks resulting from machining dust became a point of discussion when a HSE (Health and Safety Inspectorate) inspector slipped on the workshop floor during a routine visit. The inspector was not hurt but the company did agree that processing dust finding its way onto the floor in that area did make it rather slippery. Workers too said that the walkways and working area floors were very slippery; even more vulnerable were visitors to the workshops (such as staff from the offices) as they were often taken unawares by the slippery nature of the floors.

The painted concrete floors of the workshop could not be completely prevented from becoming contaminated with fine dust (up to 10 microns) from the cutting and machining of graphite components. Extract ventilation at machines was effective up to a point but the filtration systems did not seem to be able to capture as much of the dust as was needed, allowing some to be deposited on surfaces. This was compounded by the system of emptying by hand the bags holding the filtered-out dust; the manual process resulted in some dust being re-released and contaminating walkways.

The company set about dealing with this in two ways. Improving the floor grip so that it was better able to cope with the conditions and reducing dust contamination finding its way onto walkways.

Tests were carried out on various areas of the workshop floor to measure its microroughness and its slip resistance. When the floor surfaces were free of dust contamination they actually offered reasonable grip for pedestrians but when they got any dust on them, as they inevitably would, their slip resistance became very low. These were exactly the results that the company had expected the tests to reveal.

Trial treatments were carried out on various parts of the floor using epoxy paints with 'inclusions' of various sorts to give some surface roughness and grip. The best seemed to be gritty particles in a two-part epoxy – workers found it gave secure footing whether clean or with dust on it. Tests confirmed that the surface (with about 33 microns of surface roughness) did indeed give very good slip resistance when clean and still performed well when deliberately coated with carbon dust. The treatment was progressively extended throughout the workshop. Workers, who were somewhat sceptical to start with, quickly realised how well the treatment worked and were soon asking "When is my work area going to be done?"

The company even found the treatment worked on chequer plate metal stairs that, although only occasionally used, had been said to be especially slippery when dusty.

Floor audits are carried out as part of scheduled safety checks and any areas needing attention are identified. Indications are that the service life of the 'grit paint' finish is between 12 and 48 months, depending on the type and amount of use of the area. Treatment costs for the whole of the workshop worked out at around £1000.

Cleaning of the new floor finish is no more demanding with industrial grade dry vacuum cleaners doing the job day to day, supplemented by a period clean with a mechanical scrubber–dryer.

When the company looked at the amount of carbon dust being deposited throughout the workshop they resolved to do something about that too. They saw benefits in the contribution that it would make to preventing slips, providing a better working environment, and reducing the size of the general cleaning task. The existing dust capture and extraction system serving the workshop machines was not 'state of the art' and the filtration system was housed within the workshop. Plans were formulated to integrate all local exhaust ventilation into a single, more effective and efficient centralised system with the filtration plant located outside the workshop to avoid recontamination.

Of course, in addition to these benefits, the company hopes that the next HSE inspector's visit will pass without any 'slip ups'.

Conclusions

Sustainable production is the most important aspect to be considered by all managers and technicians in both manufacturing and service operations. Product life cycle analysis has become a tool of choice being used to establish the environmental impact of the products that we produce. Though application of a PLA is time and data intensive, it provides very clear avenues where environmental impact can be reduced. There are a number of areas within production that can benefit greatly from the adoption of green production or manufacturing practices. The three major principles to be considered are reducing the resource utilisation in the process, using environment-friendly materials, and reducing all forms of waste, reusing and recycling as much material as possible, to realise the goal of self-recovery capability of the earth. At the same time, social sustainability should be optimised by ensuring that the best OHS conditions are in place within production plants. These can be achieved through a regular assessment of the risks and implementation of interventions for the mitigation of the risks that are considered unacceptable.

References

da Silva, S. L. C., & Gonçalves Amarala, F. (2019) Critical factors of success and barriers to the implementation of occupational health and safety management systems: A systematic review of literature. *Safety Science*, *117*, 123–132.

Energy Saving Trust (2016). https://greengumption.co.uk/live/wp-content/uploads/TheRiseOfTheMachines.pdf.

Fixsen, D. L., Naoom, S. F., Blase, K. A., Friedman, R. M., Wallace, F. (2005). *Implementation Research: A Synthesis of the Literature*. Tampa: University of South Florida.

Fysikopoulos, A., Papacharalampopoulos, A., Pastras, G., Stavropoulos, P. and Chryssolouris G. (2013). Energy efficiency of manufacturing processes: A critical review. *Procedia CIRP*, 7, 628–633.

Health and Safety Executive (2007). https://www.hse.gov.uk/statistics/overall/hssh0708.pdf.

ILO (online). https://www.ilo.org/global/topics/safety-and-health-at-work/events-training/events-meetings/WCMS_DOC_ENT_HLP_OSH_EN/lang--en/index.htm.

ILO (2014). https://www.ilo.org/global/research/global-reports/world-of-work/2014/lang--en/index.htm.

ISO 14000 (n.d.). *Family: Environmental Management.* Geneve: International Organisation for Standardisation (ISO).

ISO 45001. (2018). *Occupational Health and Safety Management Systems: Requirements with Guidance for Use.* Geneve: International Organisation for Standardisation (ISO).

Lapillonne, B., Sebi, C., & Pollier, K. (2016). Energy efficiency trends in EU industry. https://www.odyssee-mure.eu/events/webinar/energy-efficiency-trends-industry-webinar-nov-2016.pdf.

Leigh, J., Macaskill, P., Kuosma, E., & Mandryk, J. (1999). Global burden of disease and injury due to occupational factors. *Epidemiology*, 626-631.

Loke, Y., Tan, J., Manickam, K. et al. (2013). Economic cost of work-related injuries and ill-health in Singapore. Singapore: WSH Institute. https://www.wsh-institute.sg/~/media/wshi/past%20publications/2013/economic%20cost%20of%20work-related%20injuries%20and%20ill-health%20in%20singapore.pdf?la=en. Accessed 5 June 2018.

Meyers, D. C., Durlak, J. A., & Wandersman, A. (2012). The quality implementation framework: a synthesis of critical steps in the implementation process. *American journal of community psychology, 50*(3), 462–480.

Nielsen, K., Randall, R., Holten, A. L., Rial-González, E. (2010). Conducting organizational-level occupational health interventions: What works? *Work Stress, 24*, 234–259. DOI: 10.1080/02678373.2010.515393 [CrossRef] [Google Scholar] [Ref list]

Nytrø, K., Saksvik, P. Ø., Mikkelsen, A., Bohle, P., Quinlan, M. (2000). An appraisal of key factors in the implementation of occupational stress interventions. *Work Stress, 14*, 213–225.

OECD (2016). https://stats.oecd.org/.

Schenkel, M., Caniëls, M., Krikke, H., & Van Der Laan, E. (2015). Understanding value creation in closed loop supply chains: Past findings and future directions. *Journal of Manufacturing Systems, 37*(April), 729–745.

Sheldon, M. R. (2007). Evidence-based practice in occupational health: description and application of an implementation effectiveness model. *Work, 29*(2), 137–143.

US Central Intelligence Agency (2017). https://www.cia.gov/the-world-factbook/.

Weiner, B. J., Lewis, M. A., & Linnan, L. A. (2009 Apr). Using organization theory to understand the determinants of effective implementation of worksite health promotion programs. *Health Education Research, 24*(2), 292–305.

World Health Organization (2013). https://apps.who.int/iris/handle/10665/81965.

7 Process technologies and sustainable operations

Process technologies are essential resources for management and control in manufacturing and service in organisations. No organisation can operate efficiently without the help of ubiquitous technologies in manufacturing such as production, transportation, and storage equipment as well as digital technologies, particularly those used in services, such as the internet, WiFi (Wireless Fidelity) networks, and mobile telecommunication technologies. Managing technologies is therefore of strategic importance for organisations in general, as they help firms not only to meet efficiency, market, and competitiveness requirements, but also to improve operations sustainability performance.

This chapter makes the link between process technologies and sustainable operations, providing an overview of their evolution and their potential role to enable the overall sustainability of organisations.

The key learning objectives of the chapter are:

- to position process technologies in the context of operations management;
- to justify the strategic importance of technologies to organisations;
- to characterise the historical waves of technological evolution, from Industry 1.0 to Industry 4.0;
- to discuss how technologies can improve the sustainability of organisations.

Introduction to technology and its role in operations

Technological advancements have the potential to radically change the way organisations operate in terms of automation, product and service innovations, interactions with stakeholders, and sustainability performance. Technologies in general, whether they are simple internet connections or sophisticated automation systems, are of strategic importance for organisations, as they can impact competitiveness, productivity, and sustainability (economic, social, and environmental). It is therefore crucially important to understand the role that technologies can play in operations, what advantages they can bring to the company and what constraints they might impose on an organisation. Managers do not usually need to know the technical details of all technologies, but they must have a good understanding of what a technology can do for their operations, the functionalities it brings, the advantages of adopting it, and the main difficulties with its adoption and deployment in the organisation.

DOI: 10.4324/9781003009375-9

Process technology

The term 'technology' can be viewed from two main perspectives, a tangible perspective and an intangible one. From a tangible perspective, technology usually refers to 'hard' objects such as machines, instruments, devices, and tools that are of practical use to humans and organisations. But technology also refers to 'soft', intangible, elements such as systems, methods, techniques, and the overall 'know-how' that can be applied to help organisations execute their activities. These two technological perspectives (tangible and intangible) are not necessarily separated, since the efficient utilisation of some technological machines or devices will require adequate methods and techniques for their operation. The tangible and intangible elements of technology can also be integrated in the same complete technological solution. For example, computers and smart mobile telephones (tangible hardware) can only work with software applications and systems (intangible technologies) installed in them.

In operations management, technologies can be considered particularly in relation to the role they play in supporting the production and service delivery processes. This is why they are referred to as 'process technologies'. In practice, companies can either embed technology in the products or services they provide for customers or use technology to support the production and delivery of their products or services (Brown et al., 2018). Process technology refers to this latter form of technology. Therefore, process technology can be defined as the equipment, machine, device, or system that enables and helps the production of goods and delivery of services (Slack and Brandon-Jones, 2018).

Some process technologies are directly applied in the production and delivery of goods and services. For example, a machine that controls the precise volume of a liquid when filling bottles (e.g. soft drinks) is directly supporting the production of the end-product. This type of technology is termed '*direct*' process technology. Other technologies have a peripheral role in supporting production and delivery processes. They assist and control production and delivery processes, rather than contributing directly to the creation and delivery of goods and services. Examples include computer systems to help managers to purchase the input materials for the production processes. These types of technology are called '*indirect*' process technologies and they play an important role in facilitating and supporting the operations activities.

Main types of process technologies

Process technologies can be classified according to the type of resource they process. In general, companies process the three basic resources of materials, information, or customers. Thus, process technologies can be classified as *materials-processing* technologies, *information-processing* technologies or *customer-processing* technologies. This classification helps managers to understand the main functionalities of different process technologies.

Modern technologies can in fact integrate functionalities for processing materials, information, and customers simultaneously. For example, the check-out technologies supporting supermarket cashiers integrate the moving belts that transfer the items close to the cashier, scanners to capture information from the barcode of products, and Electronic Point of Sale (EPOS) systems to process customers' payments and update the stock records of the items sold. More advanced process technologies are constantly being developed that integrate increasing numbers of functionalities.

There are so many different process technologies that it would be impossible to discuss all of them in this chapter. But regardless of the technology in question, they are all developed with the purpose of processing materials and information or processing (managing) customers in support of the production of goods or delivery of services.

Materials-processing technologies

Materials-processing technologies are those that manipulate, move, shape, or change the composition of one or more types of materials. Thus, the operations activities that these technologies support may involve materials transformations (transformation of raw materials into parts and finished goods), materials movement (transportation of materials from one place to another), and/or materials storage (automated storage, location, and retrieval of stored items).

Consequentially, materials-processing technologies are more commonly used in manufacturing operations where products are the main focus rather than service operations where the focus is mainly on customers. For example, industrial robots are commonly used in car manufacturing plants, where they automatically and flexibly perform a variety of repetitive tasks such as paint spraying, loading and unloading, welding, etc. for long periods of time. Usually robots need to be programmed only once and then will repeat the same task for many years. They are also especially useful for reducing operator fatigue, for working in places that are difficult for humans to reach or for handling hazardous substances, such as hot steel ingots, explosives, or radioactive materials. They can also work autonomously in hazardous environments, such as inside furnaces or for underground mining of minerals. With the advent of smart technologies such as AI (Artificial Intelligence), cameras and sensors are equipping robots with the capacity to emulate judgement and sensory feedback.

Information-processing technologies

Information technology (IT) usually involves the use of computers or smart devices (hardware) as well as software programs or applications that are combined together to form information systems that process data and aid decision making. The integration of electronic communication technologies into computers has considerably increased the networking capabilities of IT and the acronym ICT (information and communications technology) is commonly used to refer to IT within this context.

ICT is changing many aspects of operations, increasing their efficiency, improving sustainability and allowing new business models that were previously impossible to be implemented without the enabling technology. Currently, the number of specific ICT technologies is so vast that it would be impractical to address all of them in this book.

The internet is undoubtedly the most significant ICT to have affected the way organisations operate. In practice, the internet is a worldwide, publicly accessible network of computers. It connects people and organisations around the world through various types of information and online services such as email, social media, market, and educational platforms. These functionalities have allowed the creation of many innovative operations in the past and there will certainly be many more innovations emerging in the future.

For instance, the internet enabled development of 'electronic business' (e-business), which in practice is any business process that uses internet-based technology rather than traditional methods using paper-based ordering and financial transactions. By improving existing processes or creating entirely new business opportunities through e-business operations, companies are linking their internal and external information systems to work more closely with customers, suppliers, and other key stakeholders. One of the most

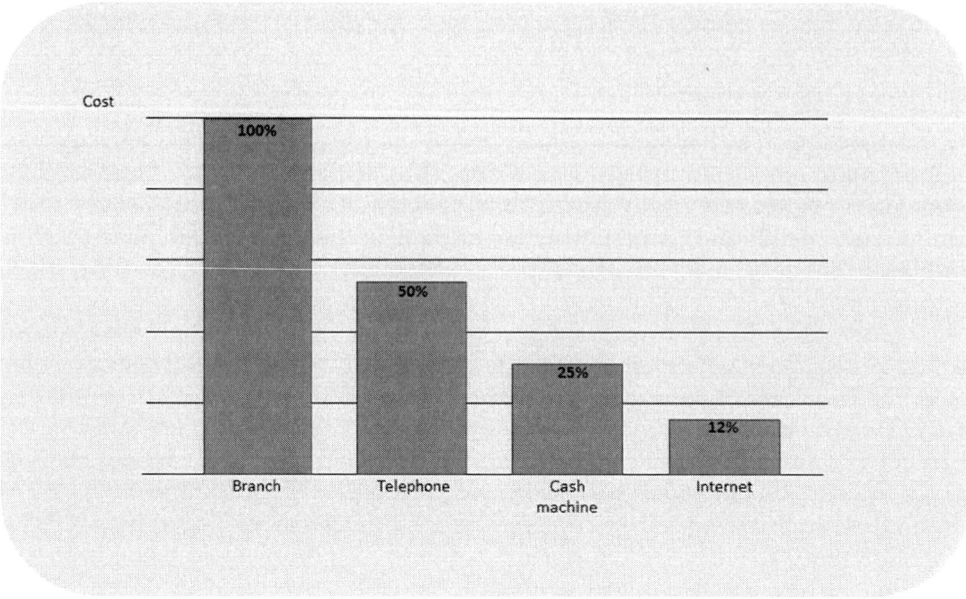

Figure 7.1 Relative cost of service delivery per channel in a retail bank (Source: Slack *et al.*, 2010, p. 214)

considerable impacts has been on operations and business processes that involve online buying and selling activities, which is a business model known as '*e-commerce*'. However, e-business is a much wider concept than e-commerce, with the latter being a subset of an overall e-business strategy. Usually, e-business involves the provision of services as well as the application of knowledge management systems to build and enhance relationships with stakeholders.

Normally, the cost of transactions conducted through the internet is significantly lower than the cost of making the same transactions through other channels of communication. Figure 7.1 shows the relative cost for a retail bank to provide its services through different channels. It can be seen that the cost of internet transactions is 88% lower than the costs of branch operations. With cost savings on this scale, internet-based services have become the preferred medium for many service operations.

Customer-processing technologies

The so-called customer-processing technologies are those that in practice are actually customer-driven. This category of technology is predominant in service operations, as they have intensive customer contacts and interactions. In general, there are three main types of customer-processing technologies: those technologies which are directly operated by the customers themselves, those operated by an intermediary, and those that discreetly capture information about customers (hidden technologies). Taking retailing as an example, customers can often self-scan items before leaving a shop and in some supermarkets customers can take portable barcode scanners with them while shopping. This will significantly speed up the check-out procedures at the end. Alternatively, when they finish shopping they can bring the non-scanned items to a cashier who will scan the products at the check-out. The cashier in this case is the intermediary agent. Supermarkets also use cameras for security purposes and for tracking customers' movements and agglomerations, although they are not necessarily visible to the customer. In-flight entertainment on aeroplanes is another example of customer-processing technology. This allows customers to interact with video terminals available by each passenger seat. The customers operate the terminals themselves and are able to choose from a range of entertainment services such as films, TV programmes, video games, music, etc. They can also be used to provide information on meal menus and airport arrival procedures etc. As well as providing such information they can also give passengers something to keep them occupied on long flights which reduces the work of the cabin crew.

Moving walkways are a type of tangible customer-processing technology commonly available at international airports. These technologies transport a large number of customers over relatively short distances through simple moving belts driven from under the floor. They are particularly useful for transporting passengers and aircraft crews to, and between, gates, so improving punctuality and speeding up the flow of people through the terminals.

In practice, many technologies are not limited to just processing materials or information or customers, but will process one or more, and often together. Taking the earlier retailing example, the check-out stations in a supermarket can concurrently process materials (the items purchased), information, and the customers.

Choice of process technology

Making decisions about which technology to choose is not a straightforward task for managers. These are important decisions and usually involve choices from a range of similar technologies or variants of the same technology. The complexity of these decisions may vary from simple technology upgrades to more strategic decisions involving technological changes that have long-term impact on the organisation's operations. Complex technology choices are generally based on three important types of evaluation: market requirement evaluation; operations resource evaluation; and financial evaluation.

Market requirement evaluation considers the potential impact of a technology on the operations' capacity to fulfil customer needs. A useful approach to this type of evaluation is to assess how a specific technology would affect the key strategic performance objectives of organisations, namely: quality, speed, dependability, flexibility, and cost. The example below illustrates the market requirement evaluation for a warehouse that stores, packs, and distributes spare parts to its customers (Slack et al., 2007).

A market requirement evaluation for a warehouse's technology choice

A warehouse is considering investing in a new 'retrieval and packing' system which converts sales orders into 'retrieval lists' and uses materials-handling equipment to automatically pick up the goods from its shelves and bring them to the packing area. The market requirements evaluation for this technology choice could be as follows:

- *Quality*: The impact on quality could be the fact that the computerised system is not prone to human error, which may previously have resulted in the wrong part being picked off the shelves.

- *Speed*: The new system may be able to retrieve items from the shelves faster than human operators can do safely.
- *Dependability*: This will depend on how reliable the new system is. If it is less likely to break down than the operators in the old system were likely to be absent, then the new system may improve the dependability of the service.
- *Flexibility*: New service flexibility is not likely to be as good as the previous manual system. For example, there will be a physical limit to the size of the products the automatic system will be able to retrieve, whereas people are capable of adapting to doing new things in new ways. Volume flexibility, however, could be better. The new system can work for longer hours when demand is higher than expected or deadlines are changed.
- *Cost*: The new system is likely to require fewer operators for the warehouse, but will need extra technical and maintenance support. Overall, however, labour costs are likely to be lower.

(Source: Slack et al., 2007, p. 241)

Operations resource evaluation concerns assessing which capabilities a process technology can bring to the operations and the potential constraints related to the application. Accordingly, this type of evaluation assesses the capabilities enabled by the process technology under consideration, together with an assessment of the constraints the technology may impose on the operations. For example, a technology that automates the production of a specific item may increase the volume capability of the operation. However, the same technology may impose a flexibility constraint if it does not produce items with different specifications such as size, colour, and shape.

Finally, *financial evaluation* is about assessing the financial value of investing in a specific process technology. There are various methods, from using the simple payback period to discounted cash flow techniques. Factors such as opportunity cost also need to be taken into account.

The three types of evaluation perspectives above (market requirement, operations, and finance) can also be considered in an evaluation framework that takes into account the *feasibility*, *acceptability*, and *vulnerability* of the process technology being assessed. Feasibility refers to the difficulties involved in acquiring and using the technology; acceptability refers to the benefits the technology will bring to the organisation and its customers; and vulnerability refers to the risks involved in acquiring and using the technology. Table 7.1 provides a useful reference for this framework, giving the evaluation criteria based on the relevant perspectives and dimensions described above. In practice, it allows managers to generate initial insights that will help them to make their decision on whether or not to adopt a process technology.

From Industry 1.0 to Industry 4.0

Technologies are continuously evolving as a result of ongoing research efforts as well as technological innovation initiatives developed by academia, industry, and governments. A historical perspective on how technology has been evolving over time shows four distinct waves of technological evolution since the first Industrial Revolution in Europe that

Table 7.1 Evaluation criteria framework for technology choice

Feasibility	*Acceptability*	*Vulnerability*
How difficult is it?	How worthwhile is it?	What could go wrong?
Do we have the skills to acquire the new technology?	Does the option satisfy market requirements?	What are the risks involved?
Do we have the financial resources to purchase it?	Will our customers want it?	Can we carry on running if things go wrong?
Do we have adequate facilities/ capacity?	Does the option give a satisfactory financial return?	Do we understand the full consequences of adopting the option?

(Source: adapted from Slack et al., 2007, p. 127)

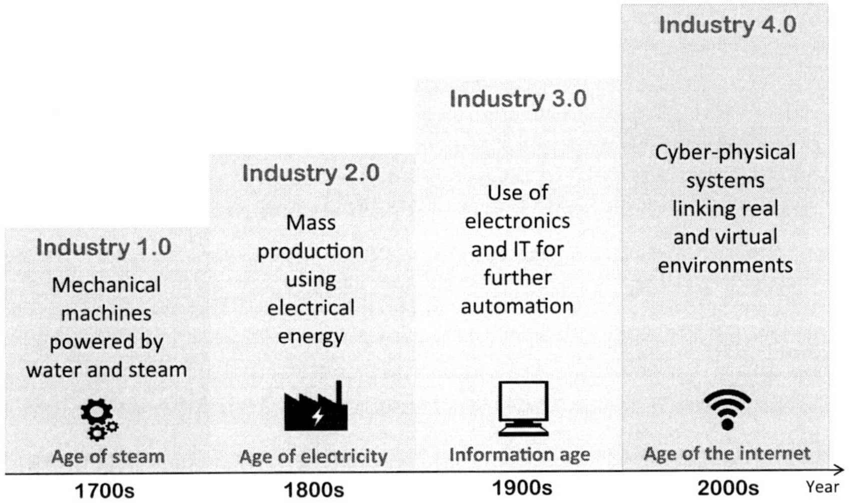

Figure 7.2 Waves of technological evolution in industry

started in the mid 1700s. The evolutionary waves are characterised by the successive types of technology that became predominant in industry. Thus, they are often termed Industry 1.0, Industry 2.0, Industry 3.0, and Industry 4.0, as illustrated in Figure 7.2.

The *Industry 1.0* wave, which started around 1760, is seen retrospectively as the first Industrial Revolution. Machines became powered by steam and enabled the mechanisation and acceleration of production activities and transportation methods (e.g. using stationary steam engines and steam powered vehicles). Machines in the textile industry were also mechanically programmed so that different patterns of cloth could be produced. Coal was used as the main fuel source, which transformed industrialisation through faster production. A large number of machines were operated together, being dependent on a single power source such as the factory's own steam engine.

The *Industry 2.0* wave started as a result of the electrification and automation of machines, i.e. with machines used in industrial activities being powered by electric motors.

The electrical technology allowed a significant increase in industrial productivity in terms of volume and speed, i.e. mass production. It also allowed machines to have their own unique power source so they could operate independently of each other. Mechanical automation also enabled the start of mass production in the engineering industries, especially for automotive manufacturing.

The emergence of electronic technologies and computers in particular enabled industrial evolution to the *Industry 3.0* wave, when information technology (IT) became predominant. Computing power allowed the development of numerically controlled machines and, later, 'intelligent' production systems that further automated a wide range of industrial activities. For example, computers are the basis behind the development of industrial robots. The first robots used in the automotive industry were developed by General Motors in the 1960s for performing spot welding activities. These robots were operated and controlled by computer systems. Such advanced electronics and information technology significantly empowered the automation of production processes.

Currently, a number of technological evolutions have shaped the *Industry 4.0* wave, where digitisation and autonomous self-behaviour of machines are becoming predominant in industry. "Smart" machines are being used in warehouse management, storage systems, and in a number of production and service operations. Smart sensors, cameras, and other types of intelligent electronic devices are able to connect and communicate with each other via the internet and exchange information autonomously, without human intervention. Such a network of interconnected devices has been called the *Internet of Things (IoT)*, which can be defined as a network of devices embedded in machines and vehicles, linked through the internet, enabling their computerised sensing, scanning, monitoring, and communication capabilities.

Cyber–physical systems are integrated systems comprising mechanical devices controlled by computer-based algorithms supported by Artificial Intelligence (AI) and are key technological systems underpinning Industry 4.0. These types of systems enable the implementation of new business models based on data-driven services and innovations such as smart products, unmanned factories, smart robots, self-driving vehicles, drone delivery systems, etc., supported by highly connected operations.

A study by the German Foundation for mechanical engineering, plant engineering, and information technology (Lichtblau et al., 2015) structured these innovations into four Industry 4.0 dimensions, which resulted from digitisation and the fusion of the physical and virtual worlds: (1) Smart factory; (2) Smart product; (3) Smart operations; and (4) Data-driven services. Lichtblau et al. (2015) provide a holistic perspective of these four dimensions and the business benefits they promote (Figure 7.3).

COLES AND WOOLWORTHS ARE MOVING TO ROBOT WAREHOUSES AND ON-DEMAND LABOUR AS HOME DELIVERIES SOAR

by Lauren Kate Kelly, RMIT University (in *The Conversation* – theconversation.com)

As lockdowns continue across Australia, many households are doing something they may not have considered just 18 months ago: ordering groceries online.

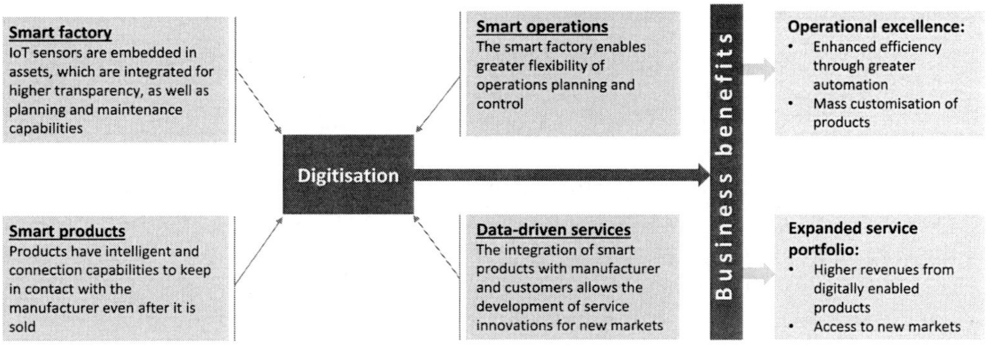

Figure 7.3 Cyber-physical Industry 4.0 innovations enabled by digitisation (Source: adapted from Lichtblau et al. (2015, p. 12)

Australia's supermarket duopoly, Coles and Woolworths, have raced to implement new technology and transform labour arrangements to keep up with the e-grocery boom.

Both are investing in "smart" warehousing and distribution systems with various degrees of automation, as well as making extensive use of app-driven gig workers for grocery picking and delivery via platforms such as Uber and Airtasker.

My research suggests a reimagining of the Australian supermarket is currently under way. And where Coles and Woolworths go, others will follow: the pair are Australia's largest private-sector employers, and their current moves seem likely to speed up the trend towards on-demand and precarious labour.

Teaming up with big tech

When the pandemic hit Australia in March 2020, Coles and Woolworths were quickly overwhelmed. Unprecedented demand for home delivery caused massive delays, and online services were paused for five weeks to prioritise shoppers with special needs.

Both supermarket giants have since partnered with food delivery platforms to solve the "last mile" problem of home delivery using a precarious, on-demand network of delivery drivers.

This week Woolworths formalised a deal with Uber, trialled in 2020, to provide one-hour delivery from selected Metro stores in Sydney and Melbourne. Woolworths staff will pick and pack the order and hand it off to an Uber driver. These drivers, and on-demand couriers Sherpa and Drive Yello, are already delivering to thousands of Woolworths customers every week.

For Coles, partnerships with the on-demand economy predate the pandemic and have only grown more important. In 2017, Coles quietly teamed up with Airtasker, encouraging shoppers to put their grocery list up for auction and have gig workers bid each other down to win the job.

Coles also released a "Netflix and Chill essentials" range for delivery via UberEats in 2019, spanning ice cream, biscuits, and other snacks. These partnerships suggest a strategy for restructuring labour relations was already under way before the pandemic.

The supermarket personal shopper

Inside the supermarket a growing number of "personal shoppers" can be found picking and packing orders for home delivery.

Some are employed by Coles or Woolworths, and they wheel around a multi-tiered workstation complete with scanner gun, measuring scales, and touch screen. Software determines the most efficient way to pick multiple orders at once and dictates the worker's route through the store, which items to pick, what bag to put them in, and how long it should take.

Other "personal shopping" is done by plain-clothed gig workers, perhaps working through Airtasker on their mobile phone, who are indistinguishable from other shoppers.

Global tech companies shake up the warehouse

Demand for online grocery shopping has also accelerated Coles and Woolworths' development of fully or semi-automated warehouses coordinated by "smart" management systems. Both supermarkets are working with global tech companies to develop billion-dollar, state-of-the-art warehouses, with some scheduled to open as soon as next year.

With UK software and robotics company Ocado, Coles is developing two data-driven "customer fulfilment centres" in Melbourne and Sydney, scheduled to open in 2022. Autonomous picking robots will retrieve items for human workers who, for now, are better able to scan goods and pack them for delivery.

The system is underpinned by the Ocado Smart Platform: end-to-end software, apps, and technology to manage online grocery demand.

Woolworths is pursuing a slightly different strategy of "micro-fulfilment", which involves smaller and more centrally located warehouses for faster home delivery.

These are hybrid warehouse–supermarket facilities developed by US company Takeoff Technologies. They cannibalise floor space in a retail store to incorporate a small warehouse with vertical racking, automation, and picking robots. As in the Ocado model, the robots retrieve items for workers to pack and deliver.

Two of these facilities are already up and running, with the second opening this week on Queensland's Sunshine Coast.

Traditional warehouses begin to close

These are just two of the new automated systems designed to replace traditional warehouses. The closure of existing warehouses will result in the loss of thousands of (mainly unionised) jobs. It is currently unclear if retrenched workers will be redeployed to automated sites, which will still require large numbers of workers to function.

Recent research led by sociologist Tom Barnes found that when unionised warehouse workers are retrenched due to automation, they are likely to continue working in warehousing, but in more insecure arrangements and for less pay. Put simply, when unionised jobs are lost, they are not recreated elsewhere.

The hidden labour of grocery home delivery

Online grocery shopping is promoted as an important measure for limiting contact between people and reducing the spread of COVID-19. However, this highlights the question of who gets to stay home and who continues to work, potentially putting themselves at risk.

Mapping of exposure sites across suburbs shows clear class divides between those who can work from home and order in, and those who cannot. Last year, as much as 80% of COVID-19 transmission in Victoria took place in insecure workplaces among precarious workers.

On-demand labour services require a stratified and unequal labour force, whereby some families outsource domestic labour to others. This outsourcing may provide an overall benefit, but it depends on workers who have been denied secure work or government assistance. By necessity, these people do the work deemed too risky by others.

The smart supermarket of tomorrow

Advances in technology and automation are not wiping out supermarket jobs but changing them. Fantasies of "lights-out" fully automated warehouses and drone deliveries are unlikely to become reality when a growing pool of precarious workers are available to do the work.

Coles and Woolworths are not straightforwardly outsourcing labour to the on-demand economy. Instead, they are bringing multiple forms of labour into their distribution networks.

Precarious workers and the more securely employed (often members of unions) work side by side in the complex labour process of grocery home delivery. Coles and Woolworths can shift risk and responsibility onto gig workers when needed, while maintaining control of the entire distribution network. This ability to outsource risk and keep control is not a new high-tech development, but a fixture of capitalist labour relations.

Partnerships with the on-demand economy and global tech companies suggest a reimagining of the Australian supermarket is currently under way. Although the supermarket may appear fixed and banal, it is an important social institution which is always changing and being renegotiated.

What will these changes mean for Coles and Woolworths, and for the rest of us? In the absence of organised labour resistance or government intervention, the trend towards an on-demand and precarious workforce seems likely to continue.

Disruptive technologies in Industry 4.0

Industry 4.0 comprises many other technological innovations such as Big Data Analytics, 3D printing, 3D sensing cameras, 5G communications, drones, blockchain, and other such innovations, which have the potential to be highly disruptive, i.e. the potential to significantly change the way that industries, consumers, and businesses operate. The Gartner Group publishes every year a report titled "*Hype Cycle for Emerging Technologies*", which identifies emerging technologies that have a significant potential to impact businesses and the society over the coming years. Many of the technologies mentioned in recent Gartner reports are shaping the next wave of technological evolution in the industry, i.e. the Industry 5.0 wave (see for example Gartner, 2019).

In relation to sustainable operations management, this chapter pays particular attention to two potentially disruptive technologies, which are already being applied in several data-driven processes in Industry 4.0, namely: UAV – Unmanned Aerial Vehicles (also known as *drones*) and *blockchain*.

UAV: Unmanned Aerial Vehicles (drones)

Unmanned Aerial Vehicles (UAVs), more popularly known as drones, initially had a limited application in industry due to the lack of sophisticated sensor technology and reduced capability of GPS (Global Positioning Systems). However, over recent years there have been considerable advancements in GPS technology and gyro stabilisation, associated with the emergence of sophisticated cameras, faster mobile telecommunications, and WiFi infrastructure. When combined with innovations in the UAV technology as a whole (e.g. design, rotors, materials, etc.) these advancements have made drones a mass-market technology, with wide application in many aspects of life and particularly in industrial operations.

Due to the commercial scale achieved through mass production, the cost of drones has decreased significantly in recent years. Such economy of scale has allowed drones to become a commercially available technology, affordable to many companies and the wider public. This has enabled the application of drones in several autonomously operated cyber–physical systems. A recent study by Hildmann and Kovacs (2019) provides some examples of advanced applications of drones in different areas. Two interesting examples they provide that relate to sustainable service operations are:

1. *Drone application in the development of Smart Cities*: Smart Cities make extensive use of ICT to reduce costs, optimise the distribution and consumption of resources, as well as improving interactivity and the overall quality of life of citizens. In this context, drones can play an important role in smart civil defence application. For example, they can be used to support civil security units such as fire fighters or police forces, providing them with real-time situational awareness and enhancing communications between agencies to coordinate their operations and improve the security of units in the field.
2. *Drone application in swarm-based services*: A common application of drones in swarm-based services is to support enhanced communications infrastructure. For example, drone swarms (i.e. groups of drones flying in a coordinated and integrated way), can significantly increase aerial communication infrastructure by expanding broadband wireless connectivity and radio wave coverage. They can also be used to assist the inspection of energy infrastructure, which is a potentially dangerous task for humans, such as when inspecting high-voltage power lines. Relevant to social sustainability, drones are also being used in humanitarian operations, assisting with localisation and evacuation efforts.

Blockchain

Blockchain is the underlying digital technology supporting cryptocurrencies such as Bitcoin. Because of the close relationship between blockchain and cryptocurrencies, many people misunderstand the two as being synonymous. However, they are different concepts because blockchain technology can support many other applications far beyond digital cryptocurrency applications such as Bitcoin.

Blockchain is a digital distributed ledger that does not need a central entity or authority to coordinate or moderate the network of users whose information systems it supports as the main repository of transaction records. Because of its shared ledger philosophy, any information recorded in the blockchain is replicated across all the computers in the network and cannot be deleted or changed. That is, no transaction can be erased or changed once published in the blockchain network. This is a typical functionality of 'append only' ledgers. As any information recorded by mistake or with an error stays in the blockchain, the corrections are made through new records rectifying the errors from previous records. Blockchain therefore keeps a historical chain of transactions between parties in the network.

The blockchain's cryptographic mechanisms, its distributed architecture, and the transparency of transactions recorded, which are visible to all users of the blockchain ledger, make the technology both 'tamper evident' and 'tamper resistant' (Yaga et al., 2018). Every transaction is cryptographically recorded as a block of information forming a chain. More specifically, every individual transaction has a pointer to the previous transaction it follows, which creates a chain of tightly linked and singled encrypted information blocks, hence the name 'blockchain'. Attempts to tamper with the information in one block of the chain are not successful because it would break the chain by creating a link inconsistency with the previous block, which would also have to be tampered with, and so forth for the whole blockchain and for each one of the network users.

The blockchain functionalities described above provide attractive and powerful resources to support a number of operations management applications where transparency (visibility) and trust in the recorded information/transactions are critical. Besides supporting cryptocurrency applications, the blockchain technology is increasingly being adopted to support applications involving, for example, smart contracts (automated recording of transactions without third party interference, following pre-established agreements between parties), supply chain visibility and communications, and proof of provenance. The applications to supply chains can be particularly important when validating the origin of material, parts, and products because of environmental, safety, or ethical concerns. These benefits regarding sustainability will be discussed in more detail in the next section. To improve the efficiency and functionality of the blockchain technology there has been an ongoing stream of developments, with new blockchain-based platforms being frequently introduced.

Technologies as enablers of operations sustainability

Process technologies can undoubtedly benefit several aspects of an organisation's operations across strategic performance objectives such as speed, dependability, flexibility, quality, and cost. As well as these performance objectives, another important capability that organisations can improve with the support of process technologies is *sustainability*.

This section illustrates how some of the Industry 4.0 disruptive technologies can enable the sustainability of businesses. The examples discussed here focus on the two disruptive technologies described in the previous section: UAVs (drones) and blockchain technology.

Drones and operations sustainability

Drones have become increasingly popular over the last few years, with many organisations adopting and integrating this technology in their operations. Since Google (through its parent company Alphabet) launched its GoogleWing and Amazon its Air drone delivery service a few years ago, the number of businesses using drones in their operations has been growing fast.

From simply delivering pizza to more complex applications like aiding search and rescue missions or defusing explosive devices, drones have a significant disruptive potential, sparing humans from repetitive and hazardous work that previously put millions of lives at risk.

The potential of drones to improve sustainability of operations is particularly important in all parts of the economy. In the agricultural sector for example, drones enable innovative ways of managing farming operations and the utilisation of valuable natural resources such as water. More specifically, drones are being used to monitor agricultural production through environmental scanning of crop fields for better execution of irrigation processes. To reduce the wasting of water, drones enable smart irrigation by providing data to support the diagnostics of specific areas in the field where crops need irrigation and calculating the appropriate amount of water necessary for the area.

Another area where drones can improve sustainability is in delivery logistics, where the potential for drone use is increasing steadily. From a sustainability perspective, the use of drones for deliveries in long or short (last-mile) distances can be more energy efficient and less polluting than traditional transportation solutions using road vehicles. The delivery of medicines to remote regions or areas of difficult access for traditional vehicles is a good example of the role that drones can play in improving social sustainability.

The application of drones in inspection operations involving potentially hazardous contexts for humans, e.g. checking of unstable tunnels, volcano craters, gas leakages, etc., are also good examples of how drones can improve the social sustainability of organisations.

AMAZON PRIME AIR

Looking at the future of its delivery system, Amazon developed a drone delivery service called "Amazon Prime Air". The service aims to deliver packages up to five pounds in 30 minutes or less. In order to achieve the best delivery of packages in a variety of operating environments, Amazon is testing different types of drone designs and associated logistics systems. Thus, the look and characteristics of Amazon Prime Air drones will continue to evolve over time over the near future. Their most recent drone design includes advances in efficiency, stability, and safety.

Safety is a critical issue in drone delivery systems. For this reason, Amazon is actively flying and testing its Prime Air drones in different environments and contexts, before the service is ready to safely run and scale. For example, Amazon drones will be built with multiple redundancies and sophisticated "sense and avoid" technology.

In August 2020, Amazon received a Part 135 Air Carrier Certificate from the United States Federal Aviation Administration (FAA), as a result of the company's systematic development of drone technology, operating guidelines, and safety measures. This certification represents an important step forward in the development of the Prime Air service, as it indicates the FAA's confidence in Amazon's operating and safety procedures for their drone delivery service.

Prime Air has a great potential to enhance package delivery to customers by providing a quick delivery service based on drones. The safety and efficiency of such transportation systems is evolving and one day Amazon expects to offer Prime Air to millions of customers around the world.

Questions:

1. How can drone technology help companies to improve their sustainability across the Triple Bottom Line (economic, environmental and social sustainability)? Use examples to illustrate some of your answer.
2. From an Operations Management perspective, what type of process technology are drones: materials-processing technology, customer-processing technology, or information-processing technology?

Blockchain and operations sustainability

The technology behind blockchains has a great potential to improve the sustainability of organisations. The resources and functionalities of blockchain are particularly useful to solve a major challenge in supply chain management: 'supply chain visibility'. Higher visibility of a supply chain allows procurement managers to check 'proof of provenance' matters concerning the environmental and the social sustainability of their supply sources.

From a social sustainability perspective, companies can check the 'social provenance' of their sources by tracing and checking the status attributed to the labour conditions of supplier organisations across several tiers of the supply chains. Blockchain can also record and make available to regulators and buyers important information for tracing and checking counterfeit items or contaminated materials concerning their original sources.

The IBM Food Trust initiative promoted by the information technology company IBM is a good example of how blockchain can help organisations to address social–environmental–economic challenges. The initiative is supported by the IBM blockchain platform (Hyperledger) and allows the connection between growers, food manufacturers, wholesalers, distributors, and retailers in a blockchain network that provides visibility and accountability in each stage of the food value chain. The network users have real-time access to shared records about food origin and processing details as well as shipping information for trace and track functionalities. Key resources of the solution with direct impact on improving the sustainability of organisations include the following (Gupta, 2020):

- identification of issues concerning food safety, recalls, and foodborne illnesses;
- recording of food compliance standards;
- prompt access to trace and track information that helps inventory optimisation and minimisation of food waste;
- verification of food quality certification and registrations throughout the supply chain;
- increased transparency of ethical practices across the food supply chain;
- access to logistics data, which help supply chain managers to avoid costly delays and losses due to missing paperwork required on border-crossing operations.

Conclusions

This chapter has introduced and discussed the main concepts and characteristics of process technologies, which are instrumentally important for operations management in all types of organisations, helping them to achieve their strategic performance objectives and in developing their sustainability capabilities. In this regard, the three main generic types of process technologies have been presented, namely: materials-processing technologies, information-processing technologies, and customer-processing technologies.

After a brief discussion of important market, operations, and financial aspects to be considered when evaluating technology choices, the chapter has provided a historical perspective of the evolutionary waves of technology, from Industry 1.0 to Industry 4.0.

The chapter developed a more detailed discussion of Industry 4.0 with specific emphasis on two technologies that have important potential to disrupt in the near future the more traditional operations, especially in the area of logistics and supply chain management. These two technologies are UAV – Unmanned Aerial Vehicles (also known as drones) and blockchain. The chapter concludes with a more detailed discussion on how these particular technologies can enable the sustainability of an organisation. A number of illustrative cases are presented to exemplify the concepts, functionalities, and resources of these technologies.

References

Brown, S., Bessant, J., & Jia, F. (2018). *Strategic Operations Management* (4th ed.). London: Routledge.

Gartner. (2019). *Hype Cycle for Emerging Technologies, Report G00370466 by Gartner Research*, August 2019. Available at www.gartner.com/en/documents/3956015/hype-cycle-for-emerging-technologies-2019. Accessed on 20/04/2021.

Gupta, M. (2020). *Blockchain for dummies, 3rd IBM Limited Edition*, Hoboken: John Wiley & Sons Inc.

Hildmann, H., & Kovacs, E. (2019). Review: Using unmanned aerial vehicles (UAVs) as mobile sensing platforms (MSPs) for disaster response, civil security and public safety. *Drones*, *3*(59). DOI: 10.3390/drones3030059.

Lichtblau, K., Stich, V., Bertenrath, R., Blum, M., Bleider, M., Millack, A., Schmitt, K., Schmitz, E., & Schröter, M. (2015 October). *Industrie 4.0 Readiness, German Foundation for Mechanical Engineering, Plant Engineering, and Information Technology*. Impuls-Stiftung des VDMA, Aachen, Cologne, Germany.

Slack, N., & Brandon-Jones, A. (2018). *Operations and Process Management: Principles and Practice for Strategic Impact* (5th ed.). Harlow, UK: Pearson.

Slack, N., Chambers, S., & Johnston, R. (2007). *Operations Management* (5th ed.). Harlow, UK: FT Prentice Hall.

Slack, N., Chambers, S., & Johnston, R. (2010). *Operations Management* (6th ed.). Harlow, UK: Pearson.

Yaga, D., Mell, P., Roby, N., and Scarfone, K. (2018). *Blockchain Technology Overview, Report NISTIR 8202*. National Institute of Standards and Technology (NIST), U.S. Department of Commerce, October 2018. Available at https://doi.org/10.6028/NIST.IR.8202. Accessed on 21/04/2021.

8 Sustainable design and product development

This chapter presents the topic of sustainable design and product development. The design function encompasses designing products (goods and services) as well as processes and business models. The elements of design for sustainable business models and production processes have already been covered in previous chapters (circular economy, sustainable production, and sustainable supply chains). Thus, the purpose of this chapter is primarily to show how environmental and social demands need to be accommodated in the product design department (or for some organisations by the R&D function). The key terminologies and techniques around sustainable product development are also discussed.

There are three key learning outcomes for this chapter. By the end of the chapter you should be:

- aware of the main challenges and opportunities around sustainable design;
- able to understand the key terminologies and techniques for sustainable product development as well as their limitations;
- competent to evaluate processes and products in terms of their sustainability performance.

Introduction to design and development within the context of sustainability

As a starting point for discussing design we need to go back to some fundamentals. The concept of sustainable development is embraced by the following statement in the report of the World Commission on Environment and Development – *Our Common Future*:

> Humanity has the ability to make development sustainable to ensure that it meets the needs of the present without compromising the ability of future generations to meet their own needs.
>
> (WCED, 1987, p. 8)

However, the paragraphs in the WCED report that follow this statement are usually neglected. They provide further elaboration on the objectives of development by adding the aspirational needs of humans (i.e. beyond the essential needs):

> The satisfaction of human needs and aspirations is the major objective of development. The essential needs of vast numbers of people in developing countries – for food, clothing, shelter, jobs – are not being met, and beyond their basic needs these

DOI: 10.4324/9781003009375-10

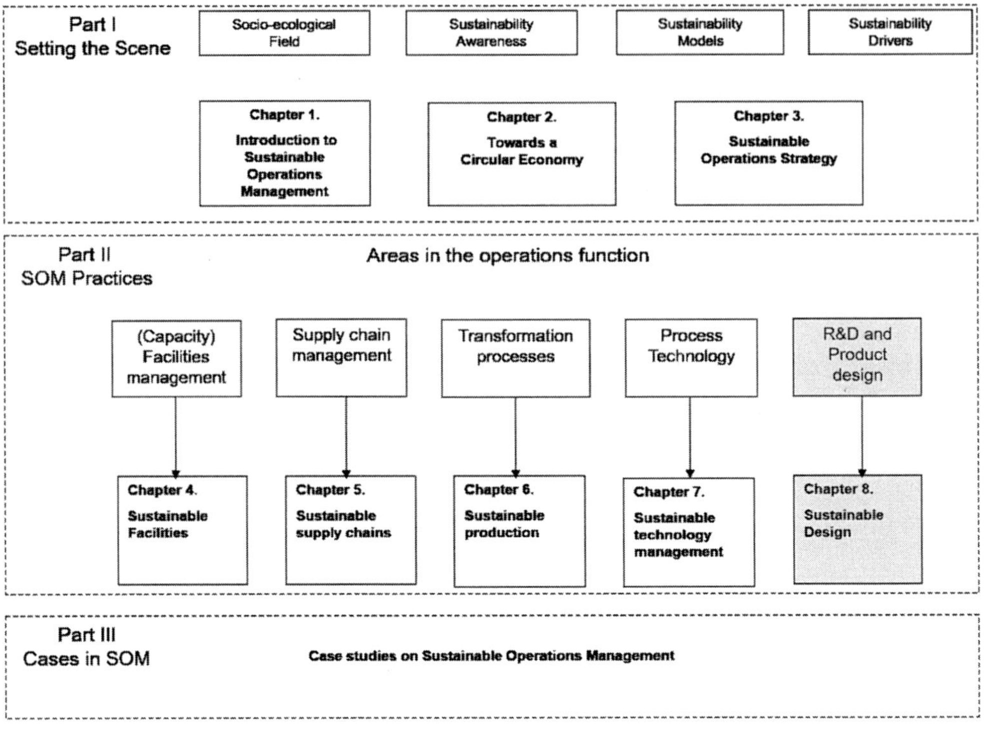

Figure 8.1 Chapter 8 within the book structure

> people have legitimate aspirations for an improved quality of life. A world in which poverty and inequity are endemic will always be prone to ecological and other crises. Sustainable development requires meeting the basic needs of all and extending to all the opportunity to satisfy their aspirations for a better life.
>
> (WCED, 1987, pp. 43–44)

In a given economic system, the majority of needs and aspirations of people will be met through the consumption of products, which can be delivered by large corporations, small companies, public organisations, or professional individuals in the form of goods or services. When societies tip the balance between essential and superfluous production and consumption, the levels of sustainability are likely to drop. Evidence of this is found in the so-called 'problems of modern societies' such as: childhood obesity, drug and alcohol abuse, high levels of anxiety and depression derived from consumerism culture.

From an environmental or ecological perspective, sustainability fitness is also negatively affected if the production, consumption, and disposal of end-of-life products have high environmental impacts. The renewal rate of natural resources such as biomass can be reduced due to over-consumption. The depletion of non-renewable resources such as precious metals or fossil fuels can be accelerated, provoking collapse or rapid increase of prices for some products (e.g. electronics or domestic gas supplies). Finally, water, land, and air contamination can be aggravated, or even become irreversible, if appropriate prevention and pollution control measures are not put in place.

In short, sustainable design is an attempt to develop consumption and production systems that address the essential needs of societies and their aspirations, and respect the limits of the environment.

BOX 8.1 MICROBEADS IN TOOTHPASTE

Colgate's approach to microbeads

www.colgate.com/en-us/oral-health/brushing-and-flossing/what-are-microbeads-in-toothpaste

Scientists are continually looking for new ways to improve oral care products, and using microbeads in toothpaste used to be a popular method of adding abrasive qualities to the product. Now that microbeads have been banned, you can rest assured that you can find a toothpaste that works effectively for you and doesn't harm the planet. Learn why the eradication of microbeads spells good news for your health and the environment's health, too.

What are microbeads?

The Australian Department of Environment and Energy defines microbeads as "small, solid, manufactured plastic particles that are less than 5 millimetres and don't degrade or dissolve in water". They are an ingredient in a variety of personal care products and have a few different purposes. Microbeads are used as an exfoliant or abrasive agent; they allow for a timed release of active ingredients, they add bulk to personal care product formulas, and they may prolong a product's shelf life. These capabilities, plus the inexpensive manufacturing costs, may account for this ingredient's popularity.

The environmental issue

Because microbeads aren't biodegradable, they pose a significant environmental concern. Research from the New York State Office of the Attorney General shows that microbeads can escape undetected into rivers and oceans after being washed down the drain, since their small size means they often aren't captured by regular sewage treatment systems. The report found that approximately 19 tons of microbeads are washed down New York drains each year!

The beads can be mistaken as food by fish, birds and other wildlife. When animals fill their stomachs with microbeads, they may spread the plastic up the food chain. This can lead to contamination of the fish we eat, since microplastics soak up pollutants in waterways, according to the Australian Department of Environment and Energy. Once in the environment, microbeads are almost impossible to remove.

The US Food and Drug Administration has addressed the issue. The Microbead-Free Waters Act of 2015 requires that the manufacturing, delivery, and sale of any rinse-off products containing microbeads smaller than 5 millimetres have been outlawed. This ban extends to cosmetics, toothpastes, and over-the-counter drugs. Many manufacturers have replaced microbeads with sustainable, biodegradable options, such as crushed nut shells and apricot kernels, according to the New Zealand Ministry for the Environment.

With microbeads banned from toothpastes for good, manufacturers are offering products that clean your teeth effectively without negatively affecting the environment.

Further readings on microbeads:

www.forbes.com/sites/carmendrahl/2016/01/09/what-you-need-to-know-about-microbeads-the-banned-bath-product-ingredients/?sh=309950a57a33
www.beatthemicrobead.org/myth-buster-toothpaste-still-contains-plastic-ingredients/

What is design?

According to the Cambridge dictionary, design is "a drawing or set of drawings showing how a building or product is to be made and how it will work and look".

For this chapter, the concept of industrial design is also useful to understand. The Industrial Designers Society of America (IDSA) defines industrial design as

> the professional practice of designing products, devices, objects and services used by millions of people around the world every day. Industrial designers typically focus on the physical appearance, functionality and manufacturability of a product, though they are often involved in far more during a development cycle. All of this ultimately extends to the overall lasting value and experience a product or service provides for end-users.

The World Design Organization (WDO) also states that industrial design is "a strategic problem-solving process that drives innovation, builds business success, and leads to a better quality of life through innovative products, systems, services, and experiences".

Relevance of design and product development for sustainability

Among characteristics such as functionality, product safety, comfort, efficiency, and aesthetics, R&D teams are also required to consider the impact of the product or process on the natural environment. Karlsson and Luttropp (2006) argue that ecodesign should also include concepts such as sustainable consumption, reduction of the volume of "desire", and should aim to enable human satisfaction in concert with a positive role in sustainable product development. As an example, power and speed have been differentiators for some car makers. Most cars available for sale allow their customers to drive at speeds much higher than those allowed by traffic law imposed by national regulatory agencies (except on German autobahns!). Furthermore, saturated markets with high ratios of cars per head of population oblige drivers to run their vehicles at very low speed in urban centres, or even ban stationary idling of engines due to the environmental pollution caused by long traffic jams.

Sustainable design is complex and potentially the riskiest sustainability practice of all. But it is also the one that is likely to return the highest yields. It is complex and risky because it usually impacts on established product features or production routines. For example, Mildenberger and Khare (2000) say about the long decision lead time in the automotive industry:

> According to the German car-maker BMW, it takes about 3–4 years to design a car, 7–8 years to manufacture it, and it would be in use for about 10–12 years; thus, in all, a decision taken today will have its effect for about a quarter of a century if it is not victim of irresponsible disposal of waste.
>
> (Mildenberger and Khare, 2000, p. 205)

Moreover, product design is often complicated by uncertainty inherent in the evolution of environmental trends and regulations (Kleindorfer et al., 2005). There is little or no guarantee for how the product will perform in the hands of a customer in respect of its absolute environmental performance. Several attempts to build sustainable product–service systems or circular economy business models are vulnerable to rebound effects, such as low economic viability, amongst other issues (Wassenhove, 2019). One of the main reasons for this is the lack of control that can be exercised in the upstream supply chain of a sustainable product – i.e. an eco-efficient vehicle may be cheaper to run, which then allows more use of it, so consequently making a larger absolute impact.

Product development fundamentals

Companies have been mainly judged by the products they make, and more recently, because of the pressures for transparency, there has also been a lot of scrutiny of production processes and practices. When companies decide to develop new products, it is considered as a total life-cycle activity and therefore the key metrics of operations performance are also applied. Slack and Lewis (2020) offer the following list of questions concerning product development:

- How long does it take to develop a new product or process? (Speed)
- How much does the development phase cost? (cost efficiency)
- Can it be finished according to the schedule? (dependability)
- Can it accommodate changes and latest ideas? (flexibility)
- Is it error-free and fulfil the market requirements? (quality)

The product development cycle starts by investigating a problem to be solved. This can be derived from a 'need' or an aspiration to be met (a 'want'). These needs and aspirations can be explicit or latent (unknown yet by consumers). In fact, organisations may use these two perspectives (*known* versus *unknown* needs or aspirations) to build their approaches to product development, which will lead respectively to market-driven or production-driven designs. Once a problem is identified it should be clearly defined in order to translate market needs into high-level product specifications and then to compose a (product development) project plan (Figure 8.2).

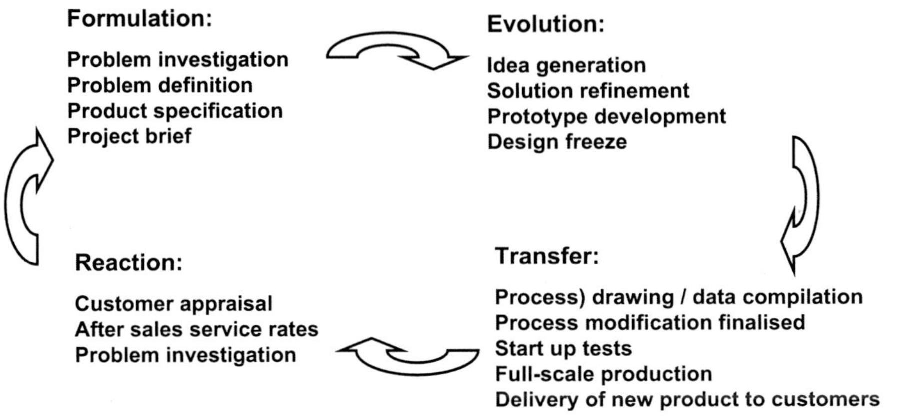

Figure 8.2 THE CYCLE OF PRODUCT DESIGN

10-Minute Exercise:

Think of an unmet need or desire and generate a few ideas that could address them.

Ex. Individual need or desire to comfortably carry more than 10 books in a long holiday trip => e-books + e-book reader

Reflection:

How many ideas did you generate?
Can you rank them in terms of production feasibility?
Can you merge two or three ideas into one?

After the problem investigation, the second step is the evolution of the design phase into solution development. Techniques such as brainstorming are usually used in this phase. It is common for design teams to generate various designs (or solutions) to the problem. A process of excluding, merging, creeping, and improving ideas will take place until the team decides the 'best' design. It is also usual to have customer or user involvement in this step to check whether their inputs (needs, aspirations, and preferences) have been correctly understood, whether the design is addressing the key priorities, and if any trade-offs are necessary (Figure 8.3).

For product development teams, a product is in practice a 'package of solutions' that organisations deliver to their customers (those who pay for the product) and consumers (those who use the product). The original view of operations management defined products as being tangible goods that could be produced for later consumption, and therefore transported and stored. However, products can be services as well as tangible goods. Services tend to be consumed at the same time as they are produced. They are intangible products and cannot be stored. However, these simple definitions of goods and services are problematic because most products, regardless of whether they are goods or services, will combine tangible with intangible elements. Very few of them will be purely goods

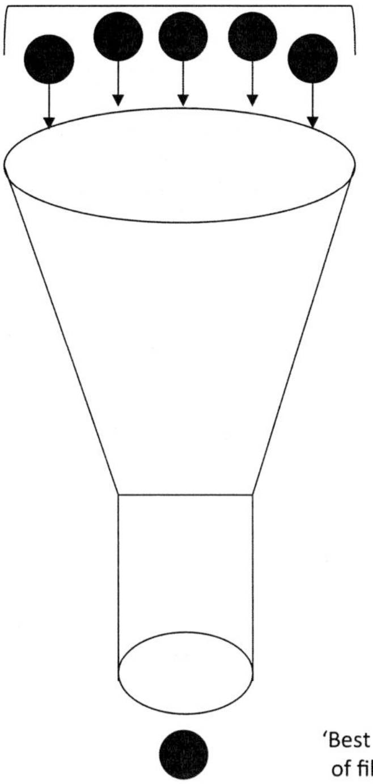

Figure 8.3 Product development funnel

(100% tangible) or purely services (100% intangible). Thus, one of the preliminary tasks of product design is to define the mix between the goods and service elements in a product. For example, a university course may comprise intangible elements such as lectures, online access to library resources, etc., but some institutions may also include a computer, books, laboratory equipment, and special clothing or a uniform as an integral part of the course. By the same logic, purchasing a car will also involve a mixed product, since it includes a warranty and service backup.

That leads to the third step in the product development cycle – transfer to production or process development. In fact, it is argued that the development of products and processes are interrelated and should be treated together (Slack and Lewis, 2020). Understanding the tangible and intangible elements of the product is a key issue at this stage because they will influence the allocation of operational resources not only during the development of the product but also during sourcing, production, use, scrappage, and disposal of the product. Once the original idea or problem solution translates into full-scale production (and if necessary is certified for use) the product is then ready to be transferred to the market.

So, the fourth step includes delivery of the product to the market and assessment of market reaction. As sales and product use increase, the company will have a chance to

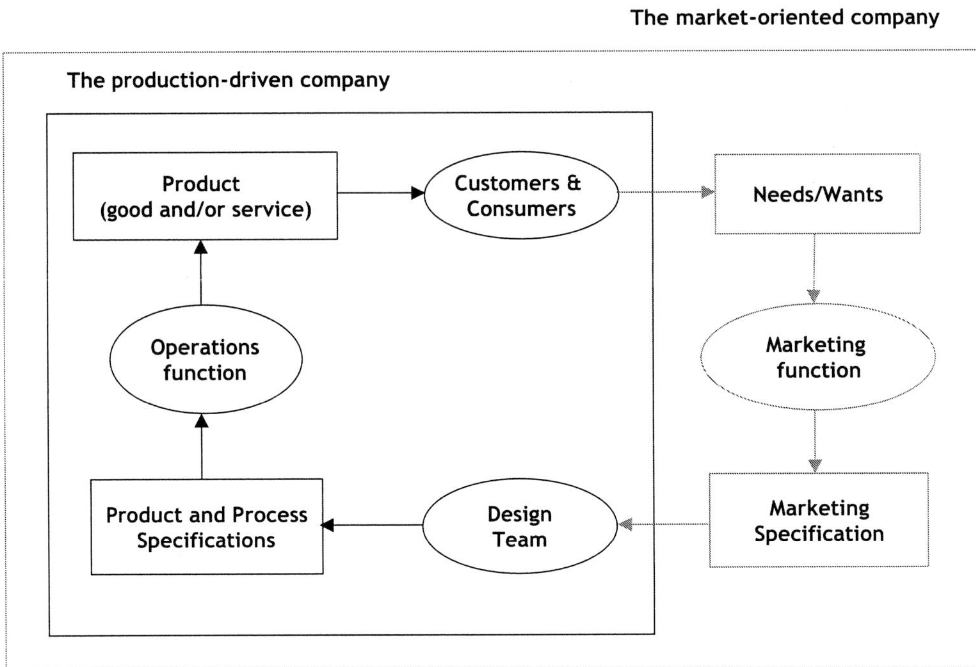

Figure 8.4 Market and production-driven design approaches

learn how the design performs in the 'real' world, and to investigate improvement opportunities from customer appraisals and after-sales services. This will frequently result in the continuation of the cycle, so information from product use will serve as an input and instruct future generations of product designs (Figure 8.4).

Developing sustainable products

The development of sustainable products is fully dependent on understanding the totality of the product's impact from original conception through to end-of-life disposal or recycling. To achieve this understanding, researchers and organisations will conduct Life Cycle Assessments (LCAs) of products for which they want to measure the environmental impact. The product's LCA, which was also described in Chapter 5 in connection with sustainable production will highlight the potential sustainability issues throughout the product's life, including the assessment of its production processes and impacts of its disposal.

In the higher levels of product development, or when considering the product architecture, the first step in the direction of achieving sustainability is to consider the essentiality of the product, i.e. how it meets the essential needs of the organisation, customers, and local communities. It is important to highlight that the essentiality of processes can be distinguished from essentiality of products that result from using these processes. For example, the production of a superfluous good could still create jobs that are essential for survival of a community or another social–ecological system.

Next, the critical resources in the environment as well as toxic materials need to be considered within the context of product design and development, and so potentially avoided in the product's bill of materials. Once product designs are approved, transferred

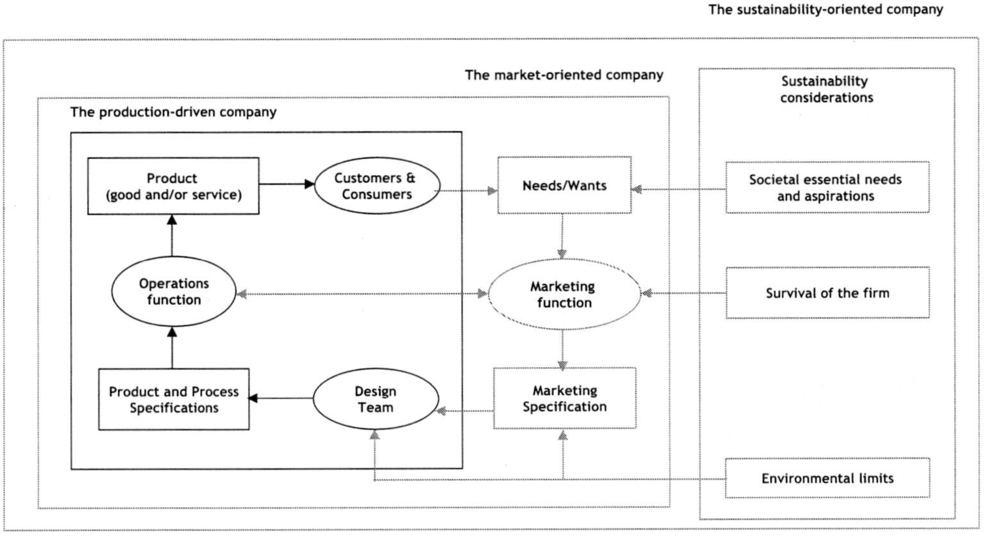

Figure 8.5 Adding sustainability considerations to market and production-driven design approaches

to production, and later sold in the market, they are usually expected to continue in production and be used for many years. For this to be considered sustainable, design teams will also have to consider today's environmental limits of, as well as the limitations imposed by, higher resource consumption and greater needs for pollution reduction in the future (Figure 8.5).

Once the decision whether a product justifies being produced from a sustainability perspective has been taken, design teams can progress towards the intermediate and detailed plans for product development (e.g. product features, aesthetics, choice of materials, etc). With the detailed designs completed, the product development team can take the approved designs through a Life Cycle Assessment.

LIFE CYCLE ASSESSMENT

According to ISO 14040:2006 – LCAs can assist in:

- identifying opportunities to improve the environmental performance of products at various points in their life cycle;
- informing decision makers in industry, government, or non-government organisations (e.g. for the purpose of strategic planning, priority setting, product or process design or redesign);
- the selection of relevant indicators of environmental performance, including measurement techniques; and
- marketing (e.g. implementing an ecolabelling scheme, making an environmental claim, or producing an environmental product declaration).

So, an LCA application starts by the definition of goals and scope of the analysis. Then an inventory list is produced and interpreted in order to produce an impact assessment. These are very useful to prevent 'avoidable' environmental and social impacts.

The scope, including the system boundary and level of detail, of an LCA depends on the subject and the intended use of the study. The depth and breadth of LCA can differ considerably depending on the goal of a particular LCA and are part of the first phase of LCA.

The life cycle inventory analysis phase (LCI phase) is the second phase of LCA. It is an inventory of input/output data with regard to the system being studied. It involves collection of the data necessary to meet the goals of the defined study.

The life cycle impact assessment phase (LCIA) is the third phase of the LCA. The purpose of LCIA is to provide additional information to help assess a product system's LCI results so as to better understand their environmental significance.

Life cycle interpretation is the final phase of the LCA procedure, in which the results of an LCI or an LCIA, or both, are summarised and discussed as a basis for conclusions, recommendations and decision making in accordance with the goal and scope definition (Figure 8.6).

BOX 8.2 KEY CONCEPTS IN SUSTAINABLE DESIGN

Life cycle: consecutive and interlinked stages of a product system, from raw material acquisition or generation from natural resources to final disposal

Life cycle assessment (LCA): compilation and evaluation of the inputs, outputs, and the potential environmental impacts of a product system throughout its life cycle

Source: www.iso.org/obp/ui/#iso:std:iso:14040:ed-2:v1:en

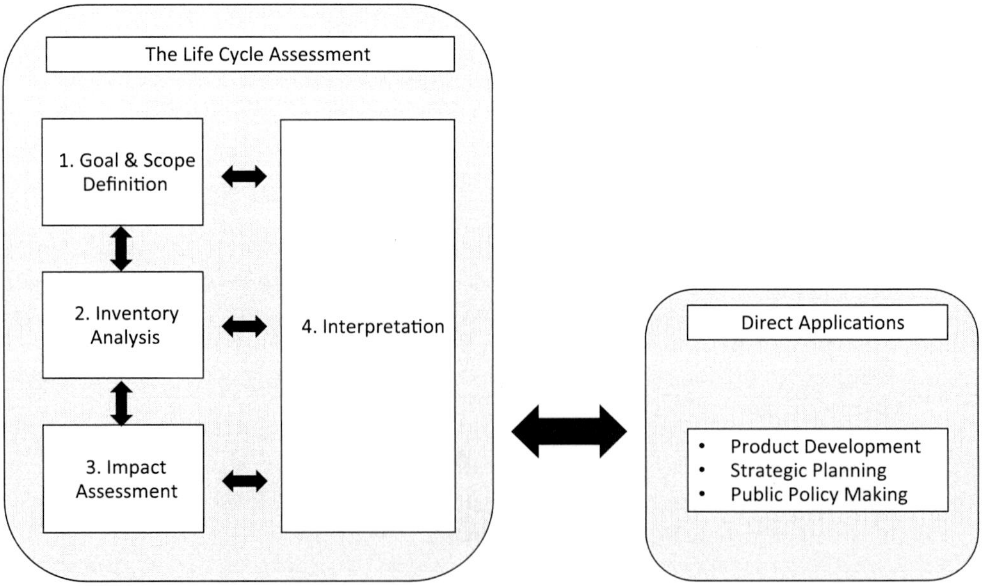

Figure 8.6 Phases of an LCA (ISO 14040, 1997) as described by ISO 14040

It is true that LCA has some limitations. And it is not necessarily the best tool to choose between competing designs (Graedel et al, 1993; Collado-Ruiz and Ostad-Ahmad-Ghorabi, 2010). For example, there is currently a weak, or no, link between the indicator scores quantified in Life Cycle Assessment (LCA) and the carrying capacity of the affected ecosystems (Bjørn and Hauschild, 2015). Also, environmental and social issues may be neglected due to bias or a narrow focus of the product development team (usually excessive on energy, carbon, and material footprints). Furthermore, it rarely includes data on product or process essentiality (Nunes et al., 2016). LCAs are also often criticised because they can be overly complicated to use, requiring extensive analysis of complex information (Orsato and Wells, 2007), as well as being vulnerable to subjectivity and lack of consistency between different product development teams.

However, these limitations are not meant to negate the application of LCAs. They simply mean that careful and additional analyses are necessary to align with wider goals of sustainable development. For instance, sensitivity analysis can be used to take account of quick technological development or progress of emerging green technologies. Currently, emergent green products and technologies tend to lack scale, which can impact on their relative economic, environmental, and social performance, so design teams should be able to use sensitivity analysis to compare them more fairly against established techniques or technologies that are already at scale.

EXERCISE: CANDLES, CHURCHES, AND LCA

Think of a very simple product like a candle. The manufacturer produces ones with no metal support or glass holder or jar. Their ordinary candle is composed only of wax (or tallow) and a cotton twisted cord called wick. Today, most candles are made from paraffin wax, a by-product of petroleum refining, but they can also be made from microcrystalline wax, beeswax (a by-product of honey collection), gel (a mixture of polymer and mineral oil), or some plant waxes (generally palm, carnauba, bayberry, or soybean wax). The candles have no individual packaging. All candles are sold to churches that use their own reusable box for collection from the local manufacturer. The priests are, however, very concerned about climate change and decided that they will implement a sustainable procurement system in all churches of the same congregation. They request the manufacturer to provide them with information on how much greenhouse gases are originated per candle and how they could reduce their environmental impact per candle.

The manufacturer then uses their request to build the goal of their LCA.

Objective: Analyse the amount of GHG emissions in the whole life cycle of a candle.

They built a rudimentary model of the key activities involved to source, produce, use, and dispose of their products. This was followed by a preliminary analysis of the material use and environmental aspects in each stage of the candle life cycle. This initial qualitative analysis is shown in Table 8.1.

The next step would be to collect information from each activity to build a complete LCA in order to quantify the contribution of each activity and each stage in the life cycle of a candle.

Do a research on the energy intensity and GHG emissions for each phase of the candle life cycle. How easy was it to find accurate information on sourcing of paraffin wax and cotton wick? What about candle manufacturing and use? How can you estimate the energy consumption and emissions for the candle disposal?
What would you recommend the candle manufacturer to do in order to meet their customer request?

One important aspect to conducting a product LCA is that it will reveal the product's bill of materials. A bill of materials (BOM) is an inventory of all the raw materials, parts, and components, and their respective quantities needed to manufacture a product. Some customers, investors, or a future legislation (e.g. on safety and health, labour conditions, or environmental) may request or require the removal of components, parts, or substances of the products.

For instance, in the above example of a candle LCA, the church was concerned about GHG emissions from purchasing and using candles. But by simply doing an initial LCA, they may perceive other sustainability issues such as emissions from burning several candles in confined spaces or even the use of solvents to clean candle holders. Discussion on the candle LCA would raise issues from reducing GHG emissions derived purchasing decisions to human health, including the provenance of cotton wicks and type of wax. While this may sound a simple decision for a candle manufacturer, this task can be very difficult for complex products where consumption of energy, materials, and water, as well as emissions need to be considered in the whole product life cycle.

For example, in the United Kingdom, the Health and Safety Executive provides a guide to Control of Substances Hazardous to Health (COSHH) in the work environment. If some of these substances of concern can be eliminated from product design or from its process the risk to human health is lowered, and their socio-economic implications improved (e.g. employee turnover, legal fines, absenteeism, low productivity, etc.).

The European Union also has a regulation on the Registration, Evaluation, Authorisation and Restriction of Chemicals (REACH).

The classification of dangerous substances is based on categories which include physical hazards (explosive, flammable, instable etc.), health hazards (all aspects of short- and long-term harm to health), and environmental hazards (aquatic, environment, etc.)

Table 8.1 Preliminary analysis of material use and environmental aspects

Sourcing raw and virgin materials	*Manufacturing*	*Use*	*Disposal*
Cotton Wax	Production of candle wick Wax production processes: • Melting wax • Building candle sticks	Emissions from burning a candle	Disposal of candle waste (e.g. transportation to landfill, incineration, etc)
Transport of transformation materials to factory	Affixing candle wick and storing finished products Transportation to Churches	Maintenance and repair of candle holders	

The health problems that can be caused by working with dangerous substances range from mild eye and skin irritation to severe effects, such as birth defects and cancer. Effects can be acute or long term, and some substances can have a cumulative effect. Some of the most common dangers are:

- allergies
- skin diseases
- cancers
- reproductive problems and birth defects
- respiratory diseases
- poisoning.

Some dangerous substances pose safety risks, such as risk of fire, explosion, or suffocation. In addition, dangerous substances normally have several of these properties.

Grant et al. (2017) list common hazardous materials found in product supply chains:

- acid and alkalis
- arsenic
- asbestos
- cadmium
- chromium
- clinical wastes
- cyanide
- dimethyl fumarate (DMFu)
- lead
- mercury
- PCBs
- POPs
- PBB and PBDE.

Many industrial, agricultural, and medical organisations use hazardous substances. The degree of hazard depends on the concentration of the chemical. In the workplace, they may be identified as:

- acids
- caustic substances
- disinfectants
- glues
- heavy metals, including mercury, lead, cadmium and aluminium
- paint
- pesticides
- petroleum products
- solvents.

Not surprisingly, it is common to find companies seeking environmental and sustainability leadership, so marketing their products as free of such hazardous substances (e.g. solvent-free and lead-free paint, organic production – free of pesticides, etc.). While this approach usually appeals to market requirements, it is important to assess the ecological and social impact of the chosen substitutes.

The next section will present the key approaches that companies can take in order to make product development more sustainable.

Design for Sustainability (DfS): approaches to making product designs more sustainable

DfS is understood to address all dimensions of sustainability, looking at bigger systems and asking more fundamental questions about consumption and production (Spangenberg et al., 2010).

Ceschin and Gaziulusoy (2016) have mapped the evolution of Design for Sustainability (DfS). Their investigation found the DfS approaches which have emerged in the past decades and they are categorised in four different innovation levels:

- **Product innovation level**: this focuses on improving existing designs or developing completely new products.
- **Product–Service System innovation level**: here the focus is beyond individual products towards integrated combinations of products and services (e.g. development of new business models).
- **Spatio-Social innovation level**: here the context of innovation is on human settlements and the spatio-social conditions of their communities. This can be addressed on different scales, from small neighbourhoods to large cities.
- **Socio-Technical System innovation level**: here design approaches focus on promoting radical changes to how societal needs, such as nutrition and transport/mobility, are fulfilled, and thus support transitions to new socio-technical systems.

The following subsections present the most commonly used approaches to accommodate or enable sustainability values and principles in design and to change the product development process so that it takes account of sustainability concerns.

Cradle-to-cradle & biomimicry

> The essential flaw remains: badly designed materials and systems that are unsuitable for indoor use.
>
> (Braungart, M. and Donough, W., *Cradle to Cradle*, 2009)

Cradle-to-cradle authors, Michael Braungart and William McDonough, advocate that industrial designers should move away from eco-efficiency to eco-effectiveness. The principle behind this idea is that although the efficiency may be seen as necessary in the short term, it may create hidden and greater impact in the long term. In times of planned obsolescence, higher efficiency associated with greater desire to consume short-life and superfluous products can lead to more consumption of natural resources. Thus, this phenomenon will eventually promote a greater, and possibly irreversible, environmental impact in the long run.

The cradle-to-cradle approach recommends being inspired by Nature in order to be eco-effective, i.e. doing the right thing from an ecological view. In this sense, it brings the concept of a circular economy in Chapter 2 to the product and process level in industrial systems.

Biomimicry is a similar concept in which solutions found in Nature should be imitated by product designers. It is a practice which starts off by asking how nature operates to satisfy aspects of life such as shelter, transport, aesthetics, etc. For example, the winglets of modern aircraft borrow from the feathered wingtips of soaring birds to improve aerodynamic efficiency. The Biomimicry Institute says that 'asking nature' has ancient roots in the indigenous communities that have passed on their observations and insights from the natural world throughout generations. Biomimicry involves learning from and emulating biological forms, processes, and ecosystems tested by the environment and refined through evolution (Benyus, 1997).

Considering the unifying theory of sustainability presented in Chapter 3, which concerned facilities, cradle-to-cradle and biomimicry approaches consider both essentiality and the limits of the environment among their principles.

Zero-waste to landfill is usually cited as one of the goals of these holistic approaches. In alignment with the industrial symbiosis concept, products and processes should play a role in their operating environment. They should benefit by using waste from other industries, which at their end-of-life should become waste that is used again by another company or industry. Their substances, materials, parts, and components will then enhance the environment where they were harvested, used, and finally, disposed of.

The Physicist Marcelo Gleiser was awarded the Best American Science Writing 2003. In his essay, he writes:

> We must learn from the way Nature operates. There is a single principle behind all existing order in Nature [...] Humans cannot escape this alliance with the rest of the cosmos. Our tensions are part of this universal trend, our creations and destructions are part of the same rhythms that permeate the Universe. However, we have distanced ourselves from Nature, and have become wasteful. [...] Our wastefulness is reflected in the way we treat our planet and ourselves. It is a cancer that grows and overwhelms what lives and what doesn't. We must learn from Nature's simple elegance, from its esthetical and economical commitment to functionality and form.
>
> (Gleiser, 2003)

The concepts of Design for Sustainability and holistic approaches, cradle-to-cradle and biomimicry will take time to be fully implemented because they involve significant changes to several materials and product components, and even the transformation of business models. In some cases, radical changes around product and process design may depend on changes to institutions and infrastructure (e.g. new legislations, government support, or centralised R&D investment, recycling infrastructure, market platforms, etc.). Alternatively, organisations might prefer to use more incremental, pragmatic, and evolutionary approaches. Also, the sustainability drivers sometimes push companies to comply with and implement sub-optimal solutions in the short-term. For example, the DfS concept is deliberately pushing the environmental and social agenda simultaneously. Nevertheless, some companies may find that the environmental agenda is more urgent, depending on the nature of their industrial sector, the characteristics of their products, and within the context of the socio-ecological systems where they operate. Such companies may therefore prefer initially to adopt Design for Environment (or Ecodesign) as described in the next section.

Alternatively, organisations may feel their role is to add extra functionalities to meet the essential needs of customers – making their product more essential. Such companies will focus on the social needs input for product development in the approach for DfS. Another example within the social dimension of sustainability is a firm that wants to expand the benefits of its products to more people. Then, the development of a more scalable and affordable design is more urgent than the reduction of environmental impact. So, those companies may prefer to consider approaches such as design for quality of life or design for the bottom of the pyramid, also described in a later section.

The alternative approaches to designing for sustainability presented in the following sections can vary in their level of risk, business benefits, as well as in their ability to create societal value and reduce environmental impacts.

Design for environment (DfE)

The concept of DfE originated from industry's effort to target specific environmental objectives for design engineers to incorporate when creating a new product (Sroufe et al. 2000). DfE incorporates environmental considerations into the original design as well as redesign of products, processes, and technical and management systems.

With respect to product interventions, DfE approaches are normally done by focusing on the most critical parts of the product life cycle and key environmental performance measures, or on critical issues for market requirements, product functionality, aesthetics, and sustainability performance. Design for environment in turn comprises other concepts or practices, namely design for eco-efficiency or eco-effectiveness, design for disassembly, and ecodesign.

Design for eco-efficiency or eco-effectiveness

Design for eco-efficiency is one approach of the DfE practice aimed at improving the overall efficiency of a product throughout its life. The term eco-efficiency was coined by the World Business Council for Sustainable Development (WBCSD), and is defined as:

> eco-efficiency is achieved by the delivery of competitively priced goods and services that satisfy human needs and bring quality of life, while progressively reducing ecological impacts and resource intensity throughout the life cycle to a level at least in line with the Earth's estimated carrying capacity.

Simple products such as carpets, or more complex ones such as wind turbines, will have their materials processing and manufacturing phases as the most dominant in terms of environmental impacts, particularly for energy consumption.

Some food and drink products, such as grains, fruits, and wine could have warehousing or transportation as their main source of energy consumption, even if not having an overall environmental impact.

On the other hand, products such as aeroplanes, heating systems, automobiles, and hairdryers are among many for which the use phase of their life cycle has the largest energy consumption. As a result, designers using design for eco-efficiency will focus on improving product performance, so they can reduce energy consumption during the overall life of the product.

Several types of cleaning materials, packaging, and batteries have their end-of-life as the most problematic phase from an environmental viewpoint. Taking plastic packaging as an example; although manufacturing is energy intensive, it is disposal that attracts more public attention because of the plastic pollution problem in landfills and water bodies, which poses a particular threat to birds and marine life.

A final group of products, which includes household appliances and electronic devices such as televisions and computers, will have a more mixed or balanced distribution of environmental impact and energy consumption throughout the life cycle, particularly between the manufacturing and use phases.

Design for disassembly

Since the 1980s the growing popularity of some national quality standards (such as the British BSI and German DIN standards), Total Quality Management, and more recently ISO 9000 have led manufacturers to pursue quality as a key differentiating competitive factor. For many years previously, and in several different sectors, product quality was mainly perceived as a function of product reliability and durability. Products were designed to have a long life, as opposed to the current idea of planned obsolescence characterised by products with short life cycles. Furthermore, they were designed for ease of repair, in contrast to today's throw-away culture. When a part or component failed it was possible to find a replacement. So, since all the other parts were still in good condition, the whole product would continue to work at the same level of performance.

Quality of materials was one of the key factors making products more durable. Another key factor for achieving longer life and durable products is a philosophy that they should not only be easy to assemble, but also easy to disassemble to allow efficient repair. Design for disassembly favours simplicity, standardised parts or components, fasteners, or screws instead of materials, parts, or components being glued together, which makes disassembly more difficult.

Design for disassembly is usually a prerequisite to adopt other forms approaches with the DfE principles, ecodesign, and improve the levels of *reusability*, *remanufacturing*, and *recyclability*. Consequently, the value capture of end-of-life products is enhanced.

Ecodesign

Ecodesign (also called green design) aims at lowering environmental impacts of individual products (Ceschin and Gaziulusoy, 2016). It is different from design for eco-efficiency because in addition to using less material and lowering energy consumption to achieve the same functionality, it incorporates waste hierarchy principles to further enable the principles of reduce–reuse–remanufacture–recycle.

The use of design for disassembly still needs to respect product characteristics. For example, a laundry power or dishwasher detergent manufacturer may also want to make its product design greener, but there may not be massive gains from disassembly (e.g. packaging materials, etc.). In this case they could therefore be more concerned with *responsible disposal* of the end-of-life product. This is why such companies might choose to green their design by developing biodegradable products.

While design for disassembly is a powerful concept, other even more radical solutions may prefer to completely dematerialise a product. This is the case for e-books and even technology convergence of office equipment. With e-books the environmental impacts of extracting and processing raw materials, printing physical books, and all the associated transportation impacts are substituted for energy consumption (and the relative environmental impacts of producing and discarding an e-book reader in addition to energy consumption from data centres because of the cloud storage). Dematerialisation (and sometimes digitalisation or miniaturisation) has also occurred where various large pieces of office equipment (photocopiers, printers, and scanners) are merged into one small device, thus substantially reducing the need for much of the materials, packaging, and transportation. Technology convergence has also enabled previously separate GPS satellite navigation devices to be incorporated into a mobile phone app (e.g. Google and Apple maps, Waze, etc.).

Design for quality of life and the bottom-of-the pyramid

The social dimension of sustainability can be the most important for some companies. Thus, product development teams will assess the socio-technical systems and needs of users to design products accordingly. However, this does not mean economic and environmental issues will be disregarded; it simply means that the social dimension is prioritised or maximised while efforts are made to maintain threshold performance for the economic and environmental dimension.

Creating products for users with special needs such as electric wheelchairs, voice-controlled devices is a good example of this. Because of their low volumes of production and potentially high level of customisation, some of these niche products can have a high ratio of design input to outcome. However, they are desirable for a society that wants to improve the quality of life for all.

The same argument can be made when products are designed with consideration of issues such as labour conditions, poverty alleviation, integration of weak and marginalised people, social cohesion, or democratic empowerment of citizens (Ceschin and Gaziulusoy, 2016). Trade-offs will exist with other dimensions of sustainability, but the product is still desirable because it addresses what is perceived to be an essential need of society.

Quality of life (and well-being) should also be a driver for sustainable product and process design (D'Anna and Cascini, 2016). The aspects of quality of life, human needs, and the aspirations of humans have been studied, classified, and listed by several authors (Maslow, 1943; Max-Neef, 1991; Felce and Perry, 1995). For example, the incorporation of essential needs such as health, nutrition, fitness, mobility, and safety are all part of physical well-being. So, the dimensions of quality of life and well-being include the following:

- physiological and physical well-being (health, nutrition, fitness, mobility, and safety);
- material well-being (wealth and ownership);
- social well-being (interpersonal relationships and community involvement);
- productive well-being (skills and competences in all areas of life);
- emotional or esteem well-being (happiness, mental state, self-esteem, spirituality, sexuality and contentment);
- civic well-being (role as citizen).

The joint UNEP and Delft University of Technology (Crul and Diehl, 2006) publication on *Design for Sustainability: a practical approach for developing economies* highlights the relevance of Design for Sustainability (or D4S) for developing economies. It recommends a 'needs assessment' to better align the D4S strategy to the context where it is developed, or is being developed for. For example, when designing products for least industrialised countries, companies may opt to use the *Design for Bottom of the Pyramid* (BOP) approach. Although sometimes controversial, the main principle of Design for BOP is providing access to essential goods and services to the poorest in society. Removing 'luxury' parts of standard products and reducing the cost of production increases the affordability of goods for BOP consumers. However, it is important to highlight that Design for BOP includes both BOP consumers as well as producers. BOP producers have the ability to develop skills and competences and increase personal income within the communities that will also benefit from consuming the essential goods they produce.

Towards an index of product sustainability fitness

The comparison of products is an inevitable aspect of competition and a relevant one for procurement departments and product development teams, among other business functions. Although benchmarking sustainability of products is an important management issue, it is very often a difficult task. In particular, sustainability is different from other mono-dimensional measures, such as cost. It is fairly easy to compare the cost of a vehicle, be it at sale price, the vehicle's operational cost (lowest fuel consumption and maintenance requirements), or even total cost of ownership (including depreciation, residual value, etc.). However, the multidimensional measurement systems of sustainability performance will require more complex assessments which often combine subjective and objective performance indicators.

As mentioned earlier, LCA is one of the most used techniques for this purpose, but it is not without limitations and consequent criticism. Furthermore, it is predominantly an environmental assessment (not a sustainability assessment) and was not originally considered to be a benchmarking tool (Graedel et al., 1993; Collado-Ruiz and Ostad-Ahmad-Ghorabi, 2010).

As an alternative, the use of product sustainability fitness (PSF) is proposed. In this approach, products can be assessed against the needs they address and the resources they use to address those needs – inspired by the sustainability fitness model by Nunes et al. (2016).

PSF is a function of how the product contributes to the survival of the firm (e.g. financially, commercially, technologically, and on learning), the level to which it addresses the essential needs of individuals, and its environmental impact.

Like the above D4S methodology, it is important to consider the critical needs of society and the criticality of resources where the product is produced and consumed. The PSF can be summarised in the following equation:

$$PSF = \frac{Product\ essentiality\ index}{Product\ environmental\ impact}$$

where,

$$Product\ Essentiality\ Index = f\left(Contibution\ to\ the\ needs\ of\ the\ firm, essential\ needs\ of\ society\right)$$

and

$$\textit{Product environmental impact} = f\left(\textit{Actual product resource consumption}, \textit{Environmental limit}\right)$$

It should not be forgotten that most products will have at least the benefit of creating jobs and developing company worker's skills when being produced, transported, sold, and repaired. While this is not necessarily a key measure to justify their production, it must be considered as part of their calculation of essentiality index.

An index for product sustainability fitness would allow organisations to measure and benchmark products in their portfolio, in different points in time, as well as for different locations. It will permit a comparison of sustainability performance of products in different sectors, and allow accommodation of contextual and complex sustainability aspects into product benchmarking and rankings.

ELECTRICAL APPLIANCES TO BE CHEAPER TO RUN AND LAST LONGER WITH NEW STANDARDS

Source: www.gov.uk/government/news/electrical-appliances-to-be-cheaper-to-run-and-last-longer-with-new-standards

Fridges, washing machines, and televisions will soon be cheaper to run, easier to repair, and will last longer thanks to plans for new energy efficiency legislation announced by the UK government today (Wednesday 10 March 2021).

Ministers are set to introduce tough new rules for electrical products to tackle 'premature obsolescence' – a short lifespan deliberately built into an appliance by manufacturers which leads to unnecessary and costly replacements for the consumer. Manufacturers will be legally obliged to make spare parts for products available to consumers for the first time – a new legal right for repairs – so that electrical appliances can be fixed easily. The move is expected to extend the lifespan of products by up to ten years – preventing appliances ending up on the scrap heap sooner than they should and reducing carbon emissions at the same time. The United Kingdom generates around 1.5 million tonnes of electrical waste every year. The changes will also set far higher energy-efficiency standards for electrical products which, overall, will save consumers an average of £75 a year on energy bills. They will cut 8 mega tonnes of carbon emissions in 2021 by reducing the amount of energy products consume over their life-time – the equivalent of removing all emissions from Birmingham and Leeds each year.

Business and Energy Secretary, Kwasi Kwarteng, said:

> Our plans to tighten product standards will ensure more of our electrical goods can be fixed rather than thrown on the scrap heap, putting more money back in the pockets of consumers whilst protecting the environment.
>
> Going forward, our upcoming energy efficiency framework will push electrical products to use even less energy and material resources, saving people

> money on their bills and reducing carbon emissions as we work to reach net zero by 2050.

The changes will provide more accurate information on energy efficiency, incentivising manufacturers to go further. They are also designed to encourage consumers to buy more energy-efficient products, and boost people's confidence in the environmental credentials of the products they are buying. Now the United Kingdom is an independent nation outside the European Union, the EU emblem on energy efficiency labels has also been replaced with the Union Flag.

Climate Change Minister, Lord Callanan, said:

> We can all play our part in ending our contribution to climate change, even when we're choosing a new electrical appliance. The new energy labels we have introduced this week will help consumers make more informed decisions about how eco-friendly one smart TV or dishwasher is over another, helping us reduce our carbon footprint and build back greener.

Head of International Collaboration at Energy Saving Trust, Emilie Carmichael, said:

> This is another positive step in raising the minimum energy performance for domestic products. Simplifying the way energy efficiency is displayed on labels will help consumers to make more informed choices to reduce their energy consumption and bills. Equally, every small step that consumers take in choosing the most efficient appliances will help the United Kingdom in reaching its net zero targets.

Summary of the chapter

Designing products and processes holds a great opportunity to improve operations sustainability performance. While the risks of product interventions can be high, so can the returns.

This chapter addressed first the economic sustainability of product and process design. Design as one of the activities in the operations function will also be judged by its cost, quality, speed, flexibility, and dependability.

In a world where sustainability pressures raise the standards beyond economic and financial requirements, designers will also be pushed to think of social and environmental sustainability. From an environmental sustainability viewpoint, LCA plays an important role in guiding environmental decision making. The social sustainability is heavily influenced by the essentiality of the goods and services designed together with the health and safety concerns for material acquisition, production process, product use, and end-of-life.

Finally, this chapter proposes a preliminary formulation of a product sustainability fitness index. This is aimed at supplementing and not necessarily replacing the current approaches such as LCA or D4S in making sustainable design a reality for organisations.

References

Benyus, J. M. (1997). *Biomimicry: Innovation Inspired by Nature* (p. 320). New York: Morrow.

Bjørn, A., & Hauschild, M. Z. (2015). Introducing carrying capacity-based normalisation in LCA: framework and development of references at midpoint level. *The International Journal of Life Cycle Assessment, 20*(7), 1005–1018.

Braungart, M., & McDonough, W. (2009). *Cradle to Cradle*. London: Penguin.

Collado-Ruiz, D., & Ostad-Ahmad-Ghorabi, H. (2010). Comparing LCA results out of competing products: developing reference ranges from a product family approach. *Journal of Cleaner Production, 18*(4), 355–364.

Crul, M. R. M., & Diehl, J. C. (2006). *Design for Sustainability: A Practical Approach for Developing Economies*. Delft: UNEP–TU.

D'Anna, W., & Cascini, G. (2016). Adding quality of life to design for Eco-Efficiency. *Journal of Cleaner Production, 112*, 3211–3221.

Felce, D., & Perry, J. (1995). Quality of life: Its definition and measurement. *Research in Developmental Disabilities, 16*(1), 51–74.

Gleiser, M. (2003). Emergent realities in the cosmos. In Oliver Sacks (Ed.), *The Best American Science Writing 2003*. New York: W. W. Norton.

Graedel, T. E., Allenby, B. R., & Linhart, P. B. (1993). Implementing industrial ecology. *IEEE Technology and Society Magazine, 12*(1), 18–26.

Grant, D. B., Wong, C. Y., & Trautrims, A. (2017). *Sustainable Logistics and Supply Chain Management: Principles and Practices for Sustainable Operations and Management*. London: Kogan Page Publishers.

Karlsson, R., & Luttropp, C. (2006). EcoDesign: what's happening? An overview of the subject area of EcoDesign and of the papers in this special issue. *Journal of Cleaner Production, 14*(15–16), 1291–1298.

Kleindorfer, P. R., Singhal, K., & Van Wassenhove, L. N. (2005). Sustainable operations management. *Production and Operations Management, 14*(4), 482–492.

Maslow, A. (1943). Theory of human motivation. *Psychological Review, 50*(4), 370–396.

Max-Neef, M., (1991). *Human Scale Development: Conception, Application and Further Reflections* (p. 114). New York: The Apex Press.

Mildenberger, U., & Khare, A. (2000). Planning for an environment-friendly car. *Technovation, 20*(4), 205–214.

Nunes, B., Alamino, R. C., Shaw, D., & Bennett, D. (2016). Modelling sustainability performance to achieve absolute reductions in socio-ecological systems. *Journal of Cleaner Production, 132*, 32–44.

Orsato, R., & Wells, P. (2007). The automobile industry and sustainability. *Journal of Cleaner Production, 15*(11–12), 989–993.

Slack, N., & Lewis, M. (2020). *Operations Strategy* (6th ed.). Harlow, UK: Pearson.

Spangenberg, J. H., Fuad-Luke, A., & Blincoe, K. (2010). Design for sustainability (DfS): The interface of sustainable production and consumption. *Journal of Cleaner Production, 18*(15), 1485–1493.

Sroufe, R., Curkovic, S., Montabon, F., & Melnyk, S. A. (2000). The new product design process and design for environment. *International Journal of Operations & Production Management*, 20, 267–291.

Van Wassenhove, L. N. (2019). Sustainable innovation: Pushing the boundaries of traditional operations management. *Production and Operations Management, 28*(12), 2930–2945.

WCED, World Commission on Environment and Development. (1987). *Our Common Future*. Oxford: Oxford University Press, 1987.

Part 3

Cases on sustainable operations management

9 Sustainable operations management in the automotive industry

PART A – SUSTAINABILITY PERSPECTIVES ON BMW'S RISE AND GLOBAL CAPACITY EXPANSION

Introduction: background to the automotive industry, internationalisation, and sustainability challenges

This part of the case considers how automotive companies develop their businesses and use an international operations strategy to expand capacity, penetrate new markets, improve cost competitiveness by increasing economies of scale, and facilitate the exchange of knowledge about innovations. It draws on the experience of BMW as an example of how automotive companies globalise their production operations and use capacity strategy and build flexibility into their international manufacturing plants as a way of dealing with uncertain markets as well as volatile political and economic environments. The case highlights specifically how environmental, economic, and social sustainability have increasingly become important considerations in the automotive industry generally and as part of BMW's operations strategy development.

Automotive production was one of the earliest industries to internationalise, with overseas production starting only a few years after the birth of the industry in the late 1800s. American companies were the first to start the trend, with General Motors establishing a joint venture in the United Kingdom in 1910. Soon after that, in 1911, Ford Motor Company also established a plant in the United Kingdom.

Beyond the United States, internationalisation of automotive companies was much slower. In the early 1900s the industry in Europe comprised a large number of smaller companies, so there was little motivation and insufficient resources for establishing foreign plants. Instead a number of European companies licensed production to newcomers elsewhere in the world. In Japan the automotive industry originally relied on European designs. For example, in 1917 the Mitsubishi Shipbuilding Company started building a car under licence from Fiat, and in 1918 the Ishikawajiama Ship Building and Engineering Company acquired the licence to build cars from the British Wolseley company. From 1934 Nissan Motor Company started building its Datsun branded cars based on a licence to produce the British Austin Seven model.

Large-scale production of European cars overseas did not start until after the Second World War, with Volkswagen establishing its plant in Brazil in 1953. Later, in the 1950s, a number of British companies opened plants in Australia, India, South Africa, and France. By the 1960s and 1970s internationalisation was becoming increasingly prevalent in the automotive industry as most of the main manufacturers started to open overseas plants. At

DOI: 10.4324/9781003009375-12

the same time more countries emerged as locations for automotive production and started to develop their own automotive industries. South Korea, and later China, became major automotive manufacturing countries with government strategy promoting the establishment of indigenous car and commercial vehicle companies.

Since the end of the 1990s internationalisation has become the main strategy of all the largest automobile manufacturers. This has been driven by market expansion and economies of scale, meaning a dramatic reorganisation of the automotive industry's worldwide production locations. In 2000 the United States, Japan, Germany, Spain, and Canada produced almost 60% of the world's motor vehicles. However, 15 years later this production share was reduced to 36%, and now almost 60% of motor vehicles are produced by Brazil, China, and India. Despite the trend towards larger integrated plants, automobile production is far more globally distributed today than in the past. In addition to the emerging country players mentioned above, there is growing automotive production in Mexico, Hungary, Romania, Czech Republic, Slovakia, Philippines, Thailand, Malaysia, Iran, and Turkey, among others.

As a consequence of internationalisation, the automobile industry has made remarkable positive contributions to the world economy and people's mobility, but its products and processes have become a significant source of environmental impact. A strong focus on lean production during the 1980s and 1990s drove down cost, leading to price reductions, and thereby market saturation and predatory price competition with low profit margins. But automotive companies can no longer rely on the benefits of lean production and production efficiencies alone as the rules of competition changed in the latter years of the 20th century. Also, more frequent materials and parts deliveries with lean production can lead to greater environmental damage as a result of the increased number of journeys by suppliers. So now, in the 21st century, the rules are changing again and there is increasing pressure for the adoption of environmentally friendly production and logistics processes as well as greener products such as cars powered by electric, hybrid, or hydrogen fuel cell engines. Environmental concerns must go beyond mere efficiency gains, and encouraging efficiency can lead to increased consumption, which increases the overall use of resources.

The history of BMW

BMW (Bayerische Motoren Werke) was established in 1917 as a result of reorganising RAPP-Motorenwerke, a German aircraft engine manufacturer founded in 1913 by the engineer Karl Rapp and financed by Julius Auspitzer. BMW based its logo on an aircraft propeller in the blue and white colours of Bavaria. But after the First World War BMW was obliged under the Versailles Treaty to stop producing aircraft engines, so in 1922 it began making small motorcycle engines for outside customers. Then in 1923 BMW started building complete motorcycles under its own brand. Car production started in 1928 when BMW acquired the Eisenach car company and its production facilities. At the time Eisenach's only model was a licence-built version of the British Austin Seven. This was developed by BMW to become its first car, known as the "Dixi". The company soon introduced several new models and enlarged its engines from 1.2 litres to 3.5 litres. During the 1930s it established a reputation as a maker of prestigious sports cars and built its sales around successes in major European road races such as Italy's "Mille Miglia".

During the Second World War BMW was requisitioned to build engines for the German air force, while at the same time all car and motorcycle production stopped. After 1945 BMW's factories were dismantled, but it survived by manufacturing small items such as cooking utensils and agricultural tools. BMW began producing motorcycles again after rebuilding its bombed-out Munich plant and in 1948 introduced a one-cylinder motorcycle, which sold well as cheap transportation. Between 1945 and 1951 "BMW" branded cars were still produced at the Eisenach plant, which was in Germany's Eastern Zone and controlled by the Soviet Union. BMW in Munich could not bring legal proceedings to protect its trade name but this situation stopped in 1952 when the Eisenach plant was transferred to the East German government and started making cars under the old Wartburg brand.

By 1958, the automotive division of BMW was in financial difficulties after several years of disappointing sales. The company survived by acquiring the rights to manufacture the Italian Iso Isetta, a three-wheeler with a single front opening door. BMW's version of these small cars was powered by a modified BMW motorcycle engine. It was moderately successful and helped with putting the company back onto a viable financial footing. Then in 1959 BMW was acquired by the German industrialist Herbert Quandt who changed its focus to production of high-performance saloon cars (sedans). The first of the BMW New Class (Neue Klasse) cars, the 1500, was launched in 1961 and sold well. This niche strategy proved successful and BMW grew considerably over the next ten years. By financial value it moved from number 69 to number 11 among the industrial companies in Germany. However, BMW was still small compared to the big US automotive companies, being a third the size of Ford and a quarter the size of General Motors. The Quandt family's 60% ownership allowed the company to accept moderate short-term returns in expectation of long-term potential profits. Between 1984 and 1994, annual sales grew nearly 8% while profits increased by approximately 1.5%. In the early 1990s BMW's profits declined, but in 1994 sales and profits increased substantially. It was at this time that BMW reassessed its international strategy and embarked on a new path that would transform the company into a major global player with increased public exposure as well as giving greater emphasis to its environmental and social responsibilities. BMW is thought to be the first automobile manufacturer to appoint its own environmental officer and the company recognises that it can directly influence the CO_2 emissions of its own plants and sites. Concerning emissions from the cars it produces, these were reduced by more than 70% between 2006 and 2019 with the aim of reducing them by a further 80% by 2030.

BMW going international

By the mid-1990s BMW had 34 wholly owned subsidiaries. Of these, 14 were in Germany and the other 20 were located around the world. It also had more than 130 foreign sales operations. BMW's manufacturing activities were still concentrated in six plants in Germany. These included a motorcycle plant in Berlin and a tooling plant in Eisenach (now a part of reunified Germany). A plant in Steyr, Austria (three hours south of Munich by car) was BMW's largest facility for production of its 4-cylinder and 6-cylinder engines. BMW also operated various so-called "kit factories" outside Europe. These factories assembled cars from either complete knockdown kits (CKDs) or semi-knockdown kits (SKDs). BMW's oldest and most sophisticated SKD plant was located in Rosslyn, South Africa (near Pretoria), which opened in 1973. Table 9.1 shows BMW's wholly owned car manufacturing plants in 1993. In addition, BMW operated a number of overseas assembly plants in partnership with local companies. In Thailand, Indonesia, Malaysia, and Mexico, local partners assembled BMW cars from kits under joint venture manufacturing agreements.

Table 9.1 BMWs Wholly-Owned Car Manufacturing Plants in 1993

Factory location	*Workforce*	*Production capability*	*Capacity (per day)*	*Plant area (square metres)*
Munich, Germany	11 ,700	3-series; 6, 8 and 12 cylinder engines	850 cars, 950 engines	450,000
Dingolfing, Germany	11 ,528	5-series, 7 and 8-series, axles and central parts supply	900 cars	1,500,000
Regensburg, Germany	7,420	3-series sedan, coupe, and convertible, components	700 cars	1,420,000
Landshut, Germany	3,056	Components and parts	n/a	320,000
Eisenach, Germany	212	Tooling	n/a	85,000
Berlin, Germany	511	R and K series engines, motorcycles and motorcycle engines	150 engines	195,000
Steyr, Austria	2,116	4 and 6 cylinder engines	1,600 engines	206,000
Rosslyn, South Africa	2,920	Parts and electronics. Kit assembly of all car models	n/a	n/a

Source: Dornier (1998).

In 1994, two new overseas assembly plants were established, one in the Philippines and another in Vietnam, so avoiding the high tariffs, taxes, and trade restrictions in those countries. The kits supplied from Germany were exempt from these restrictions because they were augmented with locally purchased components and complied with local content and value-added regulations.

By 1994 BMW's market share in Germany had increased to 6.69%, but for the United States its market share was only 0.94% (see Figure 9.1). The German market was served by 800 exclusive dealerships, while the much larger US market was served by 354 dealers, with only 30% of them exclusive.

In 1994 BMW also acquired the Rover Group in the United Kingdom, which at that time was owned by British Aerospace (BAe). BMW was looking for ways to increase volume and its board felt there were a few possible purchases available. It was attracted by many of the iconic brands such as Mini and Land Rover. At this time BMW did not make four-wheel drive (4x4) cars, although one was under development. BAe was in financial difficulties and sold Rover Group to BMW for GBP 800 million (USD 1,300 million). The deal was completed in ten days. However, the acquisition turned out to be a disaster. By 2000 the Rover Group was losing GBP 2 million each day, so BMW sold the company to a consortium of Rover managers for just GBP 10. But BMW did keep three parts of Rover, i.e. the "new" Mini model, launched in 2000 that had been under development since 1995, the new engine plant at Hams Hall near Birmingham, and a body shop at Swindon. Mini production was moved from the Rover plant in Birmingham to BMW's own manufacturing facility in Oxford. The increase in sales and income for 1994 was partly due to the acquisition of the Rover.

Another BMW acquisition around this time was Rolls-Royce. In 1998 the company called "Rolls-Royce Motors" was sold to Volkswagen including its manufacturing facilities and the Bentley brand name. However, the Rolls-Royce brand name and logo was owned by "Rolls Royce plc", the aircraft engine manufacturer (Rolls-Royce

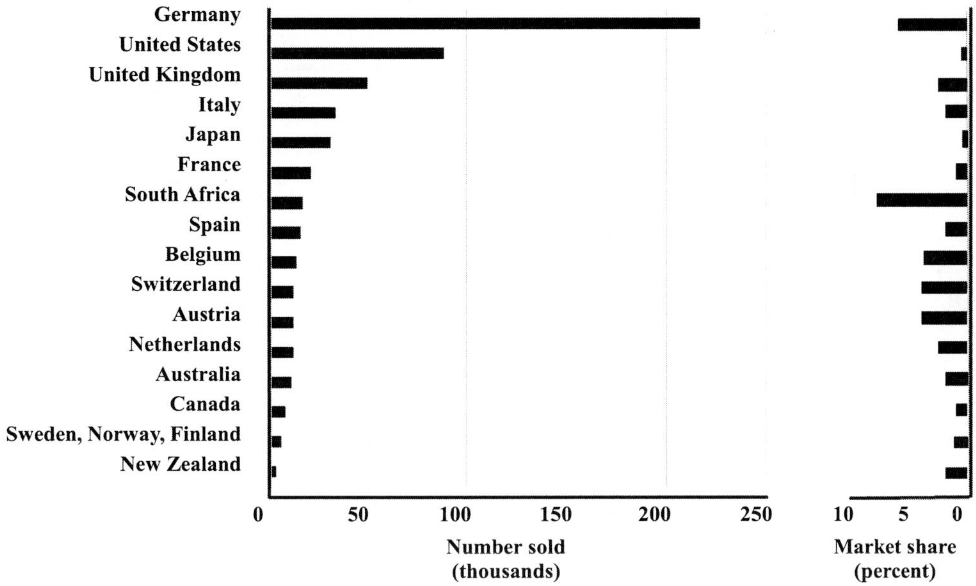

Figure 9.1 BMW Sales by Country in 1994 (Source: number sold from Dornier (1998)/Market share elaborated by the authors)

Motors and Rolls-Royce plc had been separated in 1973). Therefore only the Rolls-Royce brand and logo were acquired by BMW, through a licence bought for GBP 40 million (USD 65 million). BMW already supplied engines and other components for Rolls-Royce and Bentley cars, so this contract was cancelled and a subsidiary was created called "Rolls-Royce Motor Cars Ltd". Since 2003 all Rolls-Royce branded cars have been entirely designed and built by BMW in a new purpose-built assembly plant in the United Kingdom with major parts supplied from other BMW plants.

Making BMW economically sustainable: expansion in North America

BMW of North America Inc (BMW NA), now called BMW of North America LLC, was established in 1975 as a sales and importing company for BMW cars. The prosperous younger generation's preference for imported high performance cars in the early 1980s made the United States the fastest growing market for BMW. By 1994 the United States was the company's largest export market with 84,500 units being exported to the United States that year, 14.7% of its total production. Consequently, the trends in the US market in the late 1980s and early 1990s had a huge impact on BMW's financial performance. Between 1986 and 1991 the US automobile industry experienced a 24% decline in sales (20% between 1986 and 1989). The stock market crash of 1987 and the Tax Reform Act of the same year (which directly affected deductions and depreciation on luxury vehicles), made owning a luxury car less affordable. Also, a "luxury tax" of 10% was levied on cars selling for more than USD 30,000 and the "gas guzzler" tax (aimed at reducing fuel consumption) was doubled. By 1989, total BMW sales in the United States had fallen to 65% of the 1986 level. By 1991, BMW realised that there were serious limitations to its export strategy in the US market. Its cars were not what people were buying and exporting them from Germany to the United States made them costly.

Meanwhile, Japanese automobile manufacturers had started to introduce a new group of lower-end luxury cars. In 1986, Honda introduced the Acura, and in 1989 Nissan introduced the Infiniti and Toyota introduced the Lexus. These models were favourably reviewed, and quickly established a reputation for affordability, quality, service, and reliability among US customers. The Japanese undertook an aggressive strategy to gain market share and drastically undercut BMW's prices with similar product offerings. While BMW's least expensive 3-series in 1990 was USD 25,000 to USD 35,000, Acura's most affordable model was USD 22,000 to USD 29,000. Both Lexus and Infiniti offered a range of models priced from the low USD 20,000s to the upper USD 30,000s. The Japanese manufacturers were also overspending on BMW advertising (Lexus's 1991 advertising budget was double that of BMW). Although these luxury models were initially imported from Japan, the Japanese manufacturers started setting up factories in the United States and were soon rapidly expanding production there. Between 1979 and 1989 eight transplant factories in the United States were opened by Japanese automotive companies, these were:

Honda of America Manufacturing Inc in Marysville, Ohio (1979)
Honda of America Manufacturing Inc in East Liberty, Ohio (1982)
Nissan Motor Manufacturing Corp US in Smyna, Tennessee (1983)
New United Motor Manufacturing Inc (joint venture between Toyota and General Motors) in Fermont, California (1984)
Auto Alliance International Inc (joint venture between Mazda and Ford) in Flat Rock Michigan (1987)
Diamond Star Motors Inc (Mitsubishi), in Normal, Illinois (1988)
Toyota Motor Manufacturing (USA) Inc, in Georgetown, Kentucky (1988)
Subaru-Isuzu Automotive Inc, in Lafayette, Indiana (1989).

In 1983 Japanese vehicle production represented 1% of the total number produced in the United States and by 1993 it had grown to 15%. This growth in local production meant that by 1993 around 65% of Japanese cars sold in the US market were made in US factories. At the same time, the increasing value of the Deutsche Mark (Germany's currency at that time) and high labour costs in Germany were putting more cost pressure on BMW's US sales. The Deutsche Mark had appreciated against the dollar over the previous ten years (see Figure 9.2), so with most of its costs denominated in Deutsche Marks and virtually all of its manufacturing activities concentrated in Germany, BMW had no operational hedge, and currency changes were eating into its profit margins.

With an average of USD 22.32 per hour, wage rates in Germany were 45% higher than those in the United States (USD 15.38). Also, Germans worked an average of 1,647 hours per year, 16% fewer hours than workers in the United States. Higher fringe benefits, longer vacations, and higher absenteeism further contributed to increasing labour cost in Germany, making it among the highest in the world, and direct labour comprised about 15% of BMW's total production cost. It was estimated that BMW's production cost in Germany exceeded US production cost by 30% due to Germany's more expensive labour, materials, and overhead costs. Therefore, in the long term, BMW's growth was threatened with being undermined economically as well as depending on environmentally costly transportation of finished cars between Europe and the United States in the absence of local production.

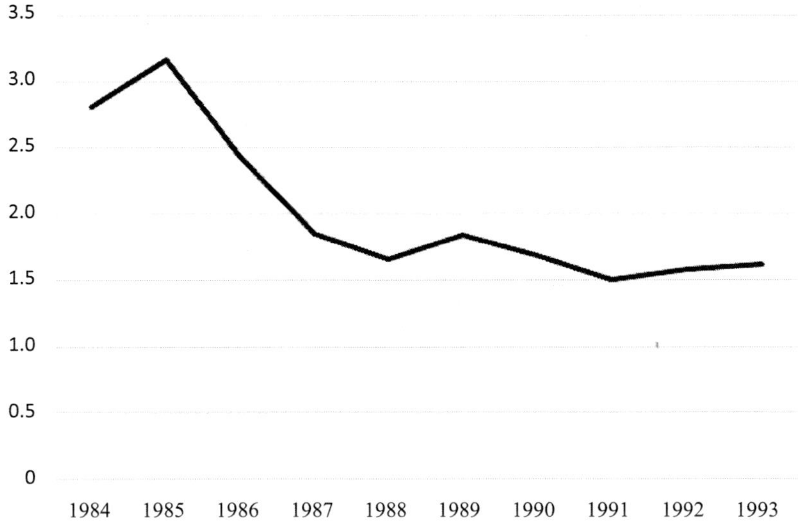

Figure 9.2 Deutsche Mark to US dollar exchange rate 1984 to 1993: The underpinning factor for BMW's economic sustainability in the United States

The situation in the early 1990s pointed to the need for more aggressive measures to maintain and increase market share in the United States. In 1991 BMW's German plants were producing 550,000 units per year, which was their full capacity, so any significant increase in output would require further capacity investment in production facilities. An American factory was a logical next step for BMW because, among other things, it would reduce exposure to exchange-rate fluctuations and, make the company more economically sustainable. Thus, plans for establishing a US factory went ahead. Meanwhile, the 5-series and 7-series luxury models were repositioned in the market by cutting prices, which reduced profitability but allowed the company to maintain its market share in the early 1990s. Then in 1994, BMW began to import its 3-series coupe (or "compact") to the United States. With a sales price of USD 20,000 this car was the least expensive BMW on the market. It was the company's first attempt to appeal to a more price sensitive customer and BMW had to sacrifice its usual high profit margins to achieve sufficient sales volumes.

Making BMW environmentally and socially sustainable: plans for a manufacturing plant in the USA

The strategic objectives for BMW's US plant went beyond reduction of short-term costs and exposure to currency fluctuations. Expanding production to the United States would help BMW maintain, secure, and build its position in the United States luxury-car market, which was the world's biggest. Since the United States had a mature industrial economy with a sophisticated workforce, a plant there could also give BMW an opportunity to implement new sustainable operations management ideas that could be tested and later implemented across plants in other countries. To achieve this position,

BMW's management believed the company should develop a flexible and technologically advanced plant and take full advantage of being close to the demanding American customer. In June 1992, BMW announced that it would set up a manufacturing plant in Spartanburg, South Carolina. The announcement was the result of a long process during which BMW narrowed its choice from 215 possible locations to four, with Spartanburg eventually chosen, partly due to an attractive incentive package from the South Carolina state government, which included reduced building and infrastructure costs. Also South Carolina was distant from the traditional automotive manufacturing state of Michigan, so there would be fewer barriers imposed by old ways of thinking and a highly unionised workforce. This had also been the rationale of the Japanese manufacturers when establishing their US plants in the 1970s and 1980s.

Moreover, the new plant was granted free-trade status as part of the free-trade zone centred on South Carolina's Greenville-Spartanburg Airport, which meant that BMW would not pay US duties on parts imported from Germany or elsewhere unless the final product was sold in the United States. The free-trade zone status would provide considerable savings on duties, which would only be paid at the vehicle's final destination, whether it be the United States or another country. Financing charges would also be reduced because duties would be paid only after the completed car had left the factory. The Spartanburg site also provided the advantage of easy access to highways and rail, as well as being close to the big seaport of Charleston and only ten minutes from the international airport. Also, the cost of living in the region was considerably lower than in many other areas in the United States.

In 1994, BMW AG (the parent company in Germany) established the BMW Manufacturing Corporation (BMW MC) as a wholly owned subsidiary with headquarters in Spartanburg, South Carolina. BMW MC was in charge of manufacturing operations and various corporate functions such as human resources, finance, and purchasing for North America. This did not affect BMW NA (headquartered in New Jersey), which was still responsible for marketing and sales in the United States. Press releases at the time, a vision statement, and interviews by several BMW officials all indicated an ambitious goal for the newly created BMW MC.

BMW initially invested USD 400 million in the plant, which included construction of a manufacturing facility covering 111,000 square metres. This was followed by an additional USD 200 million investment in tooling, bringing the total investment to USD 600 million. The Spartanburg plant was built in record time with only 17 months between the start of construction on 6 April 1993 and the first car being completed on 8 September 1994. The plant was designed with capacity to produce 300 cars per day, with future expansion to 400 cars per day. Plans were made for production of the 3-series models 318 and 328. Assembly of the 4-cylinder 318i saloon car (sedan) was scheduled for September 1994, and production of the second model, the 6-cylinder 328 sedan, was scheduled for the autumn of 1995. BMW planned gradual expansion of the plant from 100 vehicles per day at the end of 1995 to 300 vehicles by the first quarter of 1997 and 400 vehicles per day in 1998. However, this was still considerably smaller than the production capacity for a typical auto assembly plant, which was over 1,000 vehicles per day. The timeline for establishing the Spartanburg plant was as follows:

- June 1992 – Announcement made to build an assembly plant in Spartanburg, South Carolina.
- September 1992 – Groundwork for the plant starts.

- April 1993 – Construction work on buildings starts, followed by production facilities and interior.
- January 1994 – First production employee (termed an "associate") is recruited.
- June 1994 – Imported BMWs arrive at Charleston port and are prepared at the plant for delivery.
- July 1994 – Production facilities are opened.
- September 1994 – First 3-series BMW (318i Sedan) built at the Spartanburg plant.
- November 1994 – Official plant opening ceremony.
- March 1995 – First cars delivered to US dealers.

Although most automobile plants, including BMW's German plants, were built with a high degree of fixed automation, Spartanburg focused on manufacturing flexibility. The layout was designed to support a flexible team-working environment rather than using automation in body production and final assembly. This followed the trend set by some other European automotive manufacturers, especially in countries such as Sweden and the Netherlands, where social obligations meant there was a need to provide more meaningful work. Higher education levels in these countries also enabled workers to be given greater responsibilities. In a radical departure from tradition, the body shop, the paint shop, and the assembly line were all located under one roof, thereby offering greater communication and integration across the workforce. The plant layout was L-shaped to allow for a higher degree of integration between the production line, quality control and supporting functions. Also, to facilitate communication, the assembly line was in the form of a lower-case "e" (instead of the typical "s" or "u" shapes), meaning that the final part of the assembly line curved back to the middle of the shop. Testing operations were located in the middle leg of this "e" shape. In addition to bringing the assembly line workers closer to each other this layout reduced space requirements by 40% and reduced construction costs. The Spartanburg plant was designed to have limited robotics used in production with fewer than 25 robots being installed in the plant. One was used in the final assembly line (for windshield adhesive application), a few were used in welding operations that needed a high degree of speed and accuracy (much of the welding was still done manually), and the rest were in the paint shop.

Despite its limited use of automation in body production and final assembly, the new plant at Spartanburg was still state of the art, having applied all the best concepts BMW had learned from its other plants and automakers around the world. In particular, the company was able to pay special attention to measures that would make the plant more environmentally sustainable.

For example, the fully automated paint shop had a water-borne system (reducing the use of environmentally harmful solvents), which was already used in BMW's Regensburg plant in Germany. It also had an experimental paint line to test new innovations. BMW was the first car manufacturer to use water-based paint on four of the five paint layers, with only the clear top coat being solvent based. Forty per cent of the total initial investment in Spartanburg was for the paint shop and the water-borne system was difficult to commission and operate, despite being environmentally safer. The painting process involved the car body being thoroughly cleaned to remove all residues, then a special coating was applied by lowering the entire body into a water-diluted paint in a giant cathode dip bath. This layer was baked onto the body, and after cooling, the underbody protection was applied, followed by a base coat. High-speed atomisers were used to create an ultra-fine mist that was drawn to the body of the car by high-tension electrostatic charge. The final top coat was then applied and hardened in a drying oven. All paint layers were applied by robots to maintain consistent thickness. In total, BMW used 18 colours of primer and 32 base coat colours, all of which were water-based. This was a far wider colour spectrum than was usual in other auto assembly plants.

BMW had studied Harley-Davidson's success with powder coating the frames of motorcycles and GM's innovative use of an acrylic powder system, which were also less harmful to the environment. The paint shop in Spartanburg was therefore flexibly designed with provisions to allow powder coating equipment to be added later. Scheduling the daily production at the paint shop also posed a challenge. Painting was done in batches based on colours. Operations before painting (in the body shop) and after painting (final assembly) were done in series based on orders. Synchronising painting with these operations was not easy. The master production schedule at Spartanburg was based on sales orders, and suppliers delivered parts in the exact sequence in which they were used both in the body shop and the assembly line. There was a stacker (called the "post office"), which was located between the paint shop and the assembly line. The "post office" had four levels, which each held six rows of four cars to store a total of 96 car bodies. It could reshuffle the cars into the desired sequence necessary for either painting or assembly, which required sophisticated material handling and scheduling systems. All these measures meant that BMW was able to satisfy customers' demands for a wide range of paint colours, while still minimising work-in-progress inventories and making efficient use of materials in the painting process, thereby reducing the amount of waste being discharged.

As well as in the paint shop, the rest of the Spartanburg plant was also designed to be environmentally friendly. It recycled corrugated cardboard, office paper, aluminium cans, scrap metal, glass bottles, plastic bottles, solvents, rags, and used oil. In 1994 the total amount of recycled materials was 180 tonnes. It also used a cogeneration system to produce some of its own energy with gas turbine generators equipped with nitrogen oxide reduction technology which reduced emissions to less than 10% of the Federal standard for stationary gas turbines. The plant operated an on-site wastewater pre-treatment plant that cleaned the wastewater before releasing it into the community wastewater treatment system.

Once the Spartanburg plant was established, and to encourage innovation, the plant was given partial autonomy to implement projects within certain cost limits.

In 1999 the US Environmental Protection Agency (EPA) contacted BMW Spartanburg to raise awareness about the Palmetto landfill site, which was 9.5 miles away (15 km), and the possibility of taking advantage of using landfill gas as a potential power source.

At that time projects costing more than EUR 500,000 still needed approval from BMW's headquarters (note, the euro was introduced as a currency unit in January 1999). Since this was the case of the landfill gas project, a proposal was sent to Germany for approval. After receiving agreement from the headquarters in Munich, the project team spent two years planning, searching for partners, and implementing the project. Finally, in December 2002, the plant's turbines were burning landfill gas. Although costing considerably more than the amount needing headquarters approval, the investment in landfill gas facilities provided 14% of the plant's power requirements and immediately saved BMW USD 2 million per year in energy costs.

During the planning phase, BMW was conscious that it should remain a car manufacturer and did not have expertise in energy technology or waste/landfill management.

Therefore it would not be within its business scope to allocate people and effort to the landfill gas project, so long-term partners for construction and operation of the power plant were needed. The major challenge to the company was a lack of technical knowledge about the operations of an energy supply system despite energy being one of the most critical inputs for its manufacturing plant. The US clean energy company Ameresco Inc was commissioned to manage the project. BMW Spartanburg already had four 1.25 MW Dresser-Rand gas turbines sitting mainly idle, so these were re-purposed to use landfill gas. Ameresco designed and built the gas pipeline, gas processing, and gas compression facilities, which connected to the Palmetto landfill site. After completion, Ameresco took responsibility for managing the overall operations of the energy system.

As well as saving money, the landfill gas project also reduced BMW's CO_2 emissions by 60,000 tons and saved one million dollars every year. Having four turbines producing electricity and heat to the plant from the combustion of methane generated from waste, which would otherwise escape into the atmosphere, gave BMW operational stability from the financial perspective too. BMW signed a 20-year contract for landfill gas supplies, which guaranteed price stability for its operations. On the other hand, the Equipment Services associate explains that the landfill gas is produced organically and composed of 50% of methane (CH_4), producing 530 BTU per cubic foot. Due to these facts, its gas supply may vary during the day; therefore, the new system is less reliable than the former using natural gas (90% of CH_4), which produces 1,000 BTU per cubic foot. Although this operational instability does not create major difficulties, BMW keeps a "back-up" system to inject natural gas and maintain the pressure and energy supply to the plant.

The contract considers that BMW needs to have a minimal take of gas and the payment is according to energy unit. Nowadays, the turbines supply energy to co-generate approximately 4.8 MW of continuous electricity and 2,100 gallons per minute of hot water at 132 degrees Celsius, being responsible for almost two-thirds of the energy used at the BMW plant.

In 2009, BMW replaced the original four turbines with two new more efficient ones. These increased the electrical output to nearly 30% of the plant's requirements and made annual savings of USD 3.5 million. They also reduced the annual CO_2 emissions by 92,000 tons. Then in 2011, together with Ameresco and other research partners, BMW initiated a study to extract methane from landfill gas that could be used to power the company's fleet of materials handling equipment. By 2015 the Spartanburg plant had the world's largest fleet of methane fuel cell forklift trucks.

At the time of its approval the original landfill gas proposal was competing for funding against other projects. The reasons for choosing the landfill project rather than other projects were its economic and environmental benefits as well as its contribution to BMW's image of a sustainable car manufacturer. For example, the landfill gas project had very little risk to the quality of its processes and products.

BMW was aware about the importance of its quality image as an asset. Historically, this image was built partly on the German reputation for high quality manufacturing methods as well as products. The Spartanburg plant paid careful attention to this concern and, as well as focusing on the sustainability aspects, it developed several systems for maintaining good quality control. For example, suppliers were screened carefully and held responsible for meeting strict quality standards (Spartanburg did not do any incoming inspection). Within the plant, team members checked each other's work throughout the production process and final quality checks were undertaken at the end of the assembly line by workers from each shop. Production errors were referred back to the person (or the "associate", as everyone was called) who installed the system or part, so he or she was solely responsible for the rework. The quality system distinguished between person-based and system-based errors, and identified major system-wide quality problems. Spartanburg had a separate "Import Car Processing" (ICP) line that served as a final check for all imported BMWs from Germany destined for dealers in the southern United States. (BMW also had two other ICPs elsewhere in the United States.) In addition to extensive checks, installation of custom items such as radios, media players, and computer equipment was performed in the ICP.

Leveraging advantages from soft technology: production organisation at the Spartanburg plant

When production of the 3-series started at Spartanburg in July 1994, the line produced approximately 20 vehicles per week. This was ramped-up quickly to 60 vehicles per day, and reached 100 vehicles per day by February 1995.

The North American Free Trade Agreement (NAFTA) granted tariff exemption within the United States, Canada, and Mexico for all goods manufactured with a local content of at least 65%. This provided BMW with a strong incentive to develop local suppliers. Many high quality parts and components could be found in the United States at lower prices than in many other countries: stampings, frames, seats, fasteners, glass, and interior and exterior trim could all be purchased in the United States for less than in Europe. Eventually, BMW planned to import only engines and transmissions from Germany. It looked to develop an adequate US supplier base because using suppliers halfway around the world drives up costs and excessive transportation of parts pollutes the environment. But developing a local supplier base was not an easy task. Although Spartanburg wanted to choose suppliers that were also supplying BMW's other plants, it could not simply favour German-based suppliers with US operations or global suppliers with a German base. It wanted to identify the best supplier and, when appropriate, encouraged US suppliers to form joint ventures with German firms. Spartanburg also wanted to work closely with its suppliers. In late 1994, it held a two-and-a-half-day seminar for over 100 suppliers' quality control managers, and another seminar for suppliers' account managers (to handle operational details such as details of BMW's payment system). Supplier representatives were often invited to the new plant to show assembly line workers the best way to handle their parts and systems, and plant employees often visited the suppliers' plants.

The procurement office at Spartanburg had responsibility for all North American procurement activities. Although this office interacted directly with its German counterpart, it had no reporting relationship with Germany and was managed separately. Nevertheless, in 1995 a group of German engineers was still in Spartanburg to assist in the development of the supplier network and to ensure global coordination. Spartanburg's attempt to enlist local suppliers ran counter to a very strong industry trend to rationalise the network of suppliers. Like other car manufacturers, BMW faced the issue of choosing suppliers that could deliver parts and components on a global basis, thus providing more consistent quality as well as an improved bargaining position for the company. The so-called "tier-one" suppliers provided more complete sub-assemblies and helped in product development. Chrysler's LH programme used 230 parts and materials vendors and the Ford Mustang was targeting 180. BMW was aiming for 100 tier-one suppliers. More than 60 existing tier-one suppliers were already committed to Spartanburg and nearly half of these planned to set up facilities close to the plant. Among the tier-one suppliers, only a few (eight) were based in Germany. While some, like Robert Bosch Corp, were subsidiaries of large German multinationals that had operated in the United States for a long lime.

BMW enhanced the role for suppliers in the design and manufacture of its new models. This included buying more completed sub-assemblies from tier-one suppliers. To enhance the supplier's role in design, cross-functional procurement teams were formed with designers, engineers, manufacturers, and purchasers. An important objective was to build in more quality control and to work on friendlier terms with the 100 systems suppliers. The teams involved the suppliers at the concept stage of new models, and enlisted them to look for ways to reduce costs and improve manufacturability.

Suppliers also helped to change the traditional cost orientation of the purchasing function. Unlike other automakers, BMW did not mandate extreme and continuous cost-cutting by the suppliers, but instead there were clauses in the contracts for "negotiating cost adjustments". Tier-one suppliers were expected to assume responsibility for more complete sub-assemblies. Eventually, 20 of them were expected to provide 80% of all BMW's purchased parts. A sunroof, for example, which used to be assembled by BMW from 60 different purchased parts, now came semi-assembled from one supplier, with only three sub-assembled pieces. This integrated approach was estimated to yield a cost reduction of at least 20% and perhaps as much as 40% in some cases.

One of the most important objectives for Spartanburg was to develop a new atmosphere in which employees could be creative and productive. This work atmosphere would be different from that traditionally found in Germany. In a sense, Spartanburg presented BMW with a unique opportunity to experiment with a new format combining the best of German and American traditions. The entrance to the Spartanburg plant was spacious, spotless, and very well organised, to remind the visitor of a German setting. A gallery of photographs showed the development of Spartanburg, from groundwork to the present time while two receptionists took in visitor information and provided name tags. A wide corridor led to the production area and another large corridor led to the open area that housed all BMW MC corporate offices. There were three small conference rooms on this corridor, which were the only closed rooms throughout the Spartanburg plant. The open corporate office layout resembled that of a Japanese corporation with 80 desks tightly packed across a large open room creating small groups of work units. Somewhere within each, a small signboard indicated the appropriate corporate function such as finance, public relations, human resources, etc. There were no cubicles, walls, or separation between the groups. In the corner nearest to the window, at a desk with a view of the whole room, was the President of BMW MC. Everyone in the offices and the production area, including the President, was dressed in the same company clothing, a white coat with a BMW emblem. Only those employees whose specific duties required special protective clothing departed from this common dress code. There was no separation between this large office area and the rest of the plant. From their desks, managers and office workers could see part of the paint shop and some of the assembly shop. Another set of offices housed plant operations, including plant procurement and manufacturing support functions. These offices were located in the centre of the plant, surrounded by the body shop, the paint shop and the assembly line. Initially, these were also supposed to be open, but due to noise problems glass walls were erected to surround the office area. The layout of the building conveyed the message that there should be no difference between office and production workers. This philosophy of equality and a shared environment extended to every facet of work at Spartanburg. All employees used the same cafeteria, seating around 1,200 people. Three lunch shifts were necessary due to capacity constraints, but generally office workers lunched with production workers and corporate staff. Also, workers from all areas shared the same rest rooms and locker rooms.

All employees were organised into teams. A typical team had 20 members and was composed of smaller teams of four or five people. Production teams had rotating leaders who were selected democratically by the members. Each worked on a section of the car and put an identifying signature on its work. Teams were also responsible for their own quality control, with their members checking each other's work systematically and individual teams correcting their own mistakes. If an error originated outside the team, they called on the team that had signed off the part to correct the mistake. Workers who were new to automotive production were fully trained, not only in manufacturing processes, but also in team building and conflict resolution. BMW also instituted a carefully designed compensation programme at Spartanburg. Benefits were the same for production workers, staff, and managerial positions. For example, a perfect attendance bonus of USD 100 was given for every 20 consecutive workdays. All other bonuses depended on overall plant performance, regardless of the employee's rank.

An important aspect of making the Spartanburg plant sustainable in the long term was to avoid the dependence on German engineers travelling to the United States, so the company only provided external engineering support in the ramp-up phase of the plant. To this end a group of 40 German engineers was formed that was linked to BMW in Germany and its suppliers by "CATIA", an online computer-aided design (CAD) system. The German engineers worked in the United States on a rotating basis, being responsible for design, quality, and reliability tests, and export certification. Each management position in production was initially filled by two persons, a US manager and a German manager, with the latter providing expertise as well as assistance during the start-up process. Meanwhile, they also learned about the innovations that were introduced in Spartanburg and eventually, after returning to Germany, would transfer this knowledge back to other BMW plants. All the German managers at Spartanburg were expected to return home after two years, leaving the US managers in charge in accordance with the strategy of self-reliance and sustainability.

In the long term it was planned to expand the BMW MC design engineering group from 40 to 150 people. All would be networked via CATIA with the engineering headquarters in Munich. This would allow virtual real-time engineering between the United States and Germany. BMW also had a small design studio in California, which would be online with this system. Transfer of knowledge and systems between the United States and Germany also posed a cultural challenge. BMW in Germany was very hierarchical, whereas the new culture at Spartanburg emphasised a flat organisation. To ensure better communication, BMW tried to standardise managerial positions across its plants and administrative offices. In this way, everyone could easily identify his or her counterparts in other BMW operations. But since Spartanburg's organisation and culture were markedly different, it was difficult to match the positions between Germany and the United States. This required a trade-off, since imposing a hierarchy in Spartanburg would improve communication with Germany, but it would also inhibit its unique culture. There were many within BMW who felt that the repercussions of creating a US plant went beyond Spartanburg and the US market. This development had far-reaching consequences for BMW's entire manufacturing network, with the company having to reconfigure its global supplier network, to create a unique and effective work culture, and design mechanisms for essential knowledge transfer activities.

A new BMW model for Spartanburg

In July 1994, soon after the Spartanburg plant was commissioned, BMW's Head of R&D announced the introduction of a new sports car for the 1996 model year. Named "Z3", the two-seat roadster was unveiled at the Detroit Auto Show in January 1995. To benefit from modular design principles, the two-seater was based on a 3-series platform with the original model having a soft (open) top and a hard-top option to follow. Although the car's body resembled no other existing BMW, key parts of the Z3 (engine, transmission, suspension, seats, steering) were already used in other BMW models. The Z3 used the same underbody and wheelbase as the 3-series coupe. The car was powered by a 1.8 or 1.9 litre, 4-cylinder engine with 115 HP, the same as in the 318 sedan. Even the planned 6-cylinder version of the Z3 was to use an existing engine, the one used in the 328 sedan. Through the development of the Z3, BMW engineers tried to remove costs from the design and manufacturing processes. An awareness of the need to catch up with the world's leaders in overall efficiency meant the Z3 programme would spearhead BMW's drive to reduce design cost, shorten the development cycle, and increase production efficiency. An example of the improved design for manufacturability was a reduction in the number of "hits" that body panels required in the press shop, which refers to the number of times a power press must stamp a panel before it assumes its final shape, thereby also reducing energy use in production. At BMW, major body panels generally required seven hits, but for the Z3 the average was only four hits, which meant that the final shape was achieved using four shaping dies instead of seven. Dies were expensive, and reducing their numbers generated large economic and environmental savings, especially in a small-scale plant.

BMW estimated the world market for all roadsters to be 150,000 to 160,000 units per year, of which the Z3 was expected to capture 20% (around 30,000). This small number meant that the location chosen for production of the new model would have to supply the entire world market of 100 countries. Because of its flexible assembly process and lower expected costs, Spartanburg was the ideal candidate. But, if selected for the Z3, Spartanburg would have to produce the 318 sedan, the 328 sedan, and the Z3 roadster simultaneously. In addition, the Z3 had to be produced in 74 country-specific variations to accommodate the differences in exhaust systems, safety features, lights, steering, and other requirements. All this would demand enormous flexibility from the single assembly line at Spartanburg. There were also the usual concerns about the risks of producing a completely new model in a new plant, especially one located outside the "home country". There were doubts whether there would be sufficient time for Spartanburg to develop the necessary capacity and engineering competence to support the introduction of a new model, particularly one that encompassed many innovations for BMW. There were arguments that because the big Regensburg plant in Germany produced all the 3-series models, including the coupe, it was a logical place to initially make the new Z3. Regensburg could therefore solve the inevitable problems of introducing a new model while Spartanburg continued to focus on the standard 318 and 328 models. The Z3 could then be relocated to Spartanburg at a later date to take advantage of cost differences. But eventually this argument was not accepted, and BMW decided to introduce the Z3 at Spartanburg.

By September 1995 the first Z3s were leaving the assembly line at Spartanburg, but the big success of the new car had already created a new challenge. The manufacturing plan involved a gradual ramp-up of Z3 production at Spartanburg, continued production of the 318 model, and later production of the 328. But the strong demand for the Z3 was forcing major changes to this plan. Already, instead of producing the 328, Spartanburg was to focus on producing more Z3s. However, due to large differences between the Z3 and the 318 (larger than between the 318 and 328), this ramp-up would have to be slower than for the 328 model. Spartanburg's production for 1995 would therefore not reach the planned 20,000 units. Instead it would be less than 16,000 units, of which only 6,000 were Z3s. Marketing plans called for expansion of Z3 production to 35,000 units in 1996, but even that would not satisfy all the demand. The entire production planned for 1996 had already been sold by BMW's dealers.

There were also other reasons to expand production at Spartanburg. In September 1995 the newly appointed CEO of BMW AG had made an announcement that, due to pressures on margins, production volumes would need to increase to maintain profitability. Especially troublesome was the Z3 situation because the capacity at Spartanburg was limited. Not meeting the demand was problematic, especially since 1996 was the only year in which the Z3 would have only one competitor, the Mazda Miata. In 1997 Mercedes, Porsche, and Audi were all planning to introduce competing roadsters. The big question was how Spartanburg should respond to the pressure to expand the Z3's production. BMW MC knew it had to formulate a response quickly and this was the main topic of discussion in the board meeting that was to be held before the end of September 1995 at BMW headquarters in Munich. The options were narrowed to three.

The first option was to increase capacity to enable higher production rates of both the Z3 and the 3-series models. This required an additional investment of USD 200 million, bringing the total at Spartanburg to USD 800 million. This large rate of growth was unusual and demanded careful management attention. New construction would add about 29,000 square metres of manufacturing space to the 111,000 square metre plant. The expansion would increase the daily capacity of the body and assembly areas from 300 units to 400, although the plant's paint shop already had a capacity of 400 units per day. This investment would allow BMW to expand the body and assembly departments while maintaining the plant's single line production concept. Furthermore, Spartanburg would need to change to two shift working by November 1995, instead of February 1996 as originally planned.

The second option was to free capacity at Spartanburg by sending production of the 318 back to the Regensburg plant in Germany. Regensburg had recently cut back work hours and had excess capacity. By concentrating all its efforts on the Z3, Spartanburg would then become a specialised plant for the roadster. Meanwhile, Regensburg could easily increase production of the 318, although at a somewhat higher cost, but this would still be better than the first option from a sustainable operations management perspective.

The third option was to resist market pressure. The President of BMW MC understood that quality was the most important element of BMW's strategy. For 85 years BMW had been able to rely on a carefully constructed base of German engineers and had gained a leading reputation for technical excellence and quality. The risk of capitulating to market pressure and increasing production levels carried the possibility that quality problems would develop. Even the smallest failure in Spartanburg's quality would have far-reaching consequences. Corporate headquarters might lose confidence in the plant's ability to supply BMW quality vehicles. Worse, the public might decide that US-made BMWs did not deserve the premium price tag or might demand only German-made BMWs. Making fewer cars at higher prices could arguably also be better for the environment. However, it may be detrimental to the company's economic sustainability and competitors would probably still meet customers' demand, so making little difference to the environment globally when accounting for absolute emissions.

Growing from a child to a parent: BMW Spartanburg's transition to a lead plant for the X-family

The main BMW board eventually took the decision to move production of the 3-series back to the Regensburg factory in Germany, enabling the factory in Spartanburg to concentrate on expanding Z3 production. Therefore the 3-series was only made in the US plant from 1994 to 1996. Production of the Z3 continued from 1995 to 2002 when it was replaced by the Z4 model, starting in 2003. Then in 2008 production of the Z4 was transferred to Regensburg, Germany, where it was manufactured until 2016.

The Rosslyn plant in South Africa also played a role in compensating for the loss in production of the 3-series in Spartanburg. It was the first BMW production plant outside of Europe and opened in 1973, assembling all BMW models for the local market up to 1996. A change of international strategy then involved changing the South African plant to serving export markets, so Rosslyn was progressively extended from 1997 into a full-scale manufacturing facility for producing the BMW 3-series sedan. Now, more than 4,500 people at the Rosslyn plant make around 75,000 per year of the sixth generation 3-series for both the local market and export markets.

The BMW plant in Spartanburg represents a good example of the successful strategy of "production follows the market". It has developed to become BMW's largest plant, although the type of cars produced there has again changed from the roadsters that became popular in the late 1990s. The younger generation of the 1980s became the family-centred generation of the 2000s with a preference for larger, safer, but still sporty cars. BMW has followed this trend and the plant in Spartanburg became the sole global producer of several BMW X SAV (sports activity vehicle) and SAC (sports activity coupe) models within the group's global network. These models are built using the CLAR (Cluster Architecture) design platform introduced in 2015. Currently, Spartanburg produces the X3 and X3M SAV, X4 and X4M SAC, X5 and X5M SAV, X6 and X6M SAC, and X7 SAV. These vehicles are exported to more than 140 countries (see Figure 9.3).

Due to the sales success of its new models, BMW's Spartanburg plant has been expanded several times over the years, with the most recent major investment in 2017 bringing the total amount invested to USD 11.1 billion. The plant area is now enlarged to around 650,000 square metres and production capacity has been increased to 450,000 units per year. Output has also been increased by having additional shifts, introducing flexible working hours, and hiring new employees. During 2020 BMW Spartanburg produced its 5 millionth car. Daily output is now about 1,500 units and there are 11,000 employees making vehicles for customers all over the world.

The Covid-19 pandemic and beyond: the BMW response

On 7 January 2020 the Chinese authorities identified a new (novel) type of coronavirus that had emerged in the city of Wuhan (later called Covid-19 by the World Health Authority). By the end of January there were almost 15,000 confirmed cases of the disease in China and in late February nine countries in Europe had reported cases. On 12 March 2020 the World Health Organization announced there was a global pandemic. By the end of 2020 there had been more than 90 million Covid-19 cases and about 2 million

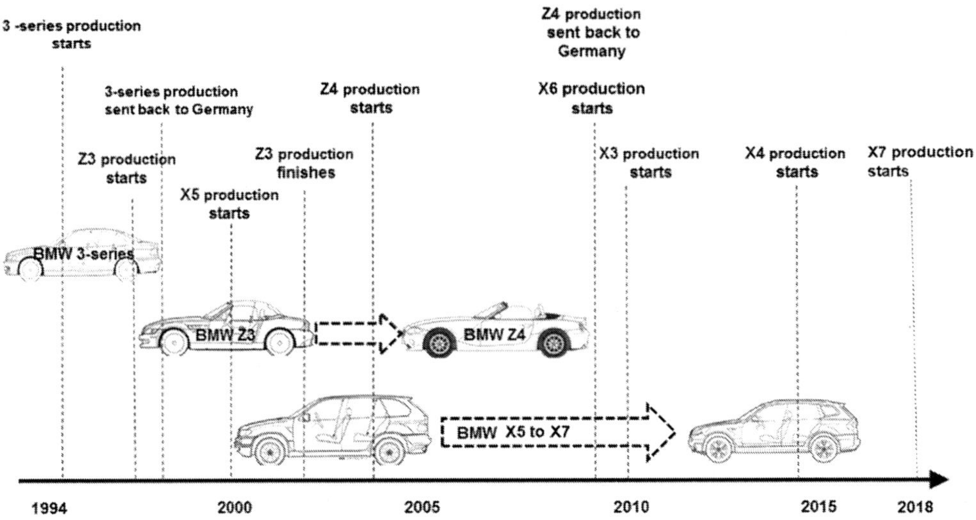

Figure 9.3 Timeline of models produced at BMW Spartanburg, South Carolina (Source: Dornier et al., 1998 and BMW company data)

deaths worldwide. The pandemic severely affected every economy and society, with the automotive sector, along with most other manufacturing industries, becoming severely disrupted. By August 2020 BMW had suffered a 25% decline in sales amounting to almost USD 800 million in lost revenues, although it should be noted that the company reported a 3.4% increase in sales of electric cars during the first half of the year.

On 20 March 2020 BMW announced the temporary closure of its Spartanburg factory, saying in its press release

> The health and protection of our associates is our top priority. At the same time, the dynamic development of the [coronavirus] pandemic is having a major impact on the global demand for cars. BMW Manufacturing is taking a flexible approach and adjusting our production volumes accordingly.

The closure of Spartanburg took place on 3 April and was expected to last until 19 April but was then extended until 30 April, and eventually the plant reopened on 4 May 2020, one week after BMW's engine manufacturing plants in Germany reopened on 27 April. However, during the summer several cases of coronavirus were diagnosed among the workforce, causing the company to adopt strict control measures within the Spartanburg plant. Around the same time BMW reported an increase in demand from certain countries, particularly China, where the economy was starting to recover from the pandemic. Being the only plant making CLAR platform vehicles, this put more pressure on Spartanburg to return to normal production levels. In June 2020 BMW produced the 5 millionth vehicle at Spartanburg, a BMW X5 M Competition model, and in January 2021 the company reported that it was making 1,500 vehicles per day, which was the same production rate as in January 2020. In February 2021 BMW once again confirmed its commitment to Spartanburg by starting construction of a new USD 20 million training centre with multiple workspaces for both professional development and technical training. The stated aim of this investment was to create a learning environment that promoted creativity, fostered innovation, and improved technical training skills among the employees of the US plant.

Summary

This case uses BMW as an example of how automotive companies develop their businesses and use an international operations strategy to expand capacity, penetrate new markets, improve cost competitiveness by increasing economies of scale, and facilitate the exchange of knowledge about innovations. The case illustrates especially how economic, environmental, and social sustainability have become important considerations when devising an international strategy and developing manufacturing capacity across different countries and regions. The core of the case focuses on BMW's manufacturing plant in the United States, which was established in the mid-1990s and has grown to become one of the company's most important production facilities in its global network. As well as demonstrating the practicalities of construction and start-up, the case shows the importance of building flexibility into international manufacturing plants as a way of dealing with uncertain markets as well as volatile political and economic environments. It also illustrates the interconnected nature of international production networks in the automotive industry and the need to find trade-offs between the different organisations, customs, and cultures that are encountered when taking operations overseas. And finally, the Covid-19 pandemic shows the need for responsiveness by manufacturing companies to unexpected events, while flexibility must allow for sudden big changes in demand volumes as well as product mix and variety differences.

Questions for discussion

1. What were BMW's options for meeting customer demand in the USA *before* the decision to build the Spartanburg plant, and from a sustainable operations management perspective what were the comparative advantages and disadvantages associated with each of these options?
2. What were the main sustainable operations management considerations when making environmental decisions about the design and operation of the Spartanburg plant?
3. What evidence does the case provide of BMW's initiatives to enhance its social sustainability performance?
4. How does BMW's sustainable operations management strategy compare with that of other major automotive companies? What is the importance of benchmarking when making long-term strategic plans about internationalising production operations?

PART B SUSTAINABILITY PERSPECTIVES ON AUTOMOTIVE DESIGN AND MANUFACTURING IN BRAZIL

Introduction

This part of the case considers how an emerging economy seeks to develop its industry by enabling involvement in international supply networks. It describes Brazil's strategy of opening the domestic market to foreign manufacturers, providing a production base for exports and creating a favourable industrial infrastructure with an attractive tax and regulatory regime. The core of the case focuses on how international automotive manufacturers enter the Brazilian market within the context of their international production and localisation strategies. The case also highlights a number of aspects of sustainable operations management relating to supply chain management, product design and the implications of corporate decision making for economic, environmental, and social sustainability.

Brazil is a large country both in terms of geographic area and population. Its most populous and commercially important states are in the south of the country, so very distant from the major industrial centres in Japan, the United States, and Europe. Therefore, it has always needed to be largely independent economically rather than relying heavily on imports. Brazil's domestic automotive industry is long established and the first car to be built in the country was a General Motors Chevrolet model produced in São Paulo in 1925. Brazil is among the ten largest automotive manufacturing countries in the world. By 2013 annual production had grown to around 3.7 million vehicles representing 4.2% of the World's total motor vehicle production. Brazil is also still a growing market for passenger cars with the fourth largest fleet in the world in 2019, having 75 million vehicles on the road, which is more than in Germany, France, or the United Kingdom. However, Brazil's population is large and the number of vehicles per person is still low compared with most developed countries such as the United States, Italy, Australia, Japan, France, Germany, and Canada, which have around 600 to 900 cars per 1,000 people. By comparison, Brazil's rate is still relatively modest, with 350 cars per 1,000 people in 2019. Therefore, there is still a big potential local market to be supplied and in 2018 Brazil had a similar number of new vehicle registrations as France and the United Kingdom. An important aspect of the automotive industry in Brazil is the use of alternative fuels. Ever since the emergence of the domestic industry in the 1920s, ethanol, which is made from sugar cane, has been used to power the internal combustion engines of vehicles as a supplement to oil-based fuels (i.e. gasoline and diesel). Engines have therefore been adapted to burn either type of fuel. Ethanol production peaked during the Second World War and again during the oil crisis in the 1970s. Today it is seen as a "clean" alternative to fossil fuels and Brazil is recognised as a leader in the production and use of biofuels.

To stimulate its domestic manufacturing industries, including the automotive sector, the Brazilian government has formulated favourable trade and investment policies to encourage foreign investments and has also provided exemptions from custom duties and other taxes on purchases of some capital goods and infrastructure. The Brazilian automotive sector is regulated by the ANFAVEA (Associação Nacional dos Fabricantes de Veículos Automotores), which was created in 1956. There are no controls on ownership, but imports were initially restricted. These restrictions were lifted in the mid-1990s. Most of the large global automotive companies are now present in Brazil and supply the majority of cars and trucks for the local market. Domestic companies are producing vehicles mainly for specialised markets (e.g. off-road vehicles, beach buggies, buses, bulk material transporters etc).

The attractions of Brazil for automotive manufacturers

Brazil has been identified by automakers as an important production base and is also known for offering good conditions to apply alternative and innovative methods of production. According to ANFAVEA, during the 1990s Brazil was the only country that hosted all the major global automotive manufacturers. A combination of government incentives, a sound industrial infrastructure, and fast-growing automotive market made Brazil an attractive testing ground for automakers to implement their strategies for new production systems, mostly in greenfield investments, but in older traditional plants as well.

Within this economic and fiscal environment Brazil became a testing ground for global automakers and served as the base for new projects targeting emerging markets. Brazil has also been an experimental base for new manufacturing strategies, particularly the modular assembly concepts that were developed as an alternative to conventional mass-production techniques. These assembly concepts have been closely aligned with the alternative production systems developed in Europe, where social obligations demanded the provision of more meaningful work. In some cases, these experimental strategies have extended beyond manufacturing and into vehicle design. After the introduction by VW of its "modular consortium" production concept in 1996, many other projects took place involving major companies such as Fiat, Ford, GM, Renault, Mercedes-Benz, and Chrysler. These have taken place both in greenfield and brownfield sites, and some suppliers have also become deeply involved in modularity. The Brazilian subsidiary of Dana, a US-based supplier of powertrain components is probably the best known due to its "rolling chassis" supplied for Chrysler's Dakota truck plant in Brazil, although many other suppliers adopted similar approaches. Modular production/supply systems tested in Brazil have been at the centre of the discussions about "transplanting" new models of production systems to traditional industrialised countries, such as in the GM case with its so-called "Yellowstone project", in Ford's modular assembly of the Focus and in Fiat's Amazon project for renewal of the Punto etc.

Brazil's recent changes to its automotive policy

From 2005 to 2011, the Brazilian automotive market averaged 12% annual growth, but imports grew by 46% annually. By 2011, imports represented 25% of domestic sales. One of the problems with the old policy was that manufacturers were including marketing, advertising, and other expenses as "local content" in order to escape from some of the taxes on imported vehicles.

In an attempt to overcome this problem and gain some of the sustainability benefits of localisation, the Brazilian government, together with automotive manufacturers and suppliers, worked together to produce a new automotive policy. Legislation was passed in April 2012 establishing Brazil's "Programme of incentives for technological innovation and densification of the automotive supply chain", more commonly known in Portuguese as "Inovar Auto" (Innovate Auto). The new requirements under Inovar Auto started in 2013 and gradually increased until 2017. Under these requirements companies should be compliant in at least three of four categories concerning: the amount of production located in Brazil; gross sales invested in local R&D; gross sales invested in local product development; conformance to INMETRO regulations (National Institute of Metrology, Quality and Technology). Brazil's automotive policy was also intended to improve social and economic sustainability by distributing the productive activity beyond the states where the industry was traditionally dominant (principally São Paulo and Minas Gerais). Figure 9.4 shows the geographic changes in car production between 1990 and 2013 and shows the relative shift towards other states during this period, particularly to Paraná.

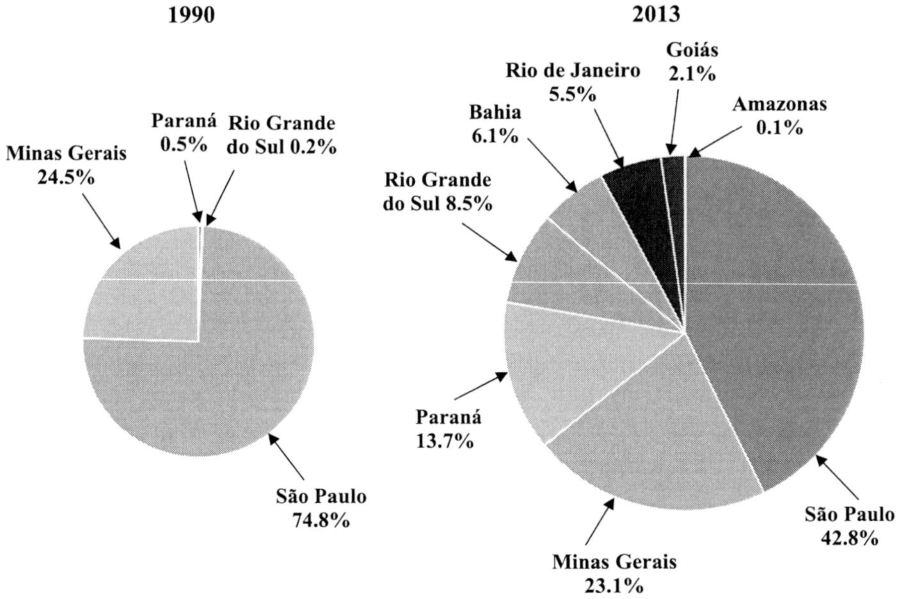

Figure 9.4 Car production by state in Brazil (1990 and 2013)

To act as a stimulus, the new policy included a 30% increase in industrial taxes (called Imposto sobre Produtos Industrializados or IPI) for vehicles sold in Brazil, but automotive companies entering the Inovar Auto programme were, in return, granted tax credits. In addition to complying with the requirements of Inovar Auto, to avoid paying the 30% increase in IPI, a company also needed to increase purchasing within Brazil, measured by its volume of strategic supplier purchases. Initially 37 companies were considered eligible to participate in Inovar Auto. Shortly after its launch, eight companies announced investments in new manufacturing facilities or expansion of existing ones. A total of BRL 5.5 billion (USD 1.73 billion) for the first three years was planned through fiscal incentives.

The success of Inovar Auto as well as that of Brazil's automotive companies depended on future market growth in the country and the region. However, in late 2014 the forecast for regional sales of cars and light commercial vehicles was cut to 5.7 million vehicles compared to 6.9 million vehicles that had previously been forecast only five months earlier. Then in August 2017 the World Trade Organisation (WTO) ruled that Inovar Auto was illegal under WTO law because the additional IPI tax on imported vehicles without having the benefit of tax credits created unfair competition. This initially caused uncertainties about a proposed 12-year extension to the Inovar Auto programme called "Rota 2030". However, when the new programme was eventually approved by Brazil's Congress in November 2018 the 30% IPI tax surcharge had been dropped to avoid complaints under WTO. The Rota 2030 programme in fact runs for 15 years from 2019 to 2034 and has tax credits over the first five years estimated to total BRL 2.1 billion (USD 560 million) in 2019 and BRL 1.5 billion in 2020. It also provides tax incentives for hybrid or "flex-fuel" motors that run both gasoline and ethanol as well as incentives for the car industry to have assembly plants in the poorer Northeast region of Brazil.

BMW's search for economic sustainability: making an automotive partnership in Brazil

BMW was very late in seeing Brazil as both a market and a manufacturing location, although in 1994 it established two joint ventures in Mexico for motorcycle and car assembly using kits to overcome import restrictions. It has had a local sales company in Brazil since 1995 and started a financing company in 1999. By the time these were established, more than 90% of Brazil's automotive production was accounted for by Volkswagen, General Motors, Ford, Mercedes-Benz, and Fiat. However, the first major investment by BMW in Brazil was not for making complete cars, but rather it was a partnership with Chrysler Motors established in 1996 for manufacturing 1.4 and 1.6 litre petrol (gasoline) engines. Being at a time when the two companies were facing financial difficulties it was driven by the need for them both to remain economically sustainable. Therefore a joint venture was formed known as "Tritec Motors Ltda", which resulted from the common need between BMW and Chrysler for producing a small displacement engine with low fuel consumption and high quality. The cost of establishing Tritec was USD 659 million shared equally between Chrysler and BMW. However, the case for building the factory was based entirely on the demand for engines outside Brazil by BMW and Chrysler for their markets in the rest of the world. There was not an in-depth study of Brazil's domestic market potential for the engines made by the joint venture.

Chrysler and BMW had decided on Brazil and the state of Paraná for the location of the joint venture after earlier studies revealed that other emerging economies were too risky. The sum of the conditions offered by the country was also an important factor. These included the availability of raw materials (smelted iron and steel), the availability of a qualified labour force, good supplier network (the rate of nationally produced components being 75%), suitable infrastructure for export by sea, and an established market presence in Mercosur. Tritec Motors received large benefits and fiscal incentives from the Paraná State Government. Neither BMW nor Chrysler had any car production in Brazil at the time the Tritec plant was being planned, although Chrysler had built cars there from 1967 to 1981 after acquiring the French company Simca that had a subsidiary "Simca Brasil".

Social sustainability was an important factor when determining the location of the Tritec plant and the quality of life in the Curitiba metropolitan area is considered to be one of the best in Brazil. It has a good infrastructure providing efficient transport and communications. The state of Paraná has established a reputation as a hub of the automotive industry, with several major international original equipment manufacturer (OEM) operations. This provided additional decisive factors that include a qualified labour force and an established service infrastructure. The location of Campo Largo is also excellent for international trade and export. The Tritec plant was located 25 kilometres from the city of Curitiba and only 110 kilometres from the shipping port of Paranáguá, which was an important factor since all its production was to be exported.

The independent construction of two self-owned plants by BMW and Chrysler would have required huge extra investments by both parties, making the separate projects unfeasible. When the plant was being planned both companies were constrained financially, so by creating a jointly owned and operated plant the partners could share costs and responsibilities. It also allowed a broad exchange of experience, and consequently an advancement in technology. In particular the two companies could share the escalating costs of implementing environmental sustainability measures in a new plant and they were also able to share European and US expertise on such matters as pollution control. During their discussions it became evident that a partnership would allow the companies to reduce their investment costs by at least 50%. BMW projected its annual demand on the plant to be about 200,000 engines and Chrysler's was about 100,000. Therefore, the brief was for an efficient engine plant with an annual capacity of 400,000 engines to allow for increasing demand and a sustainable future for the co-operative venture. Based on this brief, the design and layout of the plant was established.

Built according to strict international quality and technology standards, the 4-cylinder, 16-valve 1.6 and 1.4 litre petrol (gasoline) engines were of conventional single-fuel design and destined entirely for export, equipping all BMW Mini models worldwide, the Chrysler PT Cruiser in foreign (non-US) markets including South Africa and Europe, and an export variant of the Chrysler Neon. On completion of the plant Tritec was claimed to be among the world's best engine manufacturers due to its investment in technology, investment in human resources, modern management techniques, and extensive use of automation, which resulted in a high quality of its final products. The name Tritec was devised to signify the union of the three countries involved: Germany, the United States, and Brazil.

Human capital was arguably one of Tritec's major assets. The company sought to attract and retain the best professionals in each area by continually investing in them and enhancing working conditions. After its completion, and by the start of production, 400 people worked in the company. Tritec's employee selection process emphasised competences such as initiative, teamwork, motivation, learning capacity, communication skills, quality orientation, and planning and organisation. Within this context, Tritec sought to promote the personal and professional growth of its employees through continuous staff qualification programmes and training events.

As well as being designed with a high level of automation, the Tritec plant at the same time adopted modern management techniques based on the "Toyota Production System", ensuring simple workflow and lean production in order to avoid waste, safely and efficiently.

In 2003 Tritec Motor's achievements were endorsed by *Ward's Auto World* magazine when one of its products received the award for one of the ten best engines manufactured in the world: the 1.6L supercharged engine that powers the Mini Cooper S.

A short-lived project: economic sustainability versus commercial imperatives

At the time it was established by BMW and Chrysler, the Tritec Motors joint venture received considerable international attention. This was derived partly because in 1998, soon after it was established, Daimler-Benz AG (the owner of Mercedes-Benz) paid USD 37 billion for Chrysler Corporation and the company DaimlerChrysler was formed. Therefore, Chrysler became part of BMW's biggest rival – although in the Tritec project they were partners.

The future of Tritec Motors was consistently a subject of discussion following the merger between Daimler-Benz and Chrysler. In 2006 BMW in Germany confirmed it was studying a number of possibilities for Tritec and a DaimlerChrysler spokesman confirmed that they had been speaking directly to a Chinese automotive company, Lifan Group, after the *New York Times* had published details of the sale offer. The Russian company AvtoVAZ was also mentioned as having an interest in acquiring Tritec Motors and there were rumours of it being sold to a major Western manufacturer such as General

Motors or Fiat. However, Lifan was the only company that publicly confirmed its interest in buying Tritec Motors and, if successful, had two possible strategies open to it, i.e. to transfer the machinery and equipment to China or to continue running the plant in Brazil and export engines to the Lifan plant in China.

In May 2007 Daimler-Benz, the German partner of DaimlerChrysler, issued an announcement that it was selling an 80% stake in the loss-making US Chrysler brand to Cerberus Capital Management, a private equity investment firm, effectively ending the merger between the US and German companies. This was followed in July 2007 by BMW announcing that it was selling its 50% stake in Tritec Motors to Chrysler, at the time issuing the statement "Chrysler Group has assumed the responsibility for exploring long-term options for the Tritec operations whereby all possible alternatives for continuing the business for the long run are under analysis. This may include a sale of the facility to a third party". BMW's decision meant its withdrawal from manufacturing in Brazil only seven years after its much-publicised investment.

As well as announcing the sale of its stake in Tritec, BMW also stated that for its future Mini models the company would replace the engines made by the Brazilian company with ones supplied through a partnership with PSA Peugeot Citroen, with components made in France and engines assembled at the BMW Hams Hall engine plant in the United Kingdom that had been acquired from Rover Group. In 2006 BMW-PSA started using these new engines (codenamed "Prince" engines) in the Mini and all those made by Tritec were replaced by 2009. One automotive industry commentator at the time said that BMW abandoned the use of Tritec engines because their design was too basic and they could not adapt to current technologies.

In 2005 BMW had sold 240,000 Minis, of which 185,000 used the engines manufactured in Brazil, which meant that Tritec lost about 80% of its market. On top of this huge blow, Chrysler ended production of the Neon model, which also used Tritec engines. To keep its operations and reduce this big potential loss, Tritec signed new contracts for supplying engines to three other companies. These customers were Obvio, a Brazilian company, and two Chinese automakers. One was Lifan, the company based in Chongqing that was reported as being interested in buying Tritec, and the second was FAW-Hainan. The Brazilian company Obvio started production in 2007 and focused on exports, especially to the United States. It predicted an annual demand of 50,000 engines for its 828 and 012 models. It also planned to sell electrically powered versions of these cars, the 828E and 012E.

However, these diverse orders were not sufficient to utilise Tritec's capacity; so in June 2007 production was stopped, then re-started in July with only 114 employees compared with around 350 before the stoppage. This situation jeopardised the relationship with its new customers and Obvio threatened to sue Tritec Motors if it did not deliver the engines to meet the contract they had signed. So, by the end of 2007 Tritec's future seemed to be in the hands of potential foreign purchasers. It was set up by foreign investors to export 100% of its production. Therefore it seemed Tritec would depend more than ever on foreign investors and markets to survive, with the strongest possibility that it would be acquired by a Chinese company.

Fiat rescues Tritec

In March 2008 there was an unexpected announcement that the Fiat Powertrain Technologies (FTP), a subsidiary of Fiat, had acquired Tritec Motors from Chrysler.

Total investment in the initiative would amount to BRL 250 million (about USD 150 million) including further development costs. Its acquisition included the land, the manufacturing unit, production line, and licence to produce the current range of products.

In a press release announcing the acquisition, FPT also said it would produce at Campo Largo a new range of midsize petrol and flex-fuel engines (running on either petrol or ethylene). These engines would be developed together with Fiat's engineering centres at Betim, Brazil and Turin, Italy. It also said the acquisition of the plant was estimated to create 500 direct new jobs plus 1,500 indirect jobs, thus contributing significantly to economic growth in the city of Campo Largo, the local industrial district, and the entire state of Paraná. The investments in the plant were expected to transform it into Latin America's major production centre for midsize engines, satisfying the needs of both the local and export markets.

Fiat Powertrain Technologies, which had been set up in March 2005, pooled all of the Fiat Group's expertise in engines and transmissions, and combined all of the powertrain resources of Fiat Group Automobiles (Fiat Powertrain), Iveco (Iveco Motors), the Fiat Research Centre, and Elasis (a consortium formed by Fiat Group dedicated to research in support of development programmes in Southern Italy). FPT was one of the most significant players in the worldwide powertrain industry with an annual output of around 3.1 million engines and 2.5 million transmissions and axles. Worldwide it had 20,000 employees, 15 plants and ten research centres in seven countries. In May 2009 Fiat Powertrain Technologies announced it was starting preliminary production of new 1.4 and 1.6 litre engines at its Campo Largo, Paraná, The plant now employed 250 people and was designated an exclusive supplier of flex-fuel engines for Fiat automobiles based on the original Tritec engine as well as diesel engines for Iveco commercial vehicles. Although there had been a decline in the automotive market, FPT confirmed that the acquisition of Tritec was important to increase capacity for the supply of engines and explained that the new facility was modern and the projects for producing engines were advanced, bringing new opportunities to develop the portfolio of products for the company.

Meanwhile, Chrysler continued to struggle financially after the acquisition by Cerberus Capital Management and in 2009 it received a USD 4 billion emergency loan from the US Treasury Department, subject to submitting a restructuring plan outlining how it would become viable by 31 March 2009. However, in a surprise move at the end of January, Fiat (having previously been in a failed alliance with General Motors) agreed to acquire a 20% stake in Chrysler by providing designs of small vehicles and fuel-efficient powertrains for production at Chrysler's factories as well as distribution opportunities in key growth markets outside the United States, where Chrysler was weak. As part of the agreement Fiat would gain US manufacturing capacity for its small cars and obtain access to Chrysler's dealer network. In addition, the agreement would entitle Fiat to receive a further 15% of Chrysler in exchange for covering the cost of retooling a Chrysler plant to produce one or more Fiat models in the United States. However, before the agreement could be concluded Chrysler had to file for bankruptcy in April 2009. Chrysler and Fiat still confirmed their global strategic alliance, while Chrysler meanwhile reduced the scale of its operations and indefinitely suspended production at five of its plants in Mexico. Then in June 2009 the US Supreme Court cleared the way for Fiat to effectively take control of Chrysler by acquiring a majority of shares following its emergence from bankruptcy proceedings. By the end of 2011 Fiat had acquired a 57% share of Chrysler.

Through these complex transactions the story had come full circle with Chrysler and Tritec Motors in Brazil becoming part of the same family again only a short time after the two had parted ways, but with the ownership situation reversed. In December 2013 Fiat announced the purchase of the remaining shares so Fiat therefore had complete ownership of Chrysler. The new company, Fiat Chrysler Automobiles (FCA), is listed on the New York Stock Exchange and the Mercato Telematico Azionario (Electronic Stock Market) in Milan.

In Brazil, three aspects have determined the direction of the Campo Largo plant since its acquisition by Fiat Powertrain Technologies in 2008, i.e.

1. Fiat's transformation into a global player in the automotive industry after its own recovery from near bankruptcy in 2000 and the absorption of Chrysler's operations into its manufacturing networks.
2. Tritec's advantageous position of being a newly established factory within a burgeoning Latin American automotive market.
3. Fiat's vision of including the former Tritec plant as a key part of its supply chain investment strategy and establishing its position as probably the most modern midsize engine factory in Latin America.

The acquisition by FPT of Tritec Campo Largo brought its number of engine plants in South America to four. The largest is in Betim (Brazil) producing over 1.5 million engine and transmissions units for cars. The plant in Sete Lagoas (Brazil) produces flex-fuel engines for cars and a range of four families of diesel for light and heavy commercial vehicles, buses, agricultural and construction machinery, and power generators. The unit in Córdoba (Argentina) produces engines and transmissions for PSA Peugeot Citröen.

As well as Fiat's investment, the Government of Paraná also assisted FPT Campo Largo (Tritec) in prioritising the rehiring of former employees of Tritec Motors who had been laid-off in 2007. Funds were made available to support 150 jobs, both direct and indirect. By June 2010 the plant had 350 employees and looked on track to fulfil its initial growth plan under Fiat. With production being scaled up it could now make best use of its equipment and assembly facilities. By 2011 it had 400 employees and a production capacity of 330,000 engines per year. The plan by 2012 was to reach a capacity of 400,000 engines and employ a total of 500 employees as well as supporting approximately 1,500 indirect jobs.

When FPT completed the acquisition of Tritec the percentage of imported components in the engines was 30%. The company then went about mobilising suppliers to reduce this rate which by June 2010 was down to 10%, with a goal in 2011 to manufacture engines with 95% of Brazilian components.

In common with other FPT plants Campo Largo plant adopted the "World Class Manufacturing" (WCM) model of management. This resulted in the application of the most modern techniques and methods of manufacturing in order to achieve high levels of quality and productivity.

After FPT acquired the Campo Largo plant, it invested a total of BRL 5 million (USD 3 million) in staff training, including the spread of the Group Fiat culture and best practices. The value placed on its staff is also reflected in systems that seek to expand the ergonomics and safety at work – such as optical barriers, pedestrian crossings, totems for the verification of the correct use of Personal Protective Equipment, and mechanisms for locking machines. To make the plant "greener", FPT also improved environmental aspects and introduced total management of waste, with a recycling index of 95%. The company installed skylights in the plant for illumination, so using as much as possible of the sunlight rather than electric lighting. Moreover, the plant was also equipped with dynamometers for renewable energy generation, a system for filtering the cooling system, a mitigation area to contain leaks and production of engines with ecological features.

The engines to be produced by FPT at the Campo Largo plant were developed with both the Latin American and international automotive market in mind rather than only for the global markets, as had been the case with the BMW–Chrysler joint venture. Therefore they based the designs on the 1.6 litre 16 valve EO (ethanol free) version of the former Tritec Motors engine that was previously designed for BMW and Chrysler's own use. Based on this original engine FPT developed five new versions. The 1.6 litre 16 valve flex-fuel engine and the 1.8 litre 16 valve flex-fuel engine were both intended for sale in the Brazilian market. The 1.6 litre 16 valve and 1.8 litre 16 valve EO versions of the engine were produced for Fiat's other markets outside Brazil. While another version was specially developed for SULEV (US emission standard Super Ultra Low Emissions Vehicles). Although based on the already-proven Tritec engines, 70% of these engines were in fact new, including components such as block, crankshaft, connecting rods, pistons, intake manifold, valvetrain, electronic injection system, flywheel, water pump and power steering, valve cover, cylinder head, and gasket injectors. The new family of mid-size engines developed from the Tritec design were called "E.torQ".

All the engines in the E.torQ family were designed to deliver high torque at low revs, with the capacity to meet global limits on pollutant emissions, thereby ensuring they met the requirements of global markets. This gave FPT Campo Largo access to a much wider user base than it had for the former Tritec engine made for BMW and Chrysler. FPT engines are used in the products of all Fiat Group companies and E.torQ engines have also been incorporated into Dodge and Jeep models.

Since 2002 Fiat and General Motors in Brazil had shared a range of engines made by a Fiat–GM Powertrain joint venture company that was formed at the time Fiat and GM had its industrial alliance before it ended in 2004. Therefore from 2009 the engines from this joint venture that were used in Fiat models were replaced by E.torQ engines developed from the former Tritec design.

In November 2012 Fiat Powertrain Technologies (FPT) became part of the CNH (Case New Holland) Industrial Group, in which Fiat had a major share. CNH focuses on larger engines and powertrains for agricultural and construction equipment. Consequently, the former Tritec Campo Largo engine plant and the engine plant at Betim were transferred to direct control of Fiat Chrysler Automobiles in Latin America (FCA LATAM)

Since its acquisition from Chrysler, the Campo Largo's engine production plant has been progressively updated and in 2014 its German automation supplier made a major update to the CNC (computer numerical control) systems of 20 key machine tools in the plant that would extend the life cycle of the vital production lines. This was achieved with minimum disruption to production with each machine requiring less than the allowed four days out of service time. In November 2016 the FCA Campo Largo plant reached the Silver level of the group's World Class Manufacturing (WCM) production system implementation assessment. By the end of 2019 FCA Campo Largo had made 1.5 million E.torQ and employed 400 workers. In 2021 Fiat Chrysler Automobiles merged with PSA (Peugeot Citroen) to become the world's fourth biggest automotive company under the name Stellantis. The merger brought the number of the new company's plants in Brazil to four, with Campo Largo being the only one exclusively making engines. However, the chief executive of Stellantis' operations in the Americas, said there were no plans to close any of these plants.

Postscript: BMW makes a return to Brazil

BMW's abandonment of engine production in Brazil and sale of its share in the Tritec plant in 2007 did not signal the complete end to the company's plans to manufacture in South America. By this time it had more than ten years' experience operating its North American plant in Spartanburg and could see the economics and sustainability benefits of having a carefully considered international manufacturing network strategy. BMW's return to Brazil began at the end of 2009, although not producing cars but with its Motorrad division through a licence agreement assembling motorcycles for the local market. Located in Manaus, the capital of Amazonas state in Northwest Brazil, motorcycles were assembled in a free trade zone using parts supplied from Germany. In 2016, BMW Motorrad took full ownership of the Manaus motorcycle plant and invested BRL 42.5 million (USD 11.7 million) to build several of its models there based on CKD (complete knock down) kits shipped from the Berlin plant.

In 2012 BMW's car division announced it would start production in Brazil with a project involving an investment of BRL 520 million (USD 260 million) to build a production line in Araquari, Santa Catarina State, with a capacity to produce 32,000 cars per year. Araquari therefore became the first BMW assembly plant in Latin America. Although it is in a different Brazilian state, the Araquari plant is relatively close to where BMW had developed its experience with Tritec. The port of Paranáguá, which is used by BMW for shipping finished cars, is 200 km from Araquari and two container ports in Santa Catarina state are used to handle incoming parts and components. So, the Araquari plant also benefits from the excellent maritime logistical infrastructure of Santa Catarina and Paraná states, allowing fast and efficient inbound logistics of parts and components, and outbound logistics of finished vehicles.

Construction of the whole plant was finally completed in September 2015 by which time it had already produced 10,000 cars with the model range including the X1, X3, 1-series and Mini Countryman as well as BMW 3-series. Only final assembly was undertaken with parts supplied initially from other BMW plants outside Brazil. Welding, bodywork, painting and logistics were planned to be added later. By the beginning of 2016 the plant was only operating at one-third of capacity, so the decision was made to also build the BMW X4 crossover. In early 2017 the product range of the Brazil plant comprised the MINI Countryman, diverse models of BMW 1-series, BMW 3-series and BMW X models. All models had the eco-driving technology which combines a stop–start system with a brake energy regeneration system. By 2017 two manufacturing lines for body welding had also been established together with a painting area and body preparation with corrosion protection treatment, sealants, and acoustic insulation. The plant logistic system allowed paint and finish to be applied according to customer demand.

By the end of 2018 the BMW Araquari factory had made 50,000 cars and 65% of the company's car sales in Brazil were made in the country, although sales were still not being made to other countries in the region. The Araquari factory also started assembly of the new BMW X3 and announced that the X series vehicles accounted for 55% of its Brazilian sales. In late 2018 BMW said it would invest BRL 125 million (USD 33 million) in the Araquari factory for assembly of new versions of X4 and 3-series models. So, during 2019 the models produced in the plant were the BMW 3-series, X1, X3 and X4. By September 2019 the factory had made more than 55,000 cars and had 600 employees. In October 2019 the plant celebrated its 5-year anniversary and invested a further BRL 7 million (USD 1.7 million) in order to produce the X5 model.

Thus, following its withdrawal from the Tritec engine manufacturing project, BMW became, within a period of fewer than ten years, a fully established car and motorcycle manufacturer in Brazil. Furthermore, as part of its international manufacturing strategy, in 2014 the BMW car division announced the construction of a new plant in Mexico. This opened in 2019 with a capacity of 175,000 cars per year and acknowledged the growing importance of South America to the company both as a market and for production capacity. Furthermore, the Mexico plant's focus was on the 3-series, providing an additional source of supply of this model to the US market after its transfer from Spartanburg back to Germany.

The Covid-19 pandemic and beyond: the effect on Brazil's automotive sector

After Covid-19 was first reported in Brazil in February 2020, the country quickly became one of the worst affected globally. Being an emerging economy with a relatively weak social protection system, the country was especially vulnerable to the consequences of the pandemic. However, the Brazilian central government prioritised the economy rather than implementing disease control measures like many Western industrialised countries. Despite this, many state and city governments in Brazil imposed their own restrictions and lockdowns. In September 2020 Brazil entered a recession with gross domestic product shrinking 9.7% quarter-on-quarter, triggering a wave of corporate bankruptcies.

Within the automotive sector, new car sales in Brazil dropped more than 26% in 2020 compared to 2019. As well as causing disruptions to their operations, this prompted many automotive companies to reassess their strategies or accelerate existing restructuring plans. In late 2020 Mercedes-Benz announced it would close its Brazilian factory and in early 2021, one hundred years after opening its first factory there, Ford made the decision to stop all manufacturing in Brazil. In response to the decrease in demand, Fiat Chrysler temporarily closed all its plants in Brazil between 23 March and 18 May 2020. Also the BMW plant in Araquari did not escape the effects of the automotive sales decline and temporarily closed from 30 March to 22 April 2020, but the closure was extended to 4 May which coincided with the re-opening of its plant in Spartanburg in the United States (both plants being dependent on the slightly earlier reopening of BMW's engine manufacturing plants in Germany). However, even after this date, a plan was agreed to reduce working hours and wages while promotions and merit increases were postponed from April to October. By the time of its sixth anniversary in October 2020, the BMW Araquari plant had built around 63,600 cars, which was about 30% fewer than planned during this period.

Summary

Through the example of the automotive industry this case explores how an emerging economy seeks to develop its industry by enabling involvement in international supply networks. Strategies include opening the domestic market to foreign manufacturers, providing a production base for exports and creating a favourable industrial infrastructure with an attractive tax regime. It shows that an industrial policy is needed to avoid the market being flooded by imports and enabling the local automotive sector, including its supplier base, to be developed and integrated into international networks. The core of the case focuses on BMW's entry into Brazil through a manufacturing joint venture company with Chrysler to make engines for export. Following changes to company ownership, BMW's share of this company was sold to Chrysler and it temporarily withdrew from manufacturing in Brazil. However, only a few years later BMW returned by establishing a motorcycle plant and a car assembly plant to supply both the local and export markets. The case illustrates how plans about plant location and production operations can be disrupted by higher level corporate circumstances. It also shows how the imposition of tariffs can disrupt the export plans of automotive manufacturers in developing countries as well as how different national and local factors influence automotive manufacturers' investment decisions. Finally, it shows the serious distortions in sales and production that can occur when there is a shock to the whole industrial system, such as that caused by the Covid-19 global pandemic and the lack of a coordinated government response.

Disclaimer: This case has been researched and prepared by David Bennett, Affiliated Professor at Chalmers University of Technology and Emeritus Professor at Aston University, and Breno Nunes, Senior Lecturer at Aston University. It does not reflect the views of BMW, or any company mentioned in the case and the authors are not responsible for the accuracy or interpretation of the information or views contained in this case. This case is aimed at enriching class discussion, and it is not intended to illustrate either good or bad management practice. October 2022. Exchange rates used are those applying at the time stated.

Questions for discussion

1. What are the implications for sustainable operations management of global automotive companies choosing Brazil as a location for production within their supply networks? How have Brazil's industrial policies for the automotive sector affected their decisions?
2. To what extent did sustainability considerations influence BMW and Chrysler's decisions about the establishment and abandonment of Tritec Motors? How does Fiat Powertrain Technologies' acquisition of Tritec play a role in Fiat's sustainable operations strategy?
3. What have been the competitive priorities in recent years for global automotive companies? How do the strategies of the companies in this case address these priorities and how robust are these strategies when dealing with major disruptions such as those caused by Covid-19?

Main sources

For Part A

Dornier, P.-P., Ernst, R., Fender, M., & Kouvelis, P. (1998) BMW: Globalising manufacturing operations. In *Global Operations and Logistics: Text and Cases*. Hoboken: Wiley.

Fleischmann, B., Ferber, S., & Henrich, P. (2006). Strategic planning of BMW's global production network. *Interfaces*, 36(3), 194–208.

Henry, I. (1995). *BMW: Global Growth, AMS Automotive Manufacturing Solutions*. www.automotivemanufacturingsolutions.com (6 January).

University of South Carolina. (2014). *BMW's Impact in South Carolina, Darla Moore School of Business*. Columbia, SC: Darla Moore School of Business.

www.bmwgroup.com / www.bmwusfactory.com

For Part B

https://anfavea.com.br (ANFAEVA - Associação Nacional dos Fabricantes de Veículos Automotores / National Association of Automotive Vehicle Manufacturers).

https://www.fcagroup.com/en-US/group/regions/Pages/latam.aspxwww.stellantis.com

www.bmwgroup.com

www.fcagroup.com / www.fcagroup.com/en-US/group/plants/

www.mdic.gov.br/english (Ministério da Economia, Secretaria Especial de Comércio Exterior e Assuntos Internacionais / Brazil Ministry of Industry, Foreign Trade and Services).

www.press.bmwgroup.com/italy/article/attachment/T0162224IT/243124 (Factsheet: New BMW Group Plant in Brazil, December 2013).

10 Natura Brasil

Building sustainability leadership in the cosmetics industry[1]

Introduction to the Natura Group and its brands

Natura Cosméticos S.A. or simply Natura Brasil, is the largest manufacturer and direct selling company in the cosmetics, fragrances, skincare, and toiletries sector in Brazil. The company is now part of a group (Natura & Co) which employs around 35,000 people in its operations globally. With a strong presence in Latin America, Natura operates in Argentina, Chile, Colombia, Mexico, and Peru, and has aggressively expanded by acquiring brands in Australia and Europe. Since 2005, the company has stepped into the European market and opened an Innovation Hub Office in the United States.

The company's main commercial strategy is based on directly selling its products through a network of representatives (also called sales consultants). Currently, more than 1,300,000 sales consultants promote Natura's products to consumers all over Brazil, in other countries in Latin America, and France. In addition, since its foundation in 1969, the company has been building its activities based on sustainable development principles, being widely recognised as one of the most sustainable firms in the global beauty products industry.

Natura concentrates on developing natural-based cosmetics, with many ingredients being ethically sourced from the Amazon and the Brazilian rainforest. The company has been spearheading several sustainability initiatives in Brazil and abroad for many years, turning into the only carbon-neutral enterprise among the largest cosmetics companies.

In 2013, Natura acquired a majority stake of 65% in the Australian skincare company Aēsop for nearly USD 50 million. Not long after that, in December 2016, Natura took total ownership of Aēsop. With an urban design proposing a new concept in the beauty industry, Aēsop came to fill market spaces in which Natura was not yet present.

To continue its global expansion, Natura completed the acquisition of The Body Shop in 2017. Both brands were strongly associated with environmental causes, sustainability values, and green branding and leadership.

In May 2019, the group announced its intent to acquire Avon, and in the deal closed in January 2020 their ownership accounts for a 76% stake.

The global cosmetics industry

The global cosmetics industry is an approximate USD 277.67 billion market and on the brink of a massive, predicted expansion due to the rapid growth in emerging markets in the coming years. According to Fortune Business Insights, the market is projected to grow to USD415.29 billion in 2028. Consumers have been spending more on cosmetics

DOI: 10.4324/9781003009375-13

recently despite the economic downturn of the past years because of the global financial crisis and COVID-19 pandemic. Moreover, over those years, "Generation Y" has entered the job market, thus becoming the new big driver of trends in the cosmetics industry.

According to the data available in Statista, the global beauty market registered an average growth rate of 4.1% from 2004 to 2019. Although the cosmetics industry was directly affected by the 2009 recession, it bounced back rapidly in 2010 during the global economy recovery. The continued growth lasted until the COVID-19 global pandemic in 2020, when the market shrunk 8%. Major markets, including the United States, China, and Brazil, have been experiencing huge pressure for growth, innovation, and creativity to develop high quality products in order to expand their revenue potential (Figure 10.1).

The United States and China contribute to almost half of the global beauty market. However, the emerging markets are said to be the key to any expansion strategy of global cosmetics companies.

The United States is still by far the world's largest beauty products market, employing around 55,000 people with an estimated revenue over USD 80 billion in 2021. Brazil is the world's fifth largest market for beauty and personal care considering all segments, being number one in the fragrance and deodorant categories. China is second in the ranking, completing the top three countries for the global beauty market with Japan. India, Germany, UK, and France are also key players, being respectively the fourth, sixth, seventh, and eighth in the market-size ranking.

For nearly a hundred years only a few international corporations have been dominating global production in the cosmetics industry. Leading cosmetics companies grew at an average rate of around 5% from 2012 to 2015. Major global players such as Estée Lauder and Shiseido achieved moderate growth from 2018 to 2021. On the other hand, brands such as L'Oréal, L'Occitane, and Natura, had a sharp increase in their sales revenue, having a compound growth rate above 9% in the same period (Figure 10.2).

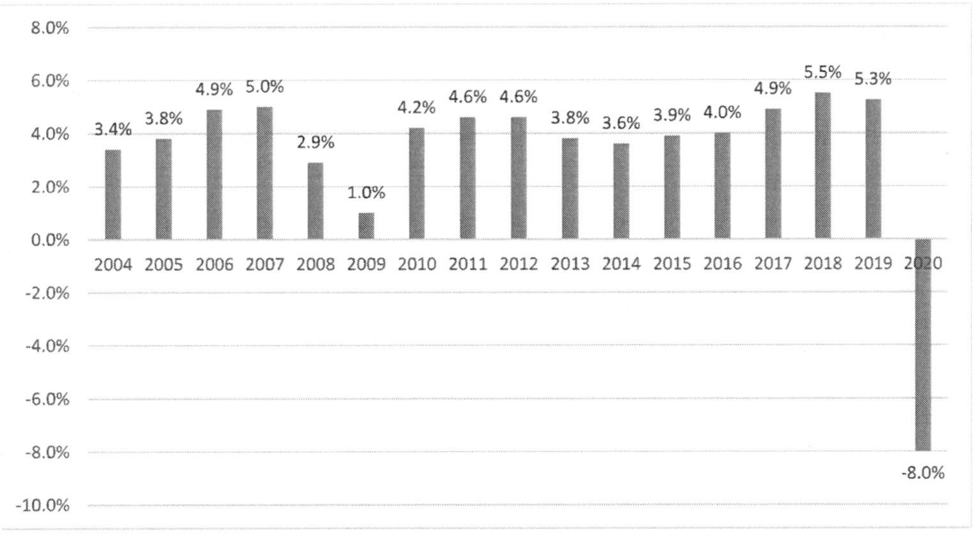

Figure 10.1 Annual growth of the global cosmetics market from 2004 to 2020 (Source: Statista)

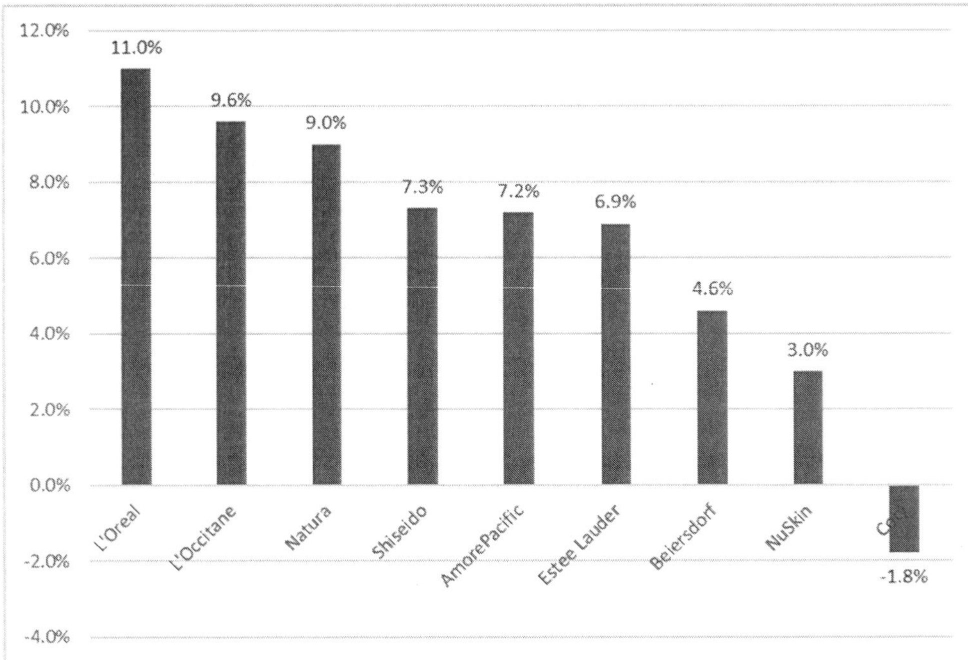

Figure 10.2 Compound annual growth rate of leading cosmetic companies between 2018 to 2021 (Source: Statista)

The beauty market classifies its products into premium and mass segments. Since 2010, the mass segment accounted for more than 70% of sales worldwide. Furthermore, the beauty industry comprises six main categories of products: skin, hair, and oral care, fragrances, colour cosmetics, and bath and shower. Skincare and haircare are the two largest categories in the global market, where skincare dominates key beauty markets such as China, Indonesia, and North America, and haircare is the main contributor for growth in Brazil, India, and Central Asian markets.

The beauty industry in Brazil

The Brazilian beauty market has seen significant growth rates despite the recent turmoil in the country's economy due to inflation and political instability. In order to continue stimulating consumption, companies have been investing in the development of high value products, making use of the "premium" concept, offering multiple benefits in one product, thus guaranteeing an increase in per capita consumption in some categories, such as haircare.

In 2014, sales revenue in Brazil's cosmetics industry amounted to USD 33 billion and a record 11% annual growth in comparison with the previous year. Accounting for almost 2% of Brazil's GDP, the beauty industry can be considered a major player in the country's economy. Being the one of the world's largest consumer market, Brazil accounts for 9.4% of global consumption. The devaluation of Brazilian Real and the prolonged economic crisis made the market to be reduced to USD18 billion in 2021.

But, the beauty market in Latin America is still to be around USD 80 billion, with Brazil contributing significantly to sales of the cosmetic industry in the region. The country's remarkable performance can be associated with major investments that have been made in important areas such as innovation and marketing, thus driving a steady industry growth.

> "Without a doubt, Brazil is a major power in Latin America. The main customers for Brazilian exports of cosmetic products are Argentina, Chile, Venezuela, Mexico and Colombia, and hair products are the most exported ones". João Carlos Basilio, President of the Brazilian Association of the Cosmetic, Toiletry and Fragrance Industry (ABIHPEC).
>
> (*Premium Beauty News*, 2015)

Brazilian consumers have a strong sense of obligation towards buying eco-friendly beauty products. A survey from GfK, a company that provides data and intelligence to the consumer goods industry, has found that over half of consumers in Brazil (the highest rate in the world) considers the product's environmental impact when acquiring cosmetics (Cosmeticobs.com, 2014), thus becoming more demanding and rigorous types of consumers. A research by a Brazilian NGO (Akatu.org.br) highlighted the five top aspects that Brazilian consumers consider when choosing a product (ABEVD, 2019):

- cruelty-free – 52%
- socially responsible – 46%
- environmentally friendly – 46%
- low energy consumption – 44%
- certified for fair labour practices – 43%.

Currently, Natura is the leading cosmetics company in Brazil followed by O Boticário, which outsells Natura in terms of revenues, and since 2013 has been the market leader in the fragrances category. In addition, O Boticário is very active in social responsibility and sustainability initiatives. In 1990, they set the foundation Groupo Boticário, which has already donated over USD 10 million to nature protection programmes, contributing to the discovery of 69 new species of plants and animals in the Brazilian rainforest.

Several international cosmetic companies such as L'Oréal and Unilever have been making investments in the booming Brazilian beauty market. Those companies have set up R&D centres in Brazil in order to develop their products based on indigenous ingredients.

Foreign investment continued in Brazil with The Body Shop, when still part of L'Oréal Group, acquiring 51% of Empório Body Store, a domestic Brazilian brand, in 2013. In this way The Body Shop intended to make use of its knowledge and retail network in the Brazilian market. After a seven-year absence, the British cosmetics retailer Lush returned to Brazil in 2014 with its world's largest stores in São Paulo. L'Occitane is gaining popularity in the Brazilian market since 2013 and the French Yves Rocher, which now has five stores in Brazil, plans to open 300 stores in the next ten years.

Brazil also boosted its growth in the cosmetics industry based on its sales in the haircare segment, in which it is the fourth largest market behind the United States, China, and Japan (Statista, 2019). Hair conditioners, hair colours, and shampoos, which together represent 90% of the segment, drive the performance of haircare in the Brazilian market.

Table 10.1 Estimated value in the beauty segments in Brazil 2020–2023 (in billion US dollars). (Elaborated by the authors)

	Personal Care	*Fragrances*	*Skin care*	*Cosmetics*
2020	12.77	4.94	2.61	2.31
2021	13.73	5.33	2.77	2.53
2022	14.46	5.63	2.88	2.72
2023	15.01	5.86	2.96	2.88

Source: Statista Research Department.

However, many cosmetic brands still struggle with competition in other aspects such as distribution due to the vast geographies of Brazil. Natura has overcome this challenge thanks to its direct sales network with more than 1.3 million consultants and O Boticário has also succeeded through its chain with almost 4,000 concept stores (Table 10.1).

> Sales of big global companies such as Unilever and Procter & Gamble have grown fast in Brazil, and luxury brands such as l'Occitane are piling in. But the country has also fostered a home-grown beauty company that dominates its bathroom shelves. Natura has a 13.4% share of the Brazilian cosmetics, perfume and hygiene market, with customers in 60% of all households. Natura is one of the world's 20 most valuable cosmetics brands according to Brand Finance consultancy even though nearly 90% of Natura sales are domestic and hardly any are outside Latin America. Now it is planning to go global.
>
> (*Economist*, 2013)

Biodiversity management as a business strategy

In the 1960s, Antonio Luiz Seabra, a Brazilian economist, discovered a passion for cosmetology (the study and application of beauty treatment) while working in a small laboratory in São Paulo, Brazil. In 1969, he founded Natura Brasil and opened a small shop in Oscar Freire Street, the main address for luxurious brand stores in São Paulo. Luiz Seabra started selling his products as well as providing beauty advice to his customers. Through this direct contact with clients, he developed his business approach, offering personal care cosmetics based on natural active substances from the Brazilian flora.

Based on two passions – for cosmetics and relationships – the company aimed at promoting the "well-being/being well" concept – an expression that embodies its essence and reason for being:

> to create and sell products and services that promote well-being/being well. Well-Being is the individual's harmonious, agreeable relationship with himself, with his body. Being well is the individual's empathetic, successful, and pleasurable relationship with others, with the nature he is part of, with the whole.
>
> (Natura's 2020 Annual Report)

> "From the start, we have been intent on building a fundamentally different kind of company, one that succeeds in the marketplace not just while integrating the

consideration of all of our stakeholders, but by integrating the interests and consideration of our people, our customers, our communities, and the natural environment". Luiz Seabra, Natura Founder.

(Management Exchange, 2012)

Natura is now a world-class beauty company and the leading direct sales business in Latin America with unique and highly valued products. Headquartered in one of the world's largest and most socially and environmentally diverse nations, Natura has more than 40 years commitment to transforming social and environmental challenges into business opportunities. The company promotes its image as being eco-friendly and sustainable through the creation of a differentiated value proposition across the triple bottom line spectrum: economic, social, and environmental dimensions.

Based on its passion for people's relationships, the company has adopted direct sales as its main commercial strategy since 1974. Natura has currently more than 1,300,000 consultants in Brazil and over 400,000 in its international operations, promoting the company's products to consumers. In 2014, Natura reported USD 2.7 billion in sales revenue and over USD 500 million of net income (EBITDA[2]). In the same year, Natura became the world's largest B Corp company.

In the global arena, Natura has a longstanding relationship with France, which has always been an important supplier of packaging, raw materials, and especially, knowledge in the beauty market for Natura. For this reason, in 2005 – the year of celebration of Brazilian culture in France – Natura opened its first flagship store in the classic neighbourhood of Saint-Germain-des-Prés in Paris, the capital of fashion in the global beauty industry.

Natura has a portfolio of more than 700 premium-mass products across eight different segments including fragrances, skincare, and haircare. The company employs more than 5,000 employees in Brazil and almost 2,000 in its international operations. Furthermore, Natura possesses five manufacturing plants, including its headquarters in Cajamar, São Paulo. In addition, the company has eight distribution centres along with five research and innovation centres all over the Brazilian territory.

Natura has been operating on the BM&F Bovespa (São Paulo Stock Exchange) since 2004. In 2014, its international operations accounted for over 19% of consolidated revenue and third-party suppliers in Latin America produced 16 million product units.

Innovation in well-being

Natura's approach to sustainable innovation is based on its founder's philosophy of the constant pursuit of innovation. The company is continuously searching for improvements that could benefit the development of its employees, organisation, and society. This approach to innovation is inherent in the company's sustainable development concept. Natura's business strategy relies on scientific and technological research to develop new concepts and products in order to improve and govern the company's relationship with its stakeholders' community.

In 1983, Natura set an innovative and pioneering initiative offering its products with a refill option, the average mass of which is 54% lower than the regular original package. Thanks to this decision, the company has subsequently avoided placing 2,200 tons of packaging in the market. In addition, Natura's consultants engage in refill sales, promoting the responsible consumption of resources.

> "For Natura, green technologies are the driving force behind business growth. Increasingly, our products will be developed in the forefront of ecodesign and eco-effectiveness, involving the entire value chain". Gerson Pinto, VP of Innovation at Natura.
>
> (Natura Annual Report, 2014)

One of the most recent examples of how the company transforms socio-environmental challenges into new business opportunities was the launch of a new product line of compressed aerosol deodorant called "Ecocompacto" in 2014. Developed in Brazil, it is a high-performance product, smaller and lighter, which incorporates innovation and environmental benefits, offering the same amount of applications in a pack with half the size of the average conventional aerosols. Consequently, its production consumes only half of the raw materials commonly used and 15% less aluminium, resulting in an environmental impact reduction of about 48% in greenhouse gas emissions. At the time, Brazil was the largest aerosol deodorant market, responsible for 22% of the global deodorant market, and was chosen as the product entry market.

Natura's research and development initiatives also rely on open innovation. Currently, 60% of the company's innovation projects are developed jointly with more than 200 partners, including other companies, universities, research institutions, test laboratories, and funding organisations. The company spends around 3% of its net annual revenue in innovation and R&D. Total investments in 2014 were over USD 60 million, including its first Innovation Hub office in New York, which is dedicated to identifying trends in the cosmetics industry in conjunction with innovation centres in Brazil.

Natura's R&D is also focused on developing environmentally friendly packaging for its products as the company prioritises the use of sustainable materials. For example, back in 2000, Natura launched the Ekos line in which products are made from raw materials such as passion fruit and Brazil nuts, harvested through sustainable methods from the Amazon and the Brazilian rainforest. Natura applies 50% recycled polyethylene terephthalate (PET) in the production of the vials in the EKOS line, which are 100% recyclable.

The company also uses 100% eco-friendly bioplastic made from sugar cane for its conditioner refills and bottles. In addition, fewer cartons have been used and they are now made from 40% recycled cardboard, being 100% recyclable. Furthermore, refills have just half the environmental impact of a classic product and are on average 20% cheaper. They are available for other product lines, helping to reduce the amount of packaging the company uses.

Responsible supply chain management

Since its foundation, Natura has been developing its business based on a commitment to sustainable management and social responsibility principles. From raw materials extraction to final products manufacturing and distribution, the company has constantly mapped the environmental impact of its activities. This unique approach has led Natura to develop its own environmental and sustainable policies over the past four decades. The company has become a pioneer in sustainable development and biodiversity management in the global cosmetics market.

In 2003, after six years of investment searching for alternative methods, Natura finally ended animal testing of its products, thus applying this commitment to its entire supply chain. The company does not purchase inputs that have been tested on animals, even throughout the research and development stages of new products. In addition, Natura also encourages its suppliers to apply this concept in their entire production system, even though those products are intended to support other companies.

To end its use of animal testing, Natura had major investment in education, training, and the search for new alternative technologies such as in vitro procedures. As a result, Nature eliminated animal testing for all finished products and for raw materials and active ingredients.

Following this philosophy, Natura was the first Brazilian company to adopt the Global Reporting Initiative's sustainability framework that provides a list of internationally developed reporting indicators. As a result, in 2014 Natura became the world's largest B Corp company – certification that associates economic growth with the promotion of social and environmental well-being.

Recognised as one of the world's top 100 most sustainable corporations, according to the Corporate Knights 2015 report (announced each year at the World Economic Forum), Natura ranks among the top five in corporate leadership in sustainability globally, together with leading global companies such as Unilever, Patagonia, and IKEA (Sustainability.com, 2021). The GlobeScan–SustainAbility Survey also shows that Natura is seen as the sustainability leader for Latin America (Figure 10.3).

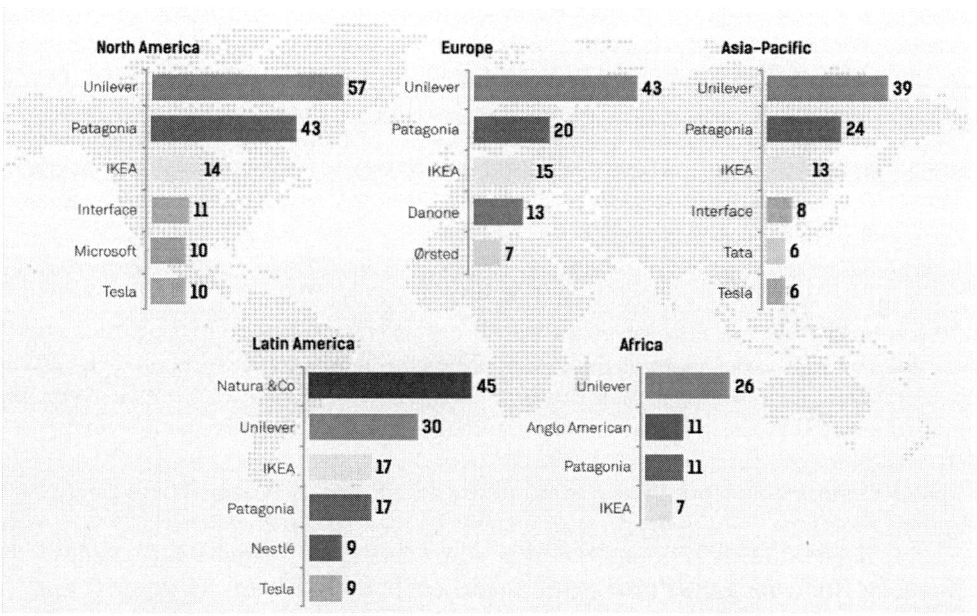

Figure 10.3 Corporate leaders in sustainability by region (Sustainability.com, 2021)

Natura works its supply chain through an integrated management culture, considering the triple bottom line dimensions in every decision. Its sustainable development policy affects every area in the business such as economic activities, society, and the environment.

Since 2007, Natura has opted to use only organic alcohol extracted from sugar cane in its products, a more environmentally friendly solution, and 30% more expensive. However, this choice of material has reduced the company's carbon emissions by 20%, thus carrying positive socio-environmental benefits. In the same year, Natura was awarded carbon-neutral certification, after reducing its CO_2 emissions by 33% in a five-year period.

Furthermore, Natura invests in dialogue with stakeholders to create a better understanding of the company's true impacts on the community and environment. To get stakeholders' feedback, a network of relationship managers works continually with communities, suppliers, and the direct sales workforce throughout Brazil.

> "More than contributing to society by adopting sustainable practices, we want to promote a growing movement to raise awareness and find solutions for a more balanced and fairer future from the economic, social and environmental standpoints". Roberto Lima, CEO of Natura.
>
> (Forbes, 2014)

Natura has also established a programme for FSC certification to guarantee that ingredients from the Brazilian flora are harvested respecting the environment. This programme governs the relationship of Natura with its 5,000 suppliers and 33 communities within its supply chain, which provide ingredients and time-honoured expertise, shaping the base to add value to every product in the company's business.

Since 1974, Natura's direct selling model has been based on its network of Natura Consultants (NCs). This unique approach was built on the opportunity for Natura to overcome some voids in the Brazilian market such as low numbers of department stores and adequate job opportunities, especially for women (currently, 50% of managers at Natura are women).

Natura invests heavily in the training of its sales force and each year around 300,000 consultants join the company. The Natura Consultants are commonly women of different ages and from different socio-economic backgrounds, truly loyal to the company's values, philosophy, and products.

These independent sales consultants are also part of the 75% of employees that participate in the company's profit sharing and stock ownership scheme.

Additionally, Natura's direct selling model has proven to be an efficient tool providing essential input for product development. The consultants are able to collect feedback, observations, and ideas from their customers. Around 95.5% of sales are delivered on time and more than 62,000 requests from NCs were received per day (almost one parcel delivered per second) (Correia da Silva, 2012).

Natura consultants work in an autonomous and not exclusive way, buying and reselling their products. To support the consultancy business, in each commercial cycle (generally 21 days) Natura distributes a new product catalogue (Natura's magazine) to the consultants, containing their products, launches, and promotions.

Their supply chains are able to respond to online and telephone orders in 4.5 days on average; 38% of deliveries are made within 48 hours. The process is fairly straightforward: sales consultants can order their products via the internet or allow their own clients to use their unique sales consultant number when shopping online. The online orders are then processed in their online system. The system informs both suppliers and production plants about the demand situation. Finished goods are sent to Cajamar distribution centre where products are sorted according to the specifications of each order. Every box is carefully organised with the right mix of product to meet the order, to avoid incorrect deliveries. The logistics department has opted to reduce the number of transportation companies (service providers) from 44 to 5. That has allowed Natura to operate with fewer strategic partners and as a result they have been able to reduce the amount of reclaimed packaging.

Natura's operations in France employ freight transport either by boat or plane for imported products from Brazil. Following the company's commitment to sustainable development, maritime transport is favoured, due to its lower energy use and the benefits in terms of greenhouse gas emissions. In 2012, 65% of Natura imports to France were made by boat, against 51% in 2011, while ensuring the best product availability for its consultants and customers.

In 2011, Natura also sought to reduce the environmental impact of its activities by optimising transport between France's port of Le Havre and the company's warehouse in Paris. Barges on the River Seine now travel for approximately 200 km, transporting containers landed from Le Havre to the inland port of Paris Gennevilliers. This choice of transportation uses 40% less fuel, allowing the company to avoid the release of three tons of CO_2.

Going global: Aēsop and The Body Shop

Aēsop, the Australia-based personal care company, was established in Melbourne In 1987. The company's mission is to create a range of the finest skin, hair, and body care products; it is committed to using different sources such as plant-based and laboratory-made ingredients with the highest quality and proven efficacy. Aēsop operates more than 98 stores in 14 countries including important locations in the cosmetics industry such as New York, London, Paris, and Tokyo. In 2016, Natura acquired complete control of Aēsop. At the time, Aēsop's CEO said:

> "We are excited to partner with Natura, a company with similar brand attributes and a culture dedicated to improving the lives of its people and the communities where it operates. This is a perfect fit with tremendous potential". Michael O'Keeffe, CEO of Aēsop
>
> (*GCI Magazine*, 2013)

Natura and Aēsop continue to operate independently, but both organisations are committed to sharing competencies and regional expertise. Natura's strategic investment in Aēsop has accelerated the growth of the Australian brand in urban centres internationally and access to complementary R&D capabilities, also leading to a potential entry in the Brazilian market, having opened the first store in São Paulo in 2015.

On the other hand, Natura benefited, gaining a highly complementary brand with common values and industry-leading expertise to explore the concept of a signature store, and, moreover, exposure to additional global markets, allowing the Brazilian brand further international expansion.

The aggressive approach to globalising its business did not stop with the acquisition of Aēsop. In a bold move, Natura acquired full ownership of The Body Shop from the French cosmetics company L'Oréal. In June 2017, L'Oréal agreed to sell its share of the company to Natura for £880 million. The Body Shop, which was started in Brighton (UK) in 1976 was strongly influenced by its founder Dame Anita Roddick, who thought that business could be a force for good. The Body Shop has more than 3,000 stores in 66 countries and employs more than 22,000 people. The company claims it delivers a "unique blend of ethical beauty with a sense of humour and serious purpose to the world".

Ethical Corporation, an independent business intelligence, publishing, and networking company founded in 2001, interviewed both sides about the acquisition. Christopher Davis, the ethical cosmetic company's international director of corporate responsibility and campaigns said, "staff were buoyed by a sense the brand will be able to return to its activist roots after 10 'challenging' years with the French cosmetics giant".

> "I joined under Anita [Roddick] over 14 years ago, and I have seen a lot of changes, but genuinely, I haven't seen or felt the place generating that amount of joy and excitement as today. It feels great", said Davis to Ethical Corporation.

According to Davis, "The Body Shop over the past ten years hasn't had the freedom to express what is still alive in the Body Shop, the human activist spirit and purpose-led philosophy". In contrast, Natura "are talking about shared purpose; they're talking about a shared vision and shared culture. The depth of the change we are going to experience here [with Natura] seems so right and so close to The Body Shop's DNA".

The excitement on Natura's side was also great. The Brazilian company's co-founders, Guilherme Leal and Antonio Luiz Seabra, told Ethical Corporation that:

> "The two companies are not only contemporaries – Natura is 47; The Body Shop 41 – they also "share the same DNA". And they both remember being hugely impressed by Anita Roddick, the human rights activist and environmental campaigner who founded The Body Shop in 1976, when they met her 13 years ago".

The *Financial Times* (*FT*) also reported on Natura's ambitions for global growth. Mr Roberto Marques, the new executive chairman told the *FT*:

> We feel there are a couple of things we want to prioritise in working with The Body Shop. The first one is this whole idea of rejuvenating the brand and make sure the brand becomes, really, its own activist voice. The second one, is the retail operation, how we can make it even more optimised, work even better.

He added:

> One of the reasons for bringing in The Body Shop, as well as acquiring Aēsop, was to create a more global footprint for Natura as a group, while also creating the possibility for Natura to expand globally with the aspiration of getting into 60 markets.

The future of the beauty sector

The prediction for the global beauty industry is optimistic for the coming years. However, the economic slowdown, inflation, and market saturation could affect the industry heavily in the near future.

The global beauty market was forecast to reach USD 415 billion in sales revenue by 2028 as result of a rise in consumer income. Moreover, this industry has been constantly influenced by different trends where, currently, first-class environmental initiatives are considered the most important for consumers. The importance of emerging markets such as Brazil, China, and India is based on their population size and cultural aspects, including consumers' passion for beauty products. Leading cosmetics manufacturers must be able to combine investments in marketing and innovation to take advantage of the sector's future market growth in developing countries.

Amidst this very dynamic sector, Natura's challenges include increasing production volume and continuing to deliver innovative products to both domestic and international markets. Also, they want to remain being seen as a world-leading company from an environmental and social perspective. Their operational excellence will be pushed to its limits with the simultaneous pressures on cost, speed, and quality. Concurrently, their plans for international expansion will require the development of key capabilities to deal with ever more complex global operations. Is Natura on the right path to position itself as a global beauty leader?

Appendix 1 Natura's timeline

- 1969 – Luiz Seabra founded Natura Brasil
- 1970 – The flower logo is born combining the perfect expression of nature and beauty
- 1974 – The company adopts direct sales as its main commercial strategy
- 1983 – Natura becomes the world's first business to offer its products in refill form
- 2000 – Launch of the Ekos range, which captures the essence of biodiversity in Brazil
- 2001 – Inauguration of the Cajamar site in São Paulo, Brazil
- 2003 – Natura begins to perform tests with synthetic material, end of animal testing
- 2004 – ISO 14001 and operations on the BM&F Bovespa (Brazilian Stock Exchange)
- 2005 – Natura Brasil arrives in France
- 2006 – Natura surpasses sales of Avon in Brazil
- 2007 – Natura initiates its carbon-neutral programme to reduce $C0_2$ emissions
- 2009 – The company celebrates 40 years and 1 million consultants
- 2010 – Natura becomes the first Brazilian company to join the WWF Climate Defenders
- 2012 – Natura acquires majority stake at Aesop
- 2013 – Natura inaugurates the Innovation Hub, an office in New York (USA)
- 2014 – Natura becomes the world's largest publicly listed company to achieve B Corp status
- 2014 – Natura launches the ecocompact deodorant
- 2015 – Recognised as one of the world's top 100 most sustainable corporations, according to the Corporate Knights 2015 report
- 2017 – Natura acquires The Body Shop from French cosmetics company L'Oréal

Appendix 2 Excerpt from Natura's sustainability reporting (Natura&Co, 2021)

A2.1 Key economic indicators (in R$ million)

	2018	*2019*	*2020*
Consolidated net revenue	13,397	14,445	18,345
Consolidated Ebitda	1,846	1,905	3,464
Consolidated net income	548	392	1,102
Average daily trading volume of shares	59	129	343

A2.2 Economic value distributed (in R$ million)

Distributed	*2018*	*2019*	*2020*
Operating costs	5,619	6,421	8,770
Employee salaries and benefits	2,813	3,011	3,500
Payments to suppliers	4,712	5,354	6,561
Payments to government	2,414	2,349	2,188
Payments to creditors	2,693	2,775	3,612
Community investments	307	312	394
Total	**18,558**	**20,223**	**25,036**

A2.3 Social indicators

Philanthropy and supplier community programme	*2018*	*2019*	*2020*
Crer Para Ver revenue (R$ million)	44.2	53.8	79.3
Families benefiting in Pan-Amazon supplier communities	4,636	5,136	7,039

A2.4 Confirmed incidents of corruption and fraud and actions taken

Confirmed incidents of corruption and fraud and actions taken	*2018*	*2019*	*2020*
Confirmed incidents of corruption	0	0	0
Confirmed incidents of fraud	23	9	7
Confirmed incidents in which employees were dismissed or punished for fraud	5	5	7
Confirmed incidents in which members of the sales force were dismissed or punished for fraud	18	1	0
% of cases addressed and resolved (punishment and/or dismissal)	100%	100%	100%

A2.5 Work-related injuries

Work-related injuries	*2018*		*2019*		*2020*	
	Employees	*People whose work and/or workplace is controlled by the organisation*	*Employees*	*People whose work and/or workplace is controlled by the organisation*	*Employees*	*People whose work and/or workplace is controlled by the organisation*
Hours worked	13,295,488	11,247,479	13,941,792	11,841,597	14,135,963	10,446,789
Severe injuries	3	5	8	2	7	9
Severe injury rate	0.23	0.44	0.57	0.17	0.5	0.86
Injuries recorded	17	24	20	23	10	12
Injury rate recorded	1.28	2.13	1.43	1.94	0.71	1.15

A2.6 Key environmental indicators

Environmental indicators	*2018*	*2019*	*2020*
Relative GHG emissions (kg CO2e/kg product billed)	3.14	3.18	2.85
GHG emissions in the value chain (tCO2e)	333,183	325,840	347,570
Water withdrawn Brazil (l/unit produced)	0.52	0.59	0.49
% post-consumer recycled material in finished product packaging – Brazil	5.4	8.6	10
% eco-efficient packaging in Brazil	22	185	18
Raw materials originating in Pan-Amazon region (% in relation to sales value)	17.8	17.7	16.5

A2.7 Emissions of ozone depleting substances (ODS) and NO_x, SO_x and other significant air emissions

Significant air emissions (tons)	*2018*	*2019*	*2020*
NO_x	8.26	7.18	3.59
SO_x	0.79	0.35	0.11
COV	Not Applicable	Not Applicable	0.34
Particulate material (PM)	18.4	13.23	12.43

A2.8 Energy consumed (MWh)

Energy consumed (MWh) by type of fuel	*2018*	*2019*	*2020*
Fuels from non-renewable sources	5,358	4,356	4,138
Fuels from renewable sources	88,968	100,330	96,606
Total	**94,325**	**104,686**	**100,745**

Energy consumed (MWh)	*2018*	*2019*	*2020*
Electricity	53,908	59,358	58,149
Heating	799	1,146	3,121
Refrigeration	13,477	14,837	14,283
Steam	26,141	29,343	25,191
Total	**94,326**	**104,686**	**100,745**

A2.9 Total waste diverted, by composition (t)

Category	*Quantity (t)*	*Waste NOT directed to disposal (t)*	*Waste directed to disposal (t)*
Non-hazardous			
Glass	373	373	–
Plastic	928	928	–
Wood	787	787	–
Metal	107	107	–
Paper/cardboard	5,933	5,933	–
Other non-hazardous	6,574	5,897	678
Total non-hazardous	**14,702**	**14,024**	**678**
Hazardous			
Hazardous	2,588	2,472	116
Total	**17,290**	**16,497**	**793**

Disclaimer

1 Note: This case has been researched and prepared by Mr Julius Silva and Dr Breno Nunes in collaboration with Dr Angela Marqui, Professor Prasanta Dey, Professor David Bennett at Aston University (UK). It does not reflect the views of Natura Brasil. The company owners, past and current directors and employees should not be responsible for the accuracy or interpretation of the information or views contained in this case. This case is aimed at enriching class discussion or assessment purposes. It is not intended to illustrate either good or bad management practices. Updated September 2022.

2 Earnings Before Interest, Taxes, Depreciation, and Amortization.

Bibliography

ABEVD. (2019). Available at: https://www.abevd.org.br/consumidores-brasileiros-consideram-o-impacto-ambiental-nos-produtos-cosmeticos/

AesopAēsop.com. (2015). About AesopAēsop. [online] Available at: http://www.aesopAēsop.com/uk/about_aesopAēsop/ [Accessed 27 Jul. 2015].

Antunes, A. (2015). Brazil's natura, the largest cosmetics maker in Latin America, becomes a B corp. [online] *Forbes*. Available at: http://www.forbes.com/sites/andersonantunes/2014/12/16/brazils-natura-the-largest-cosmetics-maker-in-latin-america-becomes-a-b-corp/ [Accessed 14 Jul. 2015].

Brazilbeautynews.com. (2014). Challenges and opportunities for sustainable cosmetics in Brazil: Brazil Beauty News. [online] Available at: http://www.brazilbeautynews.com/challenges-and-opportunities-for-sustainable,306 [Accessed 23 Jul. 2015].

Correia da Silva, I. (2012). Available at: http://pt.slideshare.net/expogestao/itamar-correia

Cosmeticobs.com. (2014). Available at: https://cosmeticobs.com/en/articles/ecoresponsability-68/going-green-to-access-the-brazilian-beauty-market-2433

Gcimagazine.com. (2015a). Natura acquires majority stake in Australian skin care company | GCIMagazine.com. [online] Available at: http://www.gcimagazine.com/marketstrends/regions/bric/Natura-Acquires-Majority-Stake-in-Australian-Skin-Care-Company-190064211.html [Accessed 27 Jul. 2015].

Gcimagazine.com. (2015b). What attracts beauty consumers in Brazil? | GCIMagazine.com. [online] Available at: http://www.gcimagazine.com/marketstrends/segments/natural/What-Attracts-Beauty-Consumers-in-Brazil-269266141.html [Accessed 24 Jul. 2015].

Harvard Business Review. (2012). The growth opportunity that lies next door. [online] Available at: https://hbr.org/2012/07/the-growth-opportunity-that-lies-next-door [Accessed 3 Jul. 2015].

http://www.ethicalcorp.com/exclusive-under-natura-body-shop-will-return-its-activist-roots

http://www.ethicalcorp.com/spirit-anita-roddick-strong-us-why-natura-bought-body-shop

https://www.ft.com/content/d4c868a0-091b-11e8-8eb7-42f857ea9f09

https://www.fortunebusinessinsights.com/cosmetics-market-102614

https://www.ibisworld.com/industry-statistics/employment/cosmetic-beauty-products-manufacturing-united-states/

https://www.statista.com/statistics/297070/growth-rate-of-the-global-cosmetics-market/

https://www.statista.com/forecasts/758635/revenue-of-the-cosmetics-and-personal-care-market-worldwide-by-country

https://www.thebodyshop.com/en-gb/about-us

Managementexchange.com. (2015). Innovation in well-beingâ€" the creation of sustainable value at natura | Management Innovation eXchange. [online] Available at: http://www.managementexchange.com/story/innovation-in-well-being [Accessed 23 Jul. 2015].

Mintel.com. (2015a). Brazil is a natural beauty hot spot | Mintel.com. [online] Available at: http://www.mintel.com/blog/beauty-market-news/brazil-is-a-natural-beauty-hot-spot [Accessed 16 Jul. 2015].

Mintel.com. (2015b). Brazilian haircare market highlights booming growth | Mintel.com. [online] Available at: http://www.mintel.com/press-centre/beauty-and-personal-care/brazilian-haircare-market-trends [Accessed 23 Jul. 2015].

Natura&Co. (2021) Natura reports. [online] Available at: https://ri.naturaeco.com/en/publications-and-documents/reports/ [Accessed 20 August 2021].

Natura.infoinvest.com.br. (2015). Natura annual report 2014. [online] Available at: http://natura.infoinvest.com.br/enu/s-15-enu.html [Accessed 3 Jul. 2015].

Naturabrasil.fr. (2015a). Cosmetics leader in Brazil | Natura Brasil. [online] Available at: https://www.naturabrasil.fr/en/about-us/cosmetics-leader-in-brazil [Accessed 3 Jul. 2015].

Naturabrasil.fr. (2015b). Environmental commitments | Natura Brasil. [online] Available at: https://www.naturabrasil.fr/en/our-values/environmental-commitments [Accessed 10 Jul. 2015].

Naturabrasil.fr (2015c). Our history | Natura Brasil. [online] Available at: https://www.naturabrasil.fr/en/about-us/our-history [Accessed 4 Jul. 2015].

Naturabrasil.fr. (2015d). Sustainable Development | Natura Brasil. [online] Available at: https://www.naturabrasil.fr/en/our-values/sustainable-development [Accessed 14 Jul. 2015].

Naturabrasil.fr. (2015e). Where do our products come from | Natura Brasil. [online] Available at: https://www.naturabrasil.fr/en/about-us/where-do-our-products-come-from [Accessed 14 Jul. 2015].

Premiumbeautynews.com. (2014a). Premium beauty news - Brazil: The cosmetics market boosted by hair care. [online] Available at: http://www.premiumbeautynews.com/en/brazil-the-cosmetics-market,6720 [Accessed 22 Jul. 2015].

Premiumbeautynews.com. (2014b). Premium beauty news: Brazilian lifestyle inspires the cosmetics industry worldwide, Mintel reports. [online] Available at: http://www.premiumbeautynews.com/en/brazilian-lifestyle-inspires-the,7198# [Accessed 16 Jul. 2015].

Premiumbeautynews.com. (2015). Premium beauty news: Brazilian cosmetics market grew by 11% in 2014. [online] Available at: http://www.premiumbeautynews.com/en/brazilian-cosmetics-market-grew-by,8021?PHPSESSID=7js9ulduo44qhjv41quinkron3 [Accessed 16 Jul. 2015].

Statista. (2015a). Annual growth rate of the cosmetics market worldwide, 2014 | Statistic. [online] Available at: http://www.statista.com/statistics/297070/growth-rate-of-the-global-cosmetics-market/ [Accessed 5 Jul. 2022].

Statista. (2015b). Sales growth of the leading global cosmetic companies between 2012–2015 | Statistic. [online] Available at: http://www.statista.com/statistics/245744/sales-growth-of-the-leading-global-cosmetic-companies/ [Accessed 20 Jul. 2015].

Statista. (2019). Revenue of the hair care market worldwide by country 2019. Available at: https://www.statista.com/forecasts/758640/revenue-of-the-hair-care-market-worldwide-by-country [Accessed 14 September 2022].

Sustainability.com. (2015). The 2015 sustainability leaders – library | SustainAbility. [online] Available at: http://www.sustainability.com/library/the-2015-sustain-ability-leaders#downloads [Accessed 12 Jul. 2015].

Sustainability.com. (2021). The 2020 sustainability leaders. *The GlobeScan-SustainAbility Survey*. Available at: https://www.sustainability.com/contentassets/b298c9248bd14c03951e8801a6880436/gss-leaders-report-2020.pdf [Accessed 20 August 2021].

USA, C. (2015). Global beauty market to reach $265 billion in 2017 due to an increase in GDP. [online] *CosmeticsDesign.com USA*. Available at: http://www.cosmeticsdesign.com/Market-Trends/Global-beauty-market-to-reach-265-billion-in-2017-due-to-an-increase-in-GDP [Accessed 28 July 2015].

WIRE, B. (2012). Natura announces strategic investment in AesopAēsop | business wire. [online] *Businesswire.com*. Available at: http://www.businesswire.com/news/home/20121220005419/en/Natura-Announces-Strategic-Investment-AesopAēsop#.VcfmdflVikp [Accessed 27 July 2015].

Index

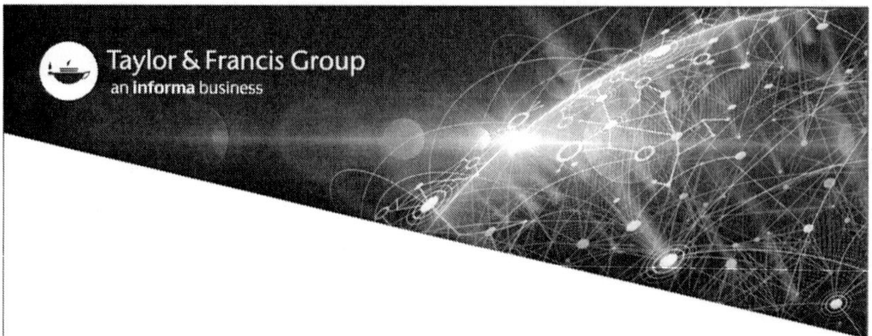

For Product Safety Concerns and Information please contact our EU representative GPSR@taylorandfrancis.com Taylor & Francis Verlag GmbH, Kaufingerstraße 24, 80331 München, Germany